1
2
3
4

ES

TEST

CHAPTER 1

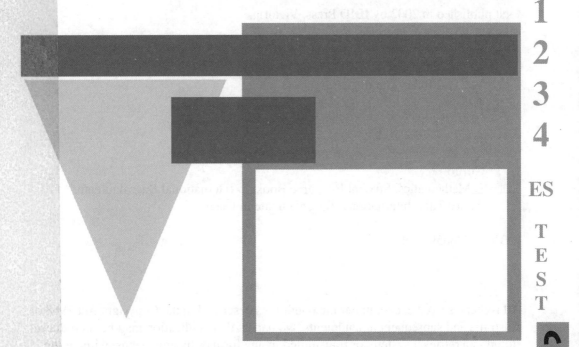

MATHEMATICAL STUDIES (SL)
STUDENT RESOURCE BOOK

Edited by Fabio Cirrito

First published in 2002 by IBID Press, Victoria,

Published by IBID Press, Victoria.
Library Catalogue:

Cirrito
1. Mathematics, Student Resource Book, 2. International Baccalaureate.
Series Title: International Baccalaureate in Detail

ISBN: 1 876659 39 4

Cover design by Adcore.

Published by IBID Press, BOX 9 CAMBERWELL, VICTORIA, 3124, AUSTRALIA.

Printed by Shannon Books Australia Pty Ltd.

PREFACE

This book has been specifically written with the student's examination preparation in mind. The questions have been written in such a way as to facilitate student consolidation of work covered throughout the year (using Level 1, 2 and 3 questions). Nearing the examination period, questions labelled at Levels 3, 4 become more accessible (and challenging). Finally, the Examinations Style and Test questions provide a solid final preparation prior to the student's final exam.

Apart from the obvious indication of the level of difficulty inherent as the student moves through Level 1 to Level 4, we make further comment regarding the purpose of the different categories.

LEVEL 1: Usually limited to basic facts or skills requiring little algebra or conceptual understanding. Questions often require only one or three lines of working. Questions relate strictly to the chapter topic.

LEVEL 2: Requires a better grasp of algebraic skills and conceptual understanding. Questions often require two to five lines of working out. Questions relate strictly to the chapter topic.

LEVEL 3: Needs a higher level of conceptual understanding with a greater demand on students' mathematical abilities. It requires a sound understanding of mathematical manipulation. Although most questions still deal with the chapter topic, some questions may require knowledge from other parts of the course. These questions are appropriate once a student has mastered the topic at hand and as a prelude to the final examination.

LEVEL 4: These questions are often challenging and although they all start with an area of the chapter topic, they will often require a working knowledge from other topics in the course and sometimes go beyond the scope of the course. These make for excellent revision towards the students' final examination preparation.

EXAMINATION STYLE:

These questions usually reflect the level and style students can be expected to confront in their final examination. The questions usually lead students through stages of a problem, with the level of difficulty increasing as they progress through each stage. These questions are suitable for final examination preparation but could also consolidate a topic just covered. Questions can include theory from a number of topics on the syllabus.

TOPIC TEST:

These tests are designed for revision of individual topics throughout the year as well as for consolidation on individual topics covered through the year as a lead up to the final examination. The level of difficulty spans Level 1 to Level 4 style questions.

This book has been synchronised to correspond to the chapters in the Mathematical Studies (SL) text book already available from IBID Press. This companion book to the text, together with a selection of past examination papers, will provide the student with an excellent preparation towards the final examination in this subject.

A word about the Answers & Solutions section: Where a solution requires a method that has been used to solve an earlier question from the same chapter, we have provided an answer to that question. However, you will find that most of the questions have a detailed solution. The setting out has sometimes been compromised for the sake of space. The solutions or mark schemes do not represent the views of the I.B.O Examination Board – they represent a guide of how marks can be allocated – which represent; Method mark, Answer or Accuracy mark and Reasoning mark.

Note: Unless otherwise stated, you should provide exact answers to the questions or answers to no less than two decimal places.

I wish you well in your studies and exams.

Fabio Cirrito

CONTENTS

QUESTIONS

LEVEL

LEVEL 1

1. Which of the following equations have solutions that are members of the set $\mathbb{Q}$?

    i. $2x - 3 = 1$ ii. $\dfrac{2}{x} = 9$ iii. $x^2 = 6.25$

    iv. $x^2 = 27$ v. $x = x + 7$ vi. $\dfrac{1}{x} = \dfrac{x}{7}$

    vii. $x^2 + 2 = 0$ viii. $\sqrt{x} = 7$ ix. $x^3 = -1$

2. Write the following numbers in standard form:

    i.   34   ii.   56700   iii.   600056

    iv.   0.4   v.   0.00438   vi.   4.0456

    vii.   0.0020   viii. $\dfrac{3}{4}$ ix.   0.0000054

    x. 100^2 xi. $\dfrac{6}{100}$ xii. $\dfrac{3}{40}$

    xiii. $\left(\dfrac{5}{200}\right)^2$ xiv. $\sqrt{\dfrac{1}{10000}}$ xv. 0.0009^2

LEVEL 2

1. If $a = 2.47 \times 10^{-2}$, $b = 7.92 \times 10^3$, $c = 4.01 \times 10^{-3}$, evaluate, giving answers in standard form, correct to three significant figures:

    i. $a + b$ ii. ab iii. $\dfrac{1}{bc}$

    iv. $\dfrac{1}{a - c}$ v. a^2c vi. $\dfrac{a + c}{a - c}$

    vii. $a(b + c)$ viii. $a + \dfrac{1}{b}$ ix. $\dfrac{1}{a^2} - b^2$

    x. a^c

2. If $x = 27 \pm 1$, $y = 155 \pm 5$, $z = 93 \pm 2$, find the percentage error, correct to two significant figures, that results from calculating:

    i. $x + y$ ii. $y - z$ iii. xy

    iv. $\dfrac{1}{y - z}$ v. x^2y vi. $\dfrac{x + z}{y - z}$

3. By writing the following numbers as fractions, prove that they are rational numbers:

    i. 1.3 ii. 0.25 iii. $0.\dot{3}$

    iv. $0.\dot{5}$ v. $0.8\dot{3}$ vi. $0.\ddot{8}\dot{3}$

    vii. $0.\dot{4}2857\dot{1}$

LEVEL **QUESTIONS**

1

2

3

4

ES

T
E
S
T

LEVEL 3

1. When an optical system forms the image of a real object that is u metres away from the lens, the image is formed v metres behind the lens. The image is also formed upside-down. The formula that relates u to v in terms of the focal length f of the lens is: $\dfrac{1}{u} + \dfrac{1}{v} = \dfrac{1}{f}$. A lens of focal length 0.4 ± 0.003 metres is used to form the image of an object that is 1.9 ± 0.06 metres from the lens.
    i.   Make v the subject of the formula.
    ii. Find the largest and smallest possible values of v.
    iii. Find the percentage error in the value of v.

2. Einstein's formula for the amount of energy (E Joules) released when matter (m kilograms) is destroyed in a nuclear reaction is $E = mc^2$ where c is the velocity of light 3.00×10^8 metres per second.
    i.   Find the energy released when 0.2 kilograms of matter is released.
    ii. A neutron weighs 1.67×10^{-27} kg. Find the amount of energy released when five million neutrons are destroyed.

3. The volume, V cm^3, of the square pyramid shown is given by the formula $V = \dfrac{1}{3}Ah$, where A is the base area.

    If $h = 12.4$ find its volume, giving the answer
    i.   correct to three significant figures.
    ii. correct to two decimal places.
    iii. to the nearest whole number.

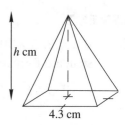

LEVEL 4

1. For what value(s) of k will $kx - 2 = \sqrt{2}$ have a rational solution when solving for x?

2. The function $f(x) = 3x + 6, \ 0 \le x \le 20$ is to be used to predict values of f throughout the domain. The maximum level of error permitted in these values is 6%. Assuming that the constant is known exactly, find the maximum percentage error allowable in the coefficient of x.

3. The diagram shows part of an engineering component. Nominally, the block has dimensions 180 by 245 by 567mm and the holes have diameter 190mm. The dimensions are known to 0.2% accuracy and the diameters of the circular holes are known to 0.1% accuracy. Find the percentage errors in the volume of metal used in making the component and in its weight.

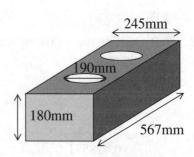

QUESTIONS

EXAMINATION STYLE QUESTIONS

1. The temperature $(O°C)$ of an industrial oven t hours after it is started is modelled by the function $O(t) = -0.9t^2 + 66t + 25, 0 \leq t \leq 50$.

   i. Copy and complete the table of values for the function giving answers in scientific form, correct to one decimal place.

t	0	10	20	30	40	50
O						

   ii. Sketch the graph of the function.

   iii. Find the average rate of change of temperature between $t = 20$ and $t = 30$.

   iv. If the coefficient of t (i.e., 66) has a 10% error, find the largest and smallest possible values of $O(20)$ and $O(30)$ and hence find the largest and smallest possible values of the average rate of change of temperature between $t = 20$ and $t = 30$.

2. The voltage, V volts, in an electrical circuit is given by the product RI, where R ohms is the total resistance of the circuit and I amps is the current flowing in the circuit.
If $R = 6$ and $I = 4$, each being correct to 1 significant figure, find the range of V.

3. The dimensions of the triangle shown are known to an accuracy of 5%.

   Find the percentage error in calculating:

   47cm

   34cm

   63cm

   i. The perimeter.

   ii. The largest angle.

   iii. The area.

4. A function is defined by $f(x) = 35 - ax^3, 0 \leq x \leq 2$. The value of the coefficient a is 3.6 ± 0.2.

   i. Find the percentage error in calculating $f(1)$.

   ii. Find the relative error in calculating $f'(1)$.

LEVEL ████████████████████████ **QUESTIONS**

1

2

TEST

1. If $a = 4.7 \times 10^3$, $b = 9.1 \times 10^{-2}$ & $c = 6.2 \times 10^4$, evaluate, giving answers in scientific form, correct to three significant figures:

3

4

i. $\dfrac{c}{ab}$ 　　　　ii. $a^3 + c^2$ 　　　　iii. $\dfrac{b}{c-a}$

[5 marks]

ES

2. Round the following quantities correct to three significant figures:

i.   4009 　　　　ii.   0.0050607 　　　　iii.   109056

[3 marks]

T
E
S
T

3. What is the percentage error in quoting a mass as being 1.50 kg?

[3 marks]

4. If $a = 3.14$, $b = 0.98$ and $c = 1.04$, calculate $a(c^2 - b)$, giving your answer
(a)   exactly.
(b)   correct to three significant figures.
(c)   correct to two decimal places.
(d)   in the form $a \times 10^k$, where $1 \leq a < 10$, $k \in \mathbb{Z}$.

[5 marks]

5. Express the recurring decimal $2.\overset{\bullet\bullet}{23}$ in the form $\dfrac{a}{b}$, where $a, b \in \mathbb{Z}$ and hence state

which of the sets $\mathbb{N}$, $\mathbb{Z}$ or $\mathbb{Q}$, the decimal belongs to.

[3 marks]

6. For the triangle shown, $x = 10.2$, $y = 3.6$ and $\theta = 32°$.
Find

i.   the range of the area, A m^2.
ii.   the percentage error in the area.

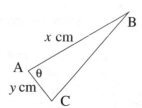

[6 marks]

Total : 25 marks

QUESTIONS   LEVEL

1
2
3
4
ES
T
E
S
T
CHAPTER 3

LEVEL 1

1. Classify the following sequences as arithmetic, geometric or neither:

i.   2   −1   −4   −7   −10   −13   −16   −19

ii. $\dfrac{1}{8}$ $\dfrac{1}{4}$ $\dfrac{3}{8}$ $\dfrac{1}{2}$ $\dfrac{5}{8}$ $\dfrac{3}{4}$ $\dfrac{7}{8}$ 1

iii.   4   9   16   25   36   49   64   81

iv.   3   −6   12   −24   48   −96   192   −384

2. Find the missing term in each of the following.

i.   4, 7, 10, x, 16, 19

ii.   1, −4, −9, −14, x, −24

iii.   2, 4, x, 8, 10, 12

iv.   2, 4, 8, x, 32, 64

3. The general term of an arithmetic sequence is given by $u_n = 8 + (n-1) \times 10$,

find   i. u_1 ii. u_5

4. Find the fifteenth term for each of the sequences in question 1.

5. Find the sum of the first ten terms for each of the sequences in question 1.

LEVEL 2

1. How many terms are there in the arithmetic sequence −12,−7, −2, ... , 208?

2. Find the number of terms in the geometric sequence 1, -5, 25, ... ,15625.

3. Find the sum of the geometric series: 2, 6, 18, 54, ... , 3188646

4. $2500 is invested at 7% annual interest with the interest compounded annually. How many years must pass before there is more than $10 000 in this account?

5. The first four terms of an A.P are given by a, b, c, d. Express b in terms of a and c.

6. Roy has a monthly salary of $5000 during his first year of employment which will increase by $500 after each year of service. Find the total amount Roy will have earnt after 5 years of service.

7. The numbers 126, x, 56 form 3 consecutive terms of a G.P. Find x.

8. Find the sum of the first 5 terms in the geometric sequence 9, 3, 1, ...

9. The first three terms of a geometric sequence are 3, 6 and 12. The sum of the first N terms is 1533. Find N.

LEVEL   **QUESTIONS**

1

2

3

4

ES

T
E
S
T

LEVEL 3

1. An arithmetic series has first term 3, 11 terms and a sum of 528. Find:
    (a)   the common difference.   (b)   the last term.   (c)   the middle term.

2. A geometric series and an arithmetic series both have first term 3 and 11 terms. The 4th term of the arithmetic series and the 6th term of the geometric are both 96. Find:
    (a)   the last term of the arithmetic series.
    (b)   the sum of the arithmetic series.
    (c)   the common ratio of the geometric series.
    (d)   the sum of the geometric series.

3. An arithmetic series has first term –50 and common difference 4. How many terms must be taken before the sum of the series first exceeds 100?

4. The first 4 terms of an A.P are a, b, c, d. Express b in terms of a and d.

LEVEL 4

1. Leo wants to save for a holiday. He needs to save a total of 1000 Euros. In the first week, Leo saves 30 Euros. In the next week he saves 32 Euros and so on in arithmetic progression. For how many weeks will Leo need to save?

2. A colony of rodents initially consists of 2700 animals. The population grows by 7% per month. How many months must pass before the population first passes ten thousand?

3. A car costs $32 000 new. After 10 years its value has fallen to $6 300. If it depreciates at $d\%$ per annum, find the value of d correct to the nearest one percent.

4. A radioactive source decays at the rate of 1% of its activity per day. On the first day, a source registered 5 000 disintegrations.
    (a)   How many disintegrations could be expected on the second day?
    (b)   On which day do the number of disintegrations first fall below 4 000?
    (c)   How many disintegrations in total could be expected to be recorded if this source is observed for 30 days?

5. Carlo saves $100 at the beginning of every month for a period of 50 months. The money is saved in an account that pays 6% annual interest calculated monthly.
    (a)   Prove that the first amount of $100 deposited becomes 100×1.005^{50} by the end of Carlo's saving period (the end of the 50th month).
    (b)   Prove that the second amount deposited becomes 100×1.005^{49} by the end of Carlo's saving period.
    (c)   Express the amounts saved and the interest received as a series and hence find the total amount Carlo has saved at the end of the 50 months.

QUESTIONS   LEVEL

EXAMINATION STYLE QUESTIONS

1. Allie is a nurse who needs to administer a drug, Zylacan, a pain killer, to a patient.
The drug is to be administered from a 'drip feeder' which will give the patient
drips of the drug dissolved in sterile water which is then fed into the patient's
bloodstream. The drip bottle contains 500 millilitres (ml.) of drug solution. The
drips of drug solution are each of 0.06 millilitres (ml). The drip does not deliver
drips at a constant rate. During the first hour there are 12 drips per minute, in the
second hour there are 11.5 drips per minute, in the third hour there are 11 drips per
minute and so on in arithmetic progression. Assume that the drip rate remains
fixed at the stated level throughout each hour. The solution contains 3 milligrams
per millilitre (mg/ml) of Zylacan.

(a) Find the total amount of Zylacan in the bottle at the start.

(b) Calculate the number of drips of drug solution, and hence the number of
millilitres, that the patient receives during each of the first three hours.

(c) Find the total volume of drug solution that the patient receives during the
first six hours and hence the amount of solution that remains in the bottle
after this time.

(d) Find the number of milligrams of Zylacan that the patient receives during
each of the first three hours.

(e) If the patient must receive at least 65 mg of Zylacan per hour, when should
the drip bottle be replaced ?

(f) If the drip is not replaced, find the number of hours (from the start) that will
pass before the solution bottle will be empty.

1
2
3
4

ES

T
E
S
T

2. The engineers who are responsible for the condition of a new bridge are trying to
calculate the future costs of corrosion protection starting from the year the bridge
was built ($t = 0$). There are two stages in corrosion protection:

Preparation, which includes the removal of flaking paint and corroded
metal. Preparation costs $180 per hour.

Painting. This involves the application of paint to the prepared metal.

The engineers estimate that by the end of the first year of operation ($t = 1$) they
will have had to spend 7 hours in preparation for painting. Because it is
anticipated that the bridge will deteriorate, they expect to have to spend 9 hours in
preparation during the second year ($t = 2$) with the time increasing by 2 hours per
year for each successive year. If P_t is the time spent on preparation in year t, then

$P_1 = 7, P_2 = 9$ etc., in arithmetic progression. A complete coat of paint costs

$6000 for the first year, but this cost is expected to rise by 7% per year.

a. Find the time expected to be spent on preparation in the tenth year (P_{10}).

b. Find a formula for the **cost** (C_t) of preparation in terms of t.

c. Find the total time spent on preparation over the first 20 years of operation
of the bridge.

d. The engineers budget to spend a total of $180,000 on preparation. How
long will this money last?

e. Find a formula for the cost of the paint in the nth year (in terms of n).

LEVEL

QUESTIONS

1
2
3
4

ES

T
E
S
T

TEST

1. Find the number of terms in the sequence –12, –7, –2, 3, ..., 123.

[2 marks]

2. Find the sum of the geometric series –5 + 10 – 20 + ... 640.

[3 marks]

3. A car costs $30,000 when new and is expected to lose 6.5% of its value each year.
   (a) How much is the car worth after 2 years?
   (b) Complete the table below

Years since purchase (t)	1	2	3	4
Value of car ($$ V$)				

   (c) Find an expression for V in terms of t.

[6 marks]

4. Chocolates are made in the shape of a sphere. They are to be marketed in triangluar boxes that contain one layer. The diagram shows a box with three rows of chocolates.

   (a) Find the number of chocolates in a box with four rows of chocolates.

   (b) Find a formula for the number of chocolates in a box with n rows.

   (c) Find the number of rows needed if the box is to contain 55 chocolates.

[5 marks]

5. A newly formed production company expects to manufacture 12 000 ratchets in their first year of operation. This is expected to grow by 8% annually.

   (a) Find the number of ratchets manufactured in the fifth year of operation.

   (b) Find the total number of ratchets manufactured by the end of the fifth year of operation.

   (c) Find the first year in which production will be more than twice that in the first year.

   (d) Find the year in which the company can expect to celebrate the manufacture of its 'millionth ratchet'.

[6 marks]
Total 22 marks

QUESTIONS

LEVEL

LEVEL 1

1. Write down, the sets represented by the number lines

(a) $\xleftarrow{\hspace{1cm}}\underset{4}{\bullet}\underset{9}{\bullet}\xrightarrow{\hspace{0.5cm}}x$ (b) $\xleftarrow{\hspace{1cm}}\underset{6}{\circ}\xrightarrow{\hspace{1cm}}x$ (c) $\xleftarrow{\hspace{1cm}}\underset{-3}{\circ}\xrightarrow{\hspace{0.3cm}}x$

i. using set notation. ii. using interval notation.

2. Represent the following sets on a real number line.

i. $[1, \infty)$ ii. $(-10,3)$ iii. $(-\infty,9)$

LEVEL 2

1. Solve the following equations for the unknown.

i. $2x = 8$ ii. $3s + 2 = 11$ iii. $9 - 7x = 2$

iv. $4 - \frac{1}{2}t = 2$ v. $2(x - 1) = 7$ vi. $1 - 3(y + 2) = 5$

2. Solve the following inequations for the unknown.

i. $1 + x > 0$ ii. $5 - x \le 9$ iii. $4 + \frac{1}{2}y < 1$

iv. $2 - 3(1 - x) > 5$ v. $\frac{2}{3}(x - 4) + 1 < 3$ vi. $3 - 2\left(1 + \frac{2}{5}x\right) < 1$

LEVEL 3

1. Solve the following for the unknown.

i. $\frac{x - 1}{3} + 1 = \frac{x}{2}$ ii. $4 - \frac{2}{5}(2 - x) = \frac{2x + 3}{4}$

iii. $\frac{5 - 2s}{3} - 1 < \frac{s}{6}$ iv. $\frac{3y - 1}{2} > \frac{y + 4}{3} + 1$

v. $\frac{2}{1 - x} + 1 = \frac{x}{1 - x}$ vi. $\frac{1}{5}(5 - 2a) \ge 2 - \frac{3}{2}(1 + a)$

2. Joseph's mother is three time as old as he is. How old is Joseph, given that their combined ages is 88.

LEVEL 4

1. Find x: i. $ax + a = ba, a \ne 0$ ii. $\frac{a}{b}x - b > a - \frac{b}{a}x, a \ne 0, b \ne 0$

2. A train departs at 1:00 pm and travels at 80 km h^{-1}. An aeroplane departs from the same area at 4:00 pm and travels at 200 km h^{-1}. How far will the aeroplane travel before it overtakes the train? What assumption have you made?

LEVEL

1
2
3
4

EXAMINATION STYLE

1. A train travels for 3 hours at a constant speed and then for the next 4 hours at 10 km h^{-1} faster than the first three hours. The train travels a total of 650 km.

   i.   If the train is travelling at $s \text{ km h}^{-1}$ during the first three hours, how far did it travel during the next four hours? Give your answer in terms of s.

   ii.   How fast did the train travel during the first three hours?

2. Find the perimeter of the triangle shown.

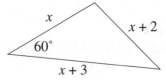

ES

T
E
S
T

3. A bag contains 10-cent and 50-cent coins. In all, there are 26 coins. The bag contains more than $ 4.50. There are x 50-cent coins and y 10-cent coins in the bag.

   i.   Write down an inequation involving x and y.

   ii.   Express y in terms of x.

   iii. Find the minimum number of 50-cent coins in the bag.

TEST

1. On a real number line, represent the set $\{x \mid 3 < x \le 8\}$.

[2 marks]

2. Solve the following equations

   i. $8h - 2 = 14$ ii. $5y - 10 = 2y + 5$ iii. $3(2x - 1) = 21$

[2 + 2 + 2 marks]

3. Solve the following

   i. $\dfrac{a-1}{2} - 2 = a + 4$ ii. $\dfrac{4x+1}{3} \le \dfrac{2-x}{5}$

[3 + 3 marks]

4. i.   Express DC in terms of x.

   ii.   Find the value of x.

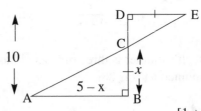

[1 + 3 marks]

5. Linley purchased some stock which, after making a profit of $y\%$ was worth $6400. A week later she sold it for $6000 making a loss of $y\%$.

   i.   Show that $\dfrac{100 + y}{100 - y} = \dfrac{16}{15}$.

   ii.   Find y.

   iii. How much did Linley pay for the stock?

[4 + 2 + 1 marks]

Total 25 marks

QUESTIONS

LEVEL

LEVEL 1

1. Which of the following are quadratic equations?

    (a) $3x + x - 7 = 0$ (b) $5x^2 - 5x + 1 = 0$ (c) $16 - y^2 = 0$

2. Factorise the following.

    (a) $x^2 + x$ (b) $2x - x^2$ (c) $4ax + ax^2$

    (d) $6y^2 + 12y$ (e) $9b^2 - 3b$ (f) $12ay^2 + 4ay$

3. Factorise the following.

    (a) $2(a + b) + a(a + b)$ (b) $z(z - 1) - 3(z - 1)$

    (c) $x(x + 1) - 2(x + 1)$ (d) $y(x - y) + x(x - y)$

LEVEL 2

1. Factorise the following.

    (a) $x^2 + 3x - 4$ (b) $y^2 - 6y + 5$ (c) $x^2 + 5x - 14$

    (d) $a^2 - 2a + 1$ (e) $a^2 - 2a - 3$ (f) $y^2 - 16y + 63$

2. Factorise the following.

    (a) $2x^2 + 5x - 3$ (b) $3x^2 + 4x + 1$ (c) $2y^2 + y - 3$

    (d) $6z^2 + 5z + 1$ (e) $12x^2 + 25x + 12$ (f) $5x^2 - 14x - 3$

3. Solve the following equations:

    i. $x^2 + 3x - 4 = 0$ ii. $x^2 - 6x + 5 = 0$

    iii. $x^2 + 5x + 6 = 0$ iv. $x^2 - 2x + 1 = 0$

    v. $x^2 + 5x - 14 = 0$ vi. $x^2 - 16x + 63 = 0$

4. Use the quadratic formula to solve these equations (give answers in exact form):

    i. $x^2 + x - 7 = 0$ ii. $2x^2 + 3x - 4 = 0$

    iii. $-x^2 - 4x + 9 = 0$ iv. $5x^2 - 3x - 4 = 0$

    v. $2x^2 - 5x + 7 = 0$ vi. $3x^2 + 5x - 9 = 0$

LEVEL 3

1. Find the turning points of the graphs of the following functions:

    i. $y = x^2 - 6x + 13$ ii. $y = x^2 + 2x + 4$

    iii. $y = 2x^2 - 4x - 1$ iv. $y = 3x^2 - 6x + 4$

    v. $y = x^2 - x + \dfrac{13}{4}$ vi. $y = 5x^2 - 10x + 5$

LEVEL

QUESTIONS

1

2

3

4

ES

T
E
S
T

2. Give equations for the functions whose graphs are shown:

i.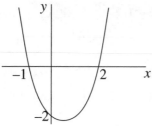

ii.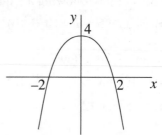

iii.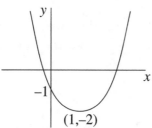

iv.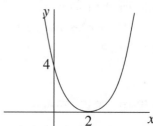

3. By making use of completing the square, find the roots of the following quadratic equations.

(a) $x^2 + x - 4 = 0$

(b) $2x^2 - 2x - 7 = 0$

(c) $x^2 - 6x - 1 = 0$

(d) $3x^2 - 12x + 3 = 0$

(e) $2x^2 - x - 2 = 0$

(f) $x^2 - 6x + 2 = 0$

4. Sketch the graph of the following functions. On your graphs indicate clearly the coordinates of the turning point and the intercepts with the y–axis.

(a) $y = (x-1)^2 + 3$

(b) $y = (x+2)^2 - 1$

(c) $y = 4 - (x-2)^2$

(d) $y = 2(x+1)^2 - 4$

(e) $y = 9 - (x+3)^2$

(f) $y = \frac{1}{2}(x+4)^2 + 2$

5. Sketch the graph of the following functions. On each graph indicate clearly all intercepts with the axes.

(a) $y = x^2 - 2x$

(b) $y = x^2 - 4x - 5$

(c) $y = 9 - x^2$

(d) $y = -x^2 + 6x - 5$

(e) $y = x^2 - 6x + 12$

(f) $y = x^2 - 6x + 9$

QUESTIONS

LEVEL

LEVEL 4

1. Find the coordinates of the turning point on the graph of the function
$y = x^2 + kx + 4$ in terms of the parameter k, where k is a real number.

2. (a) Show that $N = a^2 - 3a + 3$ is positive for all real values of a.
(b) Find the minimum value of N.

3. A stone is thrown vertically upwards so that its height, h m, above the ground,
t seconds after it is released is given by $h = 1.5 + 10t - 5t^2$.
(a) How long does it take for the stone to get back to the ground?
(b) What is the maximum height reached by the ball?
(c) How long will the stone remain above a height of 5 metres?
(d) Illustrate the path of the stone by sketching the graph of h.

4. (a) On the same set of axes, sketch the graphs of $y = x^2 - 3x + 2$ and
$y = 4 - x^2$, showing all intercepts with the axes.
(b) Solve the quadratic equation $2x^2 - 3x - 2 = 0$.
(c) Hence, find the coordinates of the points of intersection of the curves in (a).

5. What number(s) when added to its reciprocal gives 5?

6. Had Pablo walked 1 km/hr faster, he would have saved 1 hour in travelling 17 km.
How fast was Pablo walking? (Give your answer to two decimal places).

7. (a) Solve for x: $\dfrac{x}{a} + \dfrac{1}{x} + \left(1 + \dfrac{1}{a}\right) = 0$.

(b) Hence, solve the quadratic equation $0.5x^2 + 1 + 1.5x = 0$.

8. Jonathan is looking to invest money. He decides on three different investment
schemes, which he refers to as scheme A, B and C.
The details are:
Scheme A – invests $\$\,a$ paying interest at a rate of x per cent per annum,
compounded annually.
Scheme B – invests $\$\,(a + 100)$ paying simple interest at a rate of $(x - 1)$ per cent
per annum.
Scheme C – invests $\$\,(a + 50)$ paying simple interest at a rate of x per cent per
annum.
At the end of two years, scheme A earned as much interest as scheme C, which in
turn, exceeded the amount earned in scheme B by $40.00.
Find the values of x and a.

QUESTIONS

EXAMINATION STYLE

LEVEL

1

2

3

4

ES

T
E
S
T

1. The height reached by a ball thrown into the air is modelled by the function
$h = -5t^2 + 12t$ where t is the time in seconds after the ball is thrown and h is its height in metres.

    i.   Find the height of the ball after 2 seconds.

    ii.   Complete the square on the function and hence find the maximum height of the ball and the time at which this is achieved.

    iii.   Find the times at which the stone is 5 metres from the ground, correct to three significant figures.

    iv.   Find the total time that the ball is in the air.

2. A square, ABCD, of side length 5 cm is shown below.

The points X and Y are on the sides AB and AD respectively and are such that BX = CY.

(a)   If CY = x cm, write an expression for the shaded areas in terms of x.

(b)   Given that the ratio of the area of ΔDCY to the area of ΔXBY is 4:3, find x.

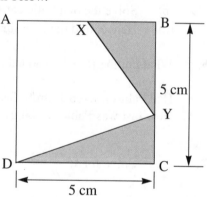

3. The graph of $y = x^2 + ax + b$ is shown.

(a)   Determine the values of a and b.

(b)   What is the minimum value of y?

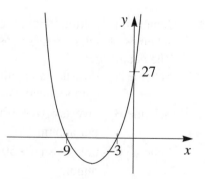

LEVEL QUESTIONS

1
2
3
4

ES

T
E
S
T

TEST

1. Solve the equation $x^2 - 6x - 7 = 0$.

Hence, sketch the graph of $y = x^2 - 6x - 7$, showing all axial intercepts.

[4 marks]

2. Factorise the following.

(a) $x^2 - 12x + 32$ (b) $x^2 - 12x + 36$ (c) $x^2 - 12x + 30$

[6 marks]

3. Find the values of x such that $5 - 3x - 3x^2 = 0$, correct to three significant figures.

[2 marks]

4. The diagram shows a quadratic graph.

Find an appropriate equation for the graph.
Hence find the coordinates of the maximum point.

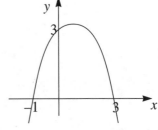

[5 marks]

5. Solve the equation $x = 1 + \dfrac{6}{x}$.

[3 marks]

6. The perimeter of a three sided rectangular enclosure is 100 metres.

(a) Find the dimensions of the rectangle in terms of x.
(b) Express the area of the enclosure in terms of x.
(c) Find the maximum area enclosed by the rectangle.

[5 marks]

7. Parts of the graphs of $y = -x^2 + 14x - 40$ and $y = 8x - x^2$ are shown below.

(a) Factorise i. $-x^2 + 14x - 40$

ii. $8x - x^2$

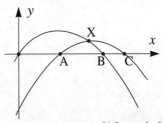

Hence, find the coordinates of A, B and C.
(b) Find the x-coordinate of the point X.
(c) Find the area of the triangle BCX.

[10 marks]
Total 35 marks

QUESTIONS

LEVEL

LEVEL 1

1. List the elements of the set $X = \{\, x \mid x \in \mathbb{N},\, 3 \le x < 8 \,\}$.

2. Let p represent " It is hot" and q represent "I will go swimming". Using p and q, write in symbolic form: "If it is hot, then I will *not* go swimming".

3. Copy the Venn diagram and shade the region
    i. $A \cap B$ ii. $A \cap B'$ iii. $A' \cap B'$

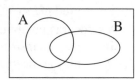

LEVEL 2

1.   i.   What is the converse of $\neg p \Rightarrow q$?
    ii.   If x represents "She is tall" and y represents "She is beautiful", write in symbolic form: "She is not tall and she is beautiful".

2. Draw a Venn diagram to display the following information:
    $n(U) = 60$, $n(A) = 28$, $n(B) = 18$ and $n(A \cap B) = 10$.

LEVEL 3

1.   i.   Copy and complete the following truth table.

p	q	$\neg p$	$\neg p \Rightarrow q$	$p \vee q$	$(\neg p \Rightarrow q) \Leftrightarrow (p \vee q)$

    ii.   Is $(\neg p \Rightarrow q) \Leftrightarrow (p \vee q)$ a tautulogy?
    iii.   Let p represent: "I do my training" and q represent: "I get into trouble".
        Write down a sentence which is equivalent to $(p \vee q)$.

2. If $x + y$ stands for x or y and xy stands for x and y, write down the following statements as simply as possible.
    i. $x + xy$ ii. $xy' + x'y + xy$

LEVEL 4

1. Using the propositions
    p: the line drawn from the vertex of a triangle to the midpoint of the opposite side does not intersect this side at a right angle.
    q: the triangle is not equilateral.
    Prove that "If a median does not intersect the third side at a right angle, the triangle cannot be equilateral".

2. Simplify the expression $A' \cup B' \cup (A \cap B \cap C')$ using the laws of sets.

LEVEL QUESTIONS

1
2
3
4

EXAMINATION STYLE

1. In a classroom of 62 students, it was found that 40 played an instrument and 25 played a sport. Seventeen of the students who play an instrument also played a sport. Use I to represent the set of students who play an instrument, S to represent the set of students who play a sport and U as the universal set.

    i.   Draw and label fully a Venn diagram to illustrate this information.

    ii.   Find n($I \cap S'$).

A student is randomly selected from the class. What is the probability that they

    iii.   play an instrument and play a sport?

    iv.   play an instrument but do not play a sport?

    v.   play a sport given they play an instrument.

ES **TEST**

T
E
S
T

1. Use the Venn diagram to shade the region

    i. $A' \cap B$ ii. $(A \cap B)'$

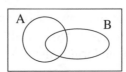

[4 marks]

2. Let x represent the statement "The number is an even integer" and y the statement "Three times the number is 18". Analyse each statement and then decide which statement(s) is(are) true if the number is 4?

    A. $x \wedge y$ B. $x \vee y$ C. y D. $x \Rightarrow y$

[5 marks]

3. Represent the following information, n(U) = 50, n(A) = 18, n(B) = 8 and n($A \cap B$) = 5 using a Venn diagram and use it to find n($A \cap B'$).

[4 marks]

4. i.   Using the following headings, complete the truth table below.

p	q	$p \Rightarrow q$	$\neg q$	$p \wedge \neg q$	$\neg(p \wedge \neg q)$	$(p \Rightarrow q) \Leftrightarrow \neg(p \wedge \neg q)$
T	T					
T	F					
F	T					
F	F					

    ii.   Let p represent the statement "Nora lives in Sydney" and let q represent the statement "Nora lives in New South Wales".

        (a)   With the aid of the table in part i., write the statement which is equivalent to

    "If Nora lives in Sydney, then Nora lives in New South Wales".

[10 marks]

5. In a class of 37 students, 20 have played volleyball and 22 have played basketball. If 25 have played at least one of these two sports,

    i.   how many played neither sport?

A student is randomly selected from the class. What are the chances that they

    ii.   have not played volleyball?

    iii.   played volleyball but not basketball?

[8 marks]

Total 31 marks

QUESTIONS

LEVEL

LEVEL 1

Find the values of the pronumerals in each of the following diagrams:

1. 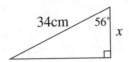 34cm 56° x

2. 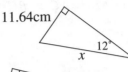 11.64cm 12° x

3. 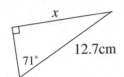 x 12.7cm 71°

4. 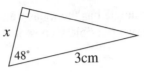 x 48° 3cm

5. 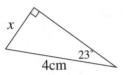 x 4cm 23°

6. 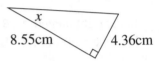 x 8.55cm 4.36cm

7. 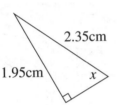 2.35cm 1.95cm x

8. 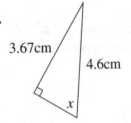 3.67cm 4.6cm x

LEVEL 2

Find the values of the pronumerals in each of the following diagrams:

1. 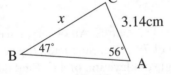 C x 3.14cm B 47° 56° A

2. 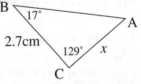 B 17° A 2.7cm 129° x C

3. 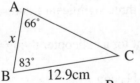 A 66° x 83° B 12.9cm C

4. 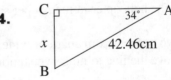 C 34° A x 42.46cm B

5. 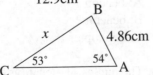 B x 4.86cm C 53° 54° A

6. 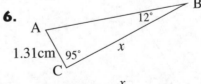 B 12° A 1.31cm 95° x C

7. 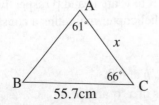 A 61° x B 66° C 55.7cm

8. 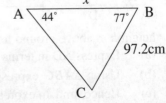 A 44° 77° B x 97.2cm C

LEVEL QUESTIONS

1

2

3

4

ES

T
E
S
T

LEVEL 3

1. For the $\triangle ABC$ shown alongside, where $AB = AC = BC = DC = 1$, find x.

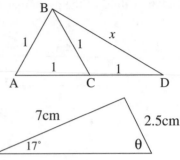

2. A triangle has the measurements shown. Find the two possible values of θ.

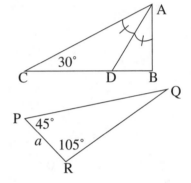

3. Solve the triangle in which $a = 2$, $b = 1.7$, $C = 63°$.

4. In the right-angled $\triangle ABC$, AD bisects $\angle BAC$. Find the ratio $BD:DC$.

5. Find the perimeter of $\triangle PQR$ giving your answer in terms of a.

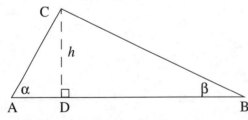

LEVEL 4

1. Andrea, Basie and Chai are standing on a sports field. Basie is standing 55 metres north of Andrea, Chai is south east of Basie and Andrea is 70 metres from Chai. Find the true bearing of Chai from Andrea.

2. A helicopter is travelling east at an altitude of 180 metres. An observer sees the helicopter east of her at an angle of elevation of 79°. A minute later, the helicopter is still east of the observer but now has an angle of elevation of 44°. Find the speed of the helicopter in metres per second correct to three significant figures.

3. Two beacons, x m apart, provide a reference point for a helicopter flying vertically above the line joining two stations A and B.

A: beacon 1
B: beacon 2
C: helicopter

The angles of elevation from A and B to C are α and β respectively. The helicopter maintains a constant height h m above ground level.

(a) Express AD in terms of h and α only.
(b) Using $\triangle ABC$ express AD in terms of x, h and β.
(c) Hence, find an expression for h in terms of x, α and β.

QUESTIONS

LEVEL

EXAMINATION STYLE

1. During a sailing race 'Team Doldrum' sail 650 metres on a bearing of 060° true. They then turn onto a bearing of 200° true and sail for another 220 metres. Next, they turn onto a bearing of 300° true and sail for 470 metres.

    i. Find the distance travelled in a north/south direction during the first leg (650 metres on a bearing of 060° true).

    ii. Find the distance travelled in a east/west direction during the first leg.

    iii. Find the distances travelled in the north/south and east/west directions during the second leg (200° true for 220 metres).

    iv. Find the distances travelled in the north/south and east/west directions during the third leg (300° true for 470 metres).

    v. Find the distances in the north/south and east/west directions that 'Team Doldrum' are from their starting point, correct to the nearest metre.

    vi. Find the distance 'Team Doldrum' are from their starting point, correct to the nearest metre.

    vii. Find the bearing that 'Team Doldrum' will need to sail if they are to return direct to their starting point.

1
2
3
4

ES

T
E
S
T

2. A piece of jewellery is in the shape of an isosceles triangle. The two equal sides are of length 5mm and the angle between them is 25°. Find the area of the piece in square centimetres, correct to three significant figures.

3.   (a) Draw a second triangle ABC based on the length measurements of the triangle PQR shown alongside.

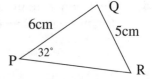

  (b) Find the two possible lengths that PR can have.

  (c) What is the difference in areas of $\triangle PQR$ and $\triangle ABC$.

Give your answers correct to three significant figures.

4. Belinda walks east from a point A for 450 metres at v m/s. She then turns 40° to her left and walks for a further 620 metres at u m/s where she reaches point B.

  (a) Draw a diagram showing Belinda's path.

  (b) Find Belinda's distance from her starting point, correct to the nearest metre.

Had Belinda walked in a staight line from A to B, her speed would have been the average of v m/s and u m/s.

  (c)   i. Find the time taken by Belinda to get to B using her original path, giving your answer in terms of u and v,

      ii. Find the time difference between the two paths.

LEVEL

1
2
3
4
ES

T
E
S
T

1. Helen stands 120 metres from the base of a tower. From ground level where Helen is standing, the angle of elevation of the top of the tower is 31°. Find the height of the tower correct to the nearest tenth of a metre.

[2 marks]

2. Find the value of a in the triangle shown, giving your answer correct to five significant figures.

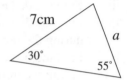

[2 marks]

3. Find the area of the triangle in the diagram, correct to four significant figures.

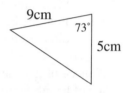

[2 marks]

4. Find, correct to the nearest degree, the largest angle in a triangle with sides of length 11cm, 12cm & 13cm.

[2 marks]

5. The bearing of D from X is N65°W and from Y it is N42°W. The point D is 50 km from the line joining XY and in a direction perpendicular to the line XY.
(a) Draw the diagram displaying the information given.
(b) Find the distance from X to Y.

[6 marks]
Total 14 marks

QUESTIONS

LEVEL

1
2
3
4

ES

T
E
S
T

CHAPTER 8

LEVEL 1

1. For the following equations, state their gradient and y–intercept.
   (a) $y = 3x - 1$ (b) $y = -(x + 1)$ (c) $2y = x + 4$

2. For the following set of points
   (a)   (3, 4) & (2, 4)   (b)   (5, 8) & (2, –2)   (c)   (2, 3) & (–2, –3), find
   i.   the measure of the distance between them.
   ii.   the gradient of the line joining them.
   iii. the coordinates of the mid-point of the line segment joining them.

3. For the following set of points
   (a)   (2, 4, 6) & (6, 4, 2)   (b)   (–1, 2, 1) & (0, –1, –2), find
   i.   the measure of the distance between them.
   ii.   the coordinates of the mid-point of the line segment joining them.

LEVEL 2

1. Find the gradient of the straight line perpendicular to each of the following.
   i. $y = 2x - 1$ ii. $y = 3 - \dfrac{1}{3}x$ iii. $5y = 2x + 10$

2. Find the equation of the straight line passing through (2, 3) with gradient 3.

3. Find the equation of the line passing through (1, 2) and perpendicular to the line with equation $2x + 3y + 1 = 0$.

4. Find the equation of the line passing through (1, 2) and parallel to the line with equation $x - 2y - 1 = 0$.

5. Find the equation of the straight lines shown.
   (a)
   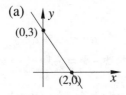
   (b)
   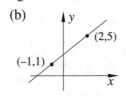
   (c)
   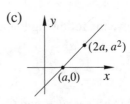

6. Find the point of intersection for each of the following linear systems.
   (a) $\begin{aligned} y &= x + 2 \\ y &= -x + 4 \end{aligned}$ (b) $\begin{aligned} x + y &= 6 \\ 2x - y &= 3 \end{aligned}$ (c) $\begin{aligned} -x + y - 1 &= 0 \\ 2x + y + 2 &= 0 \end{aligned}$

LEVEL QUESTIONS

1

2

3

4

ES

T

E

S

T

LEVEL 3

1. Find the value(s) of m for which the equations $y = mx + 1$ and $y = 2x + 4$ have
    (a)   no solution.   (b)   one real solution.

2. An initially full 500 ml water tank is leaking at a constant rate of 100 ml per hour.
    (a)   Contruct a table of values showing this relationship.
    (b)   Plot a graph using your table.
    (c)   Find an algebraic model for the amount of water, V ml, left in the tank after
         t hours.

3. For what value of k will the lines
    (a) $kx - y = 9$ (b) $2x + ky = 4$
    be   i.   parallel
         ii.   perpendicular
    to the line with equation $y = 3x + 5$?

4. Given that $4a - 5b = 2c$ and $3a + b = 3c$, find the ratio $a:b$.

5. Find the coordinates of A on the diameter AB of a circle, if B has the coordinates (–2, 4) and the centre of the circle has coordinates (1, 2).

6. (a)   On the rectangular coordinate axes Ox, Oy
         and Oz, drawn alongside, plot the points
         P(3, 2, 0), Q(0, 4, 3) and R(4, 0, 0).
    (b)   Draw the triangle PQR.
    (c)   Find the length of the side PQ.
    (d)   Find the mid–point of $\overline{PR}$.

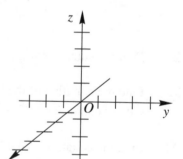

LEVEL 4

1. The points A(3, 2), B(m, 1) and C(1, –4) are collinear. Find m.

2. Solve the following linear systems:
    (a) $\begin{array}{l} y = ax - 1 \\ y = -x + a \end{array}$ (b) $\begin{array}{l} 2ax + y = 1 \\ x - ay = 1 \end{array}$ (c) $\begin{array}{l} ay = x + a \\ x - y = -1 \end{array}$

3. The vertices A, B and C of a triangle are (0, 6), (–2, 3) and (3, 4) respectively.
    i.   Draw the triangle on a set of axes.
    ii.   Show that the triangle ABC is an isosceles right-angled triangle.
    iii.   Find the coordinates of a fourth point, D, if ABCD is to be a square.

4. Find the coordinates of the point of intersection of the lines $bx + y = ab$ and
    $ax - by = a^2$, where a and b are real numbers.

QUESTIONS

5.   Find the value of a if the lines $ax + 3y = 5$ and $2x + (a+1)y = 6$ are
(a)   parallel.   (b)   perpendicular.

6.   Solve the system of equations $\begin{array}{l} ax + 2y = a \\ 8x + ay = 2a \end{array}$
for the case where (a) $a = 2$.   (b) $a = -4$.   (c) $a = 4$.

7.   Let ABC be a triangle with vertices at $A(-2a, 0)$, $B(2a, 0)$ and $C(2b, 2c)$.
i.   Draw the triangle on a set of axes.
ii.   Find the coordinates of the midpoints of AB, AC and BC and mark these on
your diagram.
iii.   Show that the equation of the median through

(a)   C is $y = \dfrac{c}{b}x$.

(b)   A is $(3a + b)y - cx - 2ac = 0$.

iv.   Prove that the medians of a triangle are concurrent.

EXAMINATION STYLE

1.   A triangle ABC is drawn on the set of axis as shown.
The slope of BX is $-\dfrac{1}{3}$ and $BX \perp AC$.

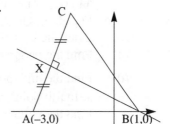

i.   Find the equation of
(a)   BX   (b)   AC
ii.   Find the coordinates of X.
iii.   Find the area of the triangle ABC.

2.   The line $ax + by + 10 = 0$ passes through the point $(-1, 2)$ and is perpendicular
to the line with equation $8x - 12y + 16 = 0$. Find the values of a and b.

3.   i.   (a)   Sketch the graph of $y = 2x^2$.
(b)   Find the gradient of this curve when $x = k$, $k > 0$.
ii.   Find the equation of the straight line which touches this curve when $x = k$.
This straight line is perpendicular to the line with equation $4y + x = 16$.
iii.   Find the value of k.
iv.   Find the area of the triangle enclosed by the straight lines and the x-axis.

LEVEL ░░░░░░░░░░░░░░░░░░░ **QUESTIONS**

1

2

3

4

ES

T
E
S
T

TEST

1. On the same set of axes, sketch the graph of the straight lines $2y - x = 8$ and
$y = 4 - x$.
The lines intersect the x–axis at A and B, how far apart are A and B?

[4 + 2 marks]

2. Using the points with coordinates (3, 5) and (5, 1) find
  i.   the measure of the distance between.
  ii.   the gradient of the line joining.
  iii.   the coordinates of their mid-point.

[2 + 2 + 2 marks]

3. Solve the system of linear equations $6x = 5y + 3$ and $8y = 12x + 6$.

[3 marks]

4. Find the relationship between p and q if the simultaneous equations $px - 3y = 8$
and $qx + y = 4$
  (a)   are perpendicular.
  (b)   have no real solution.

[4 marks]

5. (a)   On the rectangular coordinate axes Ox, Oy
            and Oz, drawn alongside, plot the points
            P(2, 2, 0), Q(–2, 0, 0) and R(0, –2, 0).
  (b)   Draw the triangle PQR.
  (c)   Find the length of the side PQ.
  (d)   Find the mid–point of $\overline{PR}$.
  (e)   A fourth point, S has coordinates (1, 1, 4).
            Find the volume of the rectangular prism
            PQRS.

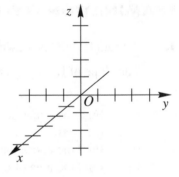

[2 + 1 + 2 + 2 + 4 marks]

6. OABC is a parallelogram as shown on the set of
    axes.
  i.   Find the coordinates of B.
  ii.   Find the midpoint of AC and OB.
  iii.   What can you deduce about the diagonals
            of a parallelogram?
  iv.   If OABC is now a rhombus, what are the coordinates of B?
  v.   Find the gradients of OB and AC for this rhombus.
  vi.   What can you deduce about the diagonals of a rhombus?

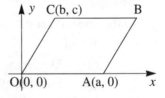

[2 + 4 + 1 + 1 + 3 + 3 marks]

Total 44 marks

QUESTIONS

LEVEL

LEVEL 1

1. For the cube of edge length 8 cm, find
  i.   the length of *DB*.
  ii. the inclination of the diagonal *BH*.

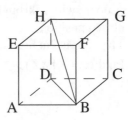

2. The right pyramid shown of vertical height 15 cm stands on a square base of edge length 5cm. Find
  i.   the length *AC*.
  ii. the inclination of the edge *AV*.

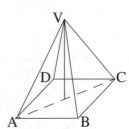

LEVEL 2

1. For the wedge shown alongside, find
  i.   the length of *BE*.
  ii. the inclination of *AE* with the base.
  iii. the ∠*AED*.

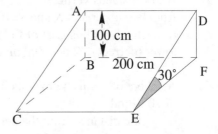

2. In the diagram alongside X is the midpoint of FG, where AB = 10 cm, BC = 6 cm and CG = 5 cm. Find the angle that AX makes with the base.

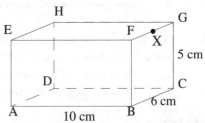

3. A square pyramid stands on a square base of side length 8cm. Each triangular face makes an angle of 60° with the base. Find the height of the pyramid.

4. A hemispherical bowl of diameter 12 cm is filled with water to a depth of 5 cm. Find the radius of the surface of the water level.

5. A book 17.6 cm wide and 24.1 cm long is opened at an angle of 30°.
  i.   Find the shortest distance between the edge BC and edge EF.
  ii. Find ∠*ECF*.

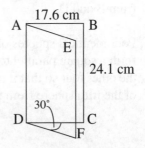

LEVEL

QUESTIONS

1

2

3

4

ES

T

E

S

T

LEVEL 3

1. A door swings through an angle of 40° from its closed position.
The door is 2m high and 1 m wide.
Find α, (∠YXZ).

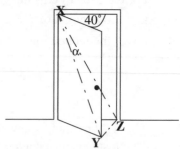

2. i. A solid sphere of radius r rests on top of a solid cylinder of radius r and height $3r$. How high from the base of the cylinder is the top of the sphere?

ii. A solid sphere rests on top of a vertical hollow cylinder having a diameter of 10 cm which is open at the top. The sphere projects 10 cm above the top of the cylinder. What is the length of the diameter of the sphere?

3. A tower stands vertically on a horizontal plane. The angles of elevations from two observers X and Y, 100m apart to the top of the tower are 45° and 30° respectively. X lies East of the tower and Y lies South of X. Find the height of the tower (correct to 2 decimal places).

4. A sphere of radius 4 cm rests in a hollow inverted cone with a semi-vertical angle of 20°. Find
i. the distance from the centre of the sphere to the vertex of the cone.
ii. how close the sphere gets to the vertex of the cone.

5. A camera is resting on a tripod. The legs of the tripod rest on a plane and even surface and form a regular tetrahedron with side lengths 1.2 m.
i. How high is the camera from the ground?
ii. Find the angles that the legs of the tripod make with the ground.

LEVEL 4

1. Calculate the angle between two adjacent faces of a regular tetrahedron.

2. A mast is erected at the corner A of a rectangular field ABCD. The angle of elevation of the top of the mast from C is $\alpha°$ and the side length of the rectangle are AB = a m and BC = b m. Find the angle of elevation of the top of the mast from B and D.

3. Four identical spheres of radius r are placed together on table so that their centers form a square parallel to the table. A fifth identical sphere is now placed on top of the other four so that it makes contact with all four spheres. How high is the centre of the fifth sphere from the table?

QUESTIONS

LEVEL

EXAMINATION STYLE

1. A sculpture has been constructed in such a way that it has a square base of side length 5 m and the surface of its top is a square base of side length 3 m. The edges are 10 m in length. The sculpture is then finished off by placing a square pyramid on top, also of side length 3 m with slant edges of length 5 m. The diagram (not drawn to scale) shows this information.

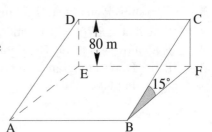

Give your answers to two decimal places.

   i.   Find the angle between the
       (a)   face BCGF and the base ABCD.
       (b)   edge GC and the base ABCD.
   ii.   How high above the plane ABCD is the plane EFGH?
   iii.   Find the angle between two opposite faces of the square pyramid EFGHV.
   iv.   How high is the vertex V from the base ABCD?
   v.   If the sculpture had been completed as a square pyramid rather than having a square pyramid postioned on top as in the diagram, which version would have resulted in the highest vertex from the base ABCD and by how much?

1
2
3
4

ES

T
E
S
T

2. (a) A hillside ABCD is sloping at an angle of 15° to the ground ABFE. The track BD makes an angle of 40° with the line of greatest slope, BC. The point D is 80 m vertically above E.

Find
   i.   the length of BC.
   ii.   the length of BD.
   iii. the angle that the track BD makes with the plane ABFE.

(b) For a similar hill, the following measurements were obtained. The angles of elevations to D' from the points A', B' and G', where A', B' and G' lie on a straight line, are given by $\tan\alpha = \frac{1}{12}$, $\tan\beta = \frac{1}{14}$ and $\tan\gamma = \frac{1}{18}$.

The distance from A' to B' is 80 m, from B' to G' it is 40 m and from D' to E' it is h m.

   i.   Show that $A'E' = 12h$, $B'E' = 14h$ and $G'E' = 18h$.

   ii.   Using $\triangle A'B'E'$, $\triangle B'G'E'$ and the fact that $\angle G'B'E' = 180° - \angle A'B'E'$, find h, giving your answer to three significant figures.

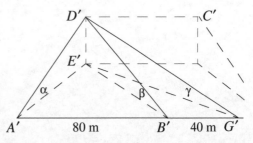

29

LEVEL QUESTIONS

1
2

TEST

1. A triangle ABC rests on a horizontal plane with a third point X vertically above the point B. Find the length of CX.

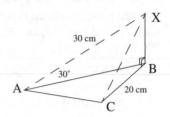

3

4

[3 marks]

ES

T
E
S
T

2. The right pyramid, ABCDV has its rectangular base ABCD on a horizontal plane and its vertex V vertically above ABCD, with AV = BV = CV = DV. Using the given dimensions, find the angle
i.   between the face ABV and the base.
ii.   between the edge AV and the base.
iii.   the plane ABV and the plane DCV.

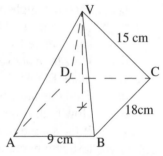

[9 marks]

3. Two ships P and Q are 1.5 km apart. From the top of a nearby lighthouse R, we have that $\angle RPQ = 61°$ and $\angle RQP = 52°$. The angle of elevation of R from P is 8° above sea level. The lighthouse is h m tall.
i.   Draw a diagram to represent this situation.
ii.   Find the value of h.

[7 marks]

4. A vertical wall in the shape of a trapezium casts a shadow on the ground when the sun is at an angle of elevation of $\theta°$. The vertical heights of the wall are x m and $1.6x$ m while its length is $\dfrac{10}{x}$ m.
i.   Represent this information using a diagram.
ii.   Find the area of the shaded region cast by the wall.

[6 marks]
Total: 25 marks

QUESTIONS

LEVEL

LEVEL 1

1. Simplify these vector expressions:

i. $\begin{pmatrix} 2 \\ 4 \end{pmatrix} + \begin{pmatrix} -7 \\ 5 \end{pmatrix}$ ii. $\begin{pmatrix} a \\ b \\ c \end{pmatrix} - \begin{pmatrix} 3a \\ -2a \\ -a \end{pmatrix}$ iii. $\begin{pmatrix} 3 \\ 2 \end{pmatrix} - \begin{pmatrix} -1 \\ 4 \end{pmatrix}$

2. Write the following in the form $a\vec{i} + b\vec{j}$ where a & b are scalars.

i. $(2\vec{i} - \vec{j}) + (3\vec{i} + 4\vec{j})$ ii. $(2\vec{i} + 8\vec{j}) + (2\vec{i} + 4\vec{j})$

iii. $(a\vec{i} - b\vec{j}) - (2a\vec{i} + 5b\vec{j})$ iv. $(\vec{i} - 5\vec{j}) + (\vec{i} + 4\vec{j}) - (\vec{i} + 5\vec{j})$

3. Consider the parallelogram OACB.
Express in terms of a and b, the vectors

i. $\overrightarrow{OC}$ ii. $\overrightarrow{BA}$

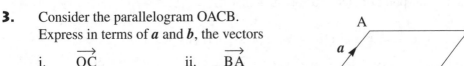

LEVEL 2

1. Find:

i. $\left\| \begin{pmatrix} 2 \\ -4 \end{pmatrix} \right\|$ ii. $5i - j + xk$ iii. $\left\| \begin{pmatrix} -3 \\ 2 \end{pmatrix} \right\|$

2. Find a unit vector in the same direction as:

i. $\begin{pmatrix} 2 \\ 3 \end{pmatrix}$ ii. $7i + 2j - k$ iii. $-2\vec{i} + 7\vec{j}$

LEVEL 3

1. M is the midpoint of AB. Find x in terms of a and b.

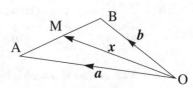

2. The vectors $a = 6i + 9j$ and $b = xi + (x + 1)j$ are parallel. Find x.

LEVEL 4

1. In the $\triangle ABC$, D and E are the mid-points of $\overline{AC}$ and $\overline{BC}$ respectively. Show that the line segment $\overline{DE}$ is parallel to and half the length of the line segment $\overline{AB}$.

2. Find a unit vector in the direction of the tangent to the curve $y = x^3$ at the point (1,1) and a unit vector in the direction of the inner normal at the same point.

CHAPTER 10

LEVEL 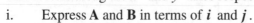 QUESTIONS

1
2
3
4

EXAMINATION STYLE

1. Forces **A** and **B** of magnitude 400 and 300 force units respectively act as shown in the diagram. If i and j are unit vectors along the x– and y– axes respectively.

    i.   Express **A** and **B** in terms of i and j.
    ii.   Find the resultant force, **R**.
    iii.   Find the magnitude of **R** and the angle it makes with the x–axis.

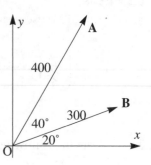

ES

**T
E
S
T**

2. On the triangle OAB, point X is such that $\overrightarrow{OX} = \frac{3}{4}\overrightarrow{OB}$, while Y is the mid-point of $\overline{AB}$ and Z is such that $\overrightarrow{OZ} = \frac{3}{2}\overrightarrow{OA}$.

    (a)   If $\overrightarrow{OA} = x$ and $\overrightarrow{OB} = y$, express, in terms of x and y

         i. $\overrightarrow{OY}$ ii. $\overrightarrow{XY}$ iii. $\overrightarrow{YZ}$
    (b)   Hence, show that the points X, Y and Z are collinear.

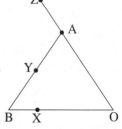

TEST

1. If $\vec{a} = 3\vec{i} + 2\vec{j}$ and $\vec{b} = 6\vec{i} - 5\vec{j}$ find:

    i. $\vec{a} + \vec{b}$ ii. $|\vec{a} - \vec{b}|$ iii. $5\vec{a} - 2\vec{b}$

                                                           [6 marks]

2. Find a unit vector in the same direction as $\begin{pmatrix} 5 \\ -2 \end{pmatrix}$.

                                                            [2 marks]

3. OABC is a trapezium, $\overrightarrow{AB}$ is parallel to $\overrightarrow{OC}$ and $\overrightarrow{AB} = 2\overrightarrow{OC}$. Express in terms of **a** and **c**

    i. $\overrightarrow{AB}$ ii. $\overrightarrow{OB}$ iii. $\overrightarrow{CB}$

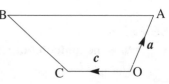

                                                            [4 marks]

4. Two forces, **A** and **B** act on a box at O as shown in the diagram. If i and j are unit vectors along the x– and y– axes respectively,

    i.   express **A** and **B** in terms of i and j.
    ii.   find the magnitude of resultant force, **R**.

                                                            [6 marks]

5. Show that the line segments joining the mid-points of the sides of any quadrilateral ABCD form a parallelogram.

                                                            [6 marks]
                                                            Total 24 marks

QUESTIONS

LEVEL

LEVEL 1

1. The diagram shows the number of children in ten families:

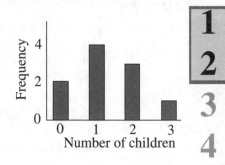

   i.   What is the modal number of children?
   ii.   What is the total number of children?
   iii. What is the mean number of children per family?
   iv. What percentage of the families have one child?

2. Tally the following data into groups 0-4, 5-9, 10-14 etc.

        12   14   24   22   18   7   4   8   19   21   13

   i.   What is the frequency of the 0-4 group?
   ii.   What is the frequency of the 20-24 group?
   iii. What is/are the modal groups?

3. The pie chart shows the proportions of a group of 200 students who play various musical instruments.

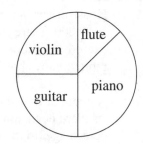

How many students play the piano?

LEVEL 2

1. Find the means of these data sets correct to three significant figures:

   i.   4   3   2   5   2   1   0   0   2   4   0
   ii.   11   9   4   8   22   31   6   3   22   19   16
   iii.   1.4   1.9   2.7   3.8   4.1   3.2   6.8   5.5   3.9   8.5   2.7
   iv.   12.8   9   14   2.6   7.2   6.8   6.8   5.9   12.8   4.8   19.4
   v.   33.9 45.2 98.7 45.7 2.9 53.8 45.1 84.2 64.7 48.2 55.9

2. Find the modes of these data sets:

   i.   3   5   6   2   6   5   7   4   4   3   4
   ii.   5   4   3   3   0   0   2   1   4   3   1
   iii. 11   14   12   12   13   14   15   11   10   12   12
   iv.   10   10   14   13   13   12   11   11   13   12   14
   v.   20   20   19   17   16   15   16   17   17   19   16

3. Find the medians of these data sets:

   i.   20   17   19   17   16   15   11   17   17   19   16
   ii.   31   62   73   11   4   15   88   45   12   6   71
   iii. 5.8   3.1   1.9   2.6   2.9   4.2   9.8   6.8   4.2   8.9   3.5
   iv.   12.3 54.9 4.6 28.5 83.5 66.7 2.1 6.7 55.9 49.1 84.8
   v.   0.1   0.8   0.4   0.7   1.9   4.1   0.4   1.1   8.2   0.4   1.4

LEVEL   QUESTIONS

1

2

3

4

ES

T

E

S

T

LEVEL 3

1. Find the quartiles of these data sets:

i.	3	7	2	8	3	5	9	1	5	2	0
ii.	19	43	91	59	83	62	77	14	82	53	22
iii.	23.5	71.4	55.8	11.8	84.6	54.9	92.6	84.2	17.9	34.8	33.8
iv.	25	11	4	5	13	19	21	6	10		
v.	5.4	6.8	3.4	8.9	3.6	2.9					

2. Find the standard deviations of these data sets, correct to three significant figures:

i.	4	6	2	5	8	1	9	4
ii.	11	75	62	89	71	82	4	68
iii.	3.4	7.9	10.1	5.1	0.3	7.4	8.2	5.3
iv.	124	638	342	836	532	539	842	44
v.	0.23	0.93	0.35	0.02	0.87	0.55	0.63	0.71

LEVEL 4

1. House prices in a particular suburb are generally in the region of $120 000 to $150 000. There are, however, a very small number of luxury homes whose values exceed $2 million. Which measure of average would you use to find a representative house value for this suburb and why?

2. A brand of tinned baked beans have a mean contents of 345 grams per tin with a standard deviation of 2.8 grams. Assuming that the distribution is normal, what percentage (to the nearest whole number) of the tins contain:
i. less than 347grams.
ii. more than 345.5 grams.
iii. between 343 and 346 grams.

If the lightest 1% of the cans are considered to be underweight:
iv. find the weight below which the cans are considered underweight.

3. The diagram shows the distribution of scores obtained by a group of 200 trainees, in an aptitude test (scored out of 10).

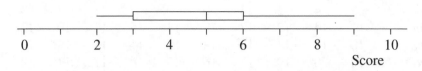

i. Find the number of students who scored more than 6 marks.
ii. Find the median mark.
iii. Find the least mark obtained by the group.
iv. Estimate the mean score.
v. Estimate the standard deviation of the distribution.

QUESTIONS

EXAMINATION STYLE

LEVEL

1

2

3

4

ES

T

E

S

T

1. The data below are the weights in grams of a sample of a species of small rodents.

3.5	5.2	6.9	2.8	8.4	12.1	9.4	5.7	1.9	6.2
4.4	5.7	4.9	8.5	9.2	9.9	4.2	7.9	3.4	6.8

i. Make a frequency table of these weights using the class intervals 0-0.9, 1.0-1.9 etc.

ii. Find the mean of these weights.

iii. Find the standard deviation of the weights correct to four significant figures.

Assuming that the weights of the population of the rodents are normally distributed with a mean and standard deviation the same as the sample, calculate:

iv. the proportion of animals that can be expected to weigh between 5 and 9 grams.

v. the percentage of animals that weigh more than 3.5 grams.

vi. the weight below which 90% of the animals might be expected to lie.

2. The diagram shows the distribution of weekly income of the employees of a small company.

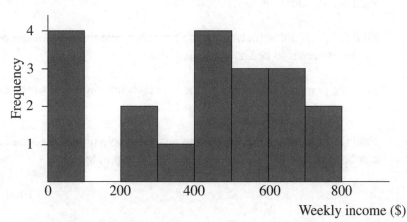

i. How many employees are recorded?

ii. Estimate the mean weekly income.

iii. Estimate the median wage.

iv. Explain the comparatively large number of employees that recive a low weekly wage.

v. If the owner of the company, who receives $1680 per week, is added to the data, which of these measures will be affected most; median or mean?

LEVEL

1

2

3

4

ES

TEST

T
E
S
T

1. The figures below are the heights (in cm, correct to the nearest cm) of a group of students:

175   179   180   179   178   181   180   177   178   180
177   180   181   178   179   179   180   178   177   181

   i.   Tally these data using no class intervals.

[2 marks]

   ii.   Show the results on an appropriate statistical graph.

[2 marks]

   iii.   Tally the data using class intervals of width 5cm. Which of the two tallies is the best for displaying the data?

[1 mark]

   iv.   Find the mode, mean and median of the data.

[3 marks]

   v.   Find the standard deviation and interquartile range of these data.

[4 marks]

2. The lengths of wooden fencing posts cut by a sawmill have a mean of 190cm and a variance of 1.44cm. Assume that the distribution is normal.

   i.   Find the standard deviation.

[1 mark]

   ii.   Find the percentage (correct to the nearest whole number) of the posts that can be expected to be shorter than 191cm.

[2 marks]

   iii.   Find the percentage (correct to the nearest whole number) of the posts that can be expected to be shorter than 188cm.

[2 marks]

   iv.   Find the percentage (correct to the nearest whole number) of the posts that can be expected to be between 189 and 192cm in length.

[2 marks]

Total 19 marks

QUESTIONS

LEVEL

LEVEL 1

1. What is the probability that a card drawn from a normal pack is a red ace?

2. A bag contains three red balls, four green balls and two white balls. If a ball is chosen at random, what is the probability that the ball is green?

3. The diagram shows a target. If projectiles are fired at this target at random, what is the probability that a single projectile hits the 3 sector?

4. If a letter is chosen at random from that word RANDOM, what is the probability that this letter is a vowel?

5. If a coin and a die are thrown together, what is the probability that the result is a head and an even number?

6. If a coin is spun twice, what is the probability that the two results are different?

LEVEL 2

1. The events A and B are such that $p(A) = 0.3$, $p(B) = 0.5$ and $p(A \cap B) = 0.1$
Find:
  i. $p(A \cup B)$ ii. $p(B')$ iii. $p(A' \cap B)$

2. A coin is tossed four times.
  i. How many outcomes are there in the sample space?
  ii. What is the probability of getting four heads?
  iii. What is the probability of getting the same number of heads as tails?
  iv. What is the probability of getting more heads than tails?

3. Two letters are randomly chosen, one after the other, from the word ARTICHOKE. What is the probability that these letters spell AT if:
  i. the same letter can be chosen twice
  ii. the same letter cannot be chosen twice?

4. In a group of 80 students, 35 play baseball, 25 play football and 30 play neither.
  i. Draw a Venn diagram to show these data.
  ii. What is the probability that a randomly selected student plays both baseball and football?
  iii. What is the probability that a randomly selected student plays baseball but not football?
  iii. What is the probability that a randomly selected student plays neither sport?

LEVEL

1
2
3
4
ES
T
E
S
T

CHAPTER 12

1
2
3
4
ES
T
E
S
T

LEVEL 3

1. Two events A and B are such that $p(A) = 0.5$, $p(B) = 0.4$ and $p(A \cap B) = 0.3$
Find:
   i. $p(A|B)$ ii. $p(B|A)$
   iii. Are the events A & B independent?

2. Two cards are drawn from a normal pack without replacement.
   i.   What is the probability that the second card is an ace given that the first card was not an ace?
   ii.   Are the two draws independent?
   iii. If we do not look at the first card, what is the probability that the second card is an ace?

3. Two letters are selected at random from the word ATTITUDE.
   (a)   If the letters are selected with the first one selected being replaced before the second one is made:
   i.   are the events independent?
   ii.   what is the probability that both letters are Ts?
   iii. what is the probability that both letters are vowels?

   (b)   If the letters are selected without replacement:
   i.   are the events independent?
   ii.   what is the probability that both letters are Ts?
   iii. what is the probability that both letters are vowels?

LEVEL 4

1. Given that $p(A) = 0.6$, $p(B) = 0.4$ and that A and B are independent events. Find the probability of the events:
   i. $A \cup B$ ii. $A \cap B$ iii. $A|B'$

2. A group of 200 language students, all of whom speak at least one language have the following languages:
Italian 99, japanese 115, german 87, italian and japanese 44, german and japanese 38 & italian and german 31.

   i.   Draw a Venn diagram to show this information.
   ii.   If a student is chosen at random, what is the probability that s/he speaks all three languages?
   iii. If a student is chosen at random, what is the probability that s/he speaks exactly two languages?
   iv.   If a student is chosen at random, what is the probability that s/he speaks italian given that she also speaks japanese?
   v.   If two students are randomly chosen to represent the group on a student council, are the selections independent of each other? Give a brief reason.

QUESTIONS   LEVEL

EXAMINATION STYLE

1. The following data represents the number of eggs laid each year by a species of
sea bird.

6	11	4	10	5	5	5	9	2	8
2	4	7	2	5	5	9	7	4	9
9	6	7	5	6	11	9	3	11	9
10	2	8	7	11	4	2	5	5	4

i.   Tally the data using class intervals of one.
ii.   What is the probability that a randomly chosen bird will lay more than 9
       eggs?
iii.   Find the mean number of eggs laid.
iv.   What is the probability that a randomly chosen bird will lay more than the
       average number of eggs?
v.   Find the standard deviation of the data, correct to four significant figures.
vi.   Find the number of eggs laid that lie within 1 standard deviation of the
       mean.
vii.   What is the probability that a randomly chosen bird will lay a number of
       eggs that is within 1 standard deviation of the mean?

2. A biassed coin has a probability of 0.6 of falling heads. The coin is spun three
times in succession and the number of heads counted.

i.   Explain why each spin is independent of the others.
ii.   Complete the following probability table:

Heads	Probability
0	
1	
2	
3	

iii.   If the first spin was a head, what is the probability that the next two throws
       will also be heads?

The coin is spun repeatedly until a tail is obtained.

iv.   What is the probability that the coin is spun ten times before the first tail in
       the sequence is obtained?

LEVEL ▮▮▮▮▮▮▮▮▮▮▮▮▮▮▮▮▮▮▮▮ **QUESTIONS**

1

2

3

4

ES

T
E
S
T

TEST

1. If a letter is chosen at random from the word SUSTENANCE, what is the probability that the letter is:

    i.   S.
    ii.   a vowel.

[3 marks]

2. If two cards are drawn from a normal pack:

    i   What is the probability that the first card is a 'club'?
    ii.   What is the probability that both cards are 'clubs'?
    iii. If the first card is black, what is the probability that the second is also black?

[5 marks]

3. Given that $p(A) = 0.2$, $p(B) = 0.8$ and that A and B are independent events.

    i.   Show the data as a Venn diagram.

Find the probability of the events:

    ii. $A \cup B$
    iii. $A \cap B$
    iv. $A|B$

[7 marks]

4. 'Weston Athletic' soccer club have a $\frac{3}{7}$ chance of winning each game. The result of each game is independent of any other games the club plays.

    i.   The club has won its last two games. What is the probability that it will win its next game?

    ii.   If the club plays four games in January, what is the probability that it will win exactly half of them?

    iii. If the club plays three games in May and has lost the first game, what is the probability that it will win the other two?

[5 marks]
Total 20 marks

QUESTIONS

LEVEL 1

1. State the domain and range of the following relations.

(a)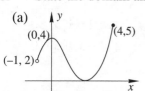

(b)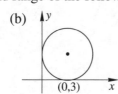

(c)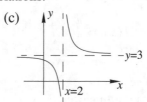

2. Which of the relations in question 1 are also functions?

3. Evaluate each of the following at $x = 2$.

(a) $y = x + 2$ (b) $y = (x + 2)^2 + 2$ (c) $f(x) = 2^x + 2$

LEVEL 2

1. Given that $f(x) = \dfrac{x}{x + 2}$, find $\{x : f(x) = 4\}$.

2. Find the largest possible set of x–values for which the following are defined.

(a) $x \mapsto \sqrt{2 - x}$ (b) $x \mapsto \sqrt{x - 3}$ (c) $x \mapsto \dfrac{1}{\sqrt{1 + x}}$

3. Given that $f(x) = 2x - 1$ and $g(x) = \dfrac{1}{x + 1}$ find

(a) $g(f(x))$ (b) $f(g(x))$

4. Sketch the graphs of the functions

(a) i. $x \mapsto x^2 + 1, \; x \in \mathbb{R}$ ii. $x \mapsto x^2 + 1, \; -1 \le x \le 2$
(b) State the range in each case.

5. For the function $f(x) = x^2 + 2x, \; x \in \mathbb{R}$, evaluate:

(a) $f(-1)$ (b) $f(2x)$ (c) $f(x - 2)$ (d) $f(x) - f(-x)$

6. Sketch the graphs of the following, clearly showing intercepts with all axes.

(a) $f : x \mapsto 4x - 2$ (b) $f : x \mapsto 5 - \dfrac{1}{2}x$ (c) $f : x \mapsto 2(3 - x)$

7. For the function $f(x) = x(x - 3), \; x \in \mathbb{R}$ find
(a) i. $f(3)$
  ii. $f(h)$
(b) $f(3 + h) - f(3)$

LEVEL

1

2

3

4

ES

T
E
S
T

CHAPTER 13

1
2
3
4

ES

T
E
S
T

LEVEL 3

1. Sketch the graphs of

(a) $f(x) = \begin{cases} x+1 & \text{if } x>1 \\ 2x & \text{if } x\le 1 \end{cases}$

(b) $f(x) = \begin{cases} 2 & \text{if } x\ge 0 \\ 1-x & \text{if } x<0 \end{cases}$

2. Given the function, $f: x \mapsto 3 + \dfrac{1}{x-2}$, $x \ne 2$, find   i. $f(3)$ ii. $f\left(\dfrac{2x+1}{x}\right)$

3. For the functions $f(x) = \dfrac{1}{x+1}$, $x \ne -1$ and $g(x) = \dfrac{1}{x} - 1$, find $g(f(x))$ and $f(g(x))$.

4. Using a graphics calculator, sketch each of the functions in question 1.

5. For the function $f(x) = \dfrac{x}{x-1}$, $x \ne 1$, find $\{x : f(x) = k\}$.

6. Sketch the graph of $f(x) = \begin{cases} \sqrt{x} & \text{if } x>4 \\ \sqrt{8-x} & \text{if } x\le 4 \end{cases}$.

LEVEL 4

1. If $f: S \mapsto \mathbb{R}$, where $f(x) = 4x - x^2$, find S, the largest subset of the positive real numbers set, such that f is an increasing function.

2. Find $\left\{x: f(x) = \dfrac{1}{f(x)}\right\}$ if $f: [0, \infty) \mapsto \mathbb{R}$, where $f(x) = x^2 - 2$.

3. Find the domain of the function $f : x \mapsto \dfrac{3}{\sqrt{9-x^2}}$. Sketch the graph of f.

4. The function f is defined by $f: x \mapsto 2x^2 - 2$, $x \in \mathbb{R}$.

(a) Find the integers a, b and c given that $f(x+2) = ax^2 + bx + c$.

(b) Find the values of x that satisfy the equation $f(x) + 2 = f(x+2)$.

5. (a) Sketch the graph of $f(x) = a + \dfrac{b}{x}$, $a > 1, b > 0$.

(b) On the same set of axes, sketch the graphs of

i. $y = f(x)$ ii. $y = (f(x))^2$

QUESTIONS

EXAMINATION STYLE

1. (a) Sketch the graph of $f(x) = x(4-x)$, $x \in \mathbb{R}$, showing all intercepts with the axes and giving the coordinates of the turning point.

(b) Define, I as the largest subset of $\mathbb{R}^+$ for which the function $f(x)$ will be a one–to–one function.

(c) i. Sketch the graph of $g: I \mapsto \mathbb{R}$ where $g(x) = f(x)$.

ii. State the range of $g(x)$.

2. Let the function f be defined by, $f(x) = \begin{cases} 4 & x < 0 \\ 4-x & 0 \le x \le 2 \\ \dfrac{4}{x} & x > 2 \end{cases}$

(a) Sketch the graph of f.

(b) State the range of f.

(c) Find the values of x for which $f'(x)$ does not exist.

3. A piecewise linear function is defined by $f(x) = \begin{cases} \dfrac{1}{2}x + k & \text{if } x > 2 \\ 2-x & \text{if } x \le 2 \end{cases}$.

(a) Sketch the graph of $f(x)$ if

i. $k = 0$ ii. $k = 2$ iii. $k = -2$

(b) Find k if the graph is to be continuous for all real values of x.

4. For the two functions, $f(x) = 9 - x^2$ and $g: [0, \infty) \mapsto \mathbb{R}$, where, $g(x) = \sqrt{x}$,

(a) Find $f(g(x))$.

(b) Let $h(x) = f(g(x))$

i. State the domain of $h(x)$.

ii. Sketch the graph of $h(x)$.

iii. Find the range of $h(x)$.

5. A relation is given by $f: x \mapsto 4 - \dfrac{3x}{4}$, for $0 \le x \le \dfrac{16}{3}$.

(a) Is this relation a function?

(b) Sketch the graph of f.

(c) For f, state

i. the domain

ii. the range.

(d) For what value of x will the image of f be 2?

LEVEL

1

2

3

4

ES

QUESTIONS

TEST

1. If $f : x \mapsto x^2 - \dfrac{1}{x} + 1$ find   i. $f(1)$ ii. $\{a : f(a) = 1\}$

[4 marks]

2. Sketch the graph of the linear piecewise function $f(x) = \begin{cases} 2x - 1 & \text{if } x > 4 \\ 4 & \text{if } x \le 4 \end{cases}$

[3 marks]

3. (a) Find the range of $f : x \mapsto 8x - x^2$, where $x \in \mathbb{R}$.

     (b) Hence, find the range of $f : x \mapsto k + 8x - x^2$, where $x \in \mathbb{R}$.

[4 marks]

T
E
S
T

4. A function is defined as $f(x) = \begin{cases} bx & 0 \le x < 1 \\ 2^{-kx} & x \ge 1 \end{cases}$, where $k > 0$.

     (a) If f is continuous in the interval $[0, \infty)$, show that $b \times 2^k = 1$.

     (b) Sketch the graph of f and state its range.

[3 + 3 marks]

5. The temperature, $T°C$ of kettle, t minutes after it is removed from the stove is

thought to be given by $T(t) = 30 + \dfrac{60}{t + 1}, t \ge 0$.

     (a) Complete the table below

t min	1	3	7	14	29	59
$T°C$						

     (b) Use your results of (a) to sketch the graph of $T(t) = 30 + \dfrac{60}{t + 1}, t \ge 0$.

     (c) What will the eventual temperature of the kettle be?

     (d) How long will it take the kettle to reach a temperature of 50°C?

[5 marks]

6. The minimum charge for a telegram is \$4.80 which includes the use of up to 10 words. Each additional word is charged at a rate of 40 cents. Show, on a graph, the cost of telegrams up to 14 words.

[4 marks]

7. Give the equations which define the graphs shown below.

(a)

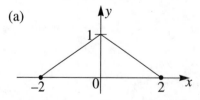

(b)

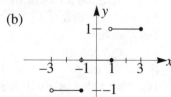

[6 marks]

Total 32 marks

QUESTIONS

LEVEL

LEVEL 1

1. Give exact values for:

    i. $\sin 90°$ ii. $\cos 30°$ iii. $\cos 45°$

    iv. $\cos 135°$ v. $\sin 120°$ vi. $\sin 300°$

2. Give values, correct to four signficant figures for:

    i. $\sin 23°$ ii. $\sin 145°$ iii. $\cos -10°$

    iv. $\sin 560°$ v. $\cos(-500°)$ vi. $\sin 15°47'$

LEVEL 2

1. State the maximum values reached by the following functions:

    i. $f(x) = 2\sin 3x$ ii. $f(x) = 1 - \cos x$ iii. $f(x) = 3 - 4\sin 2x$

    iv. $f(x) = \dfrac{1 + \cos x}{2}$ v. $f(x) = \sin\left(\dfrac{x}{4}\right)$ vi. $f(x) = 3 + \cos 4x$

2. State the period of these functions:

    i. $f(x) = 2\sin x$ ii. $f(x) = \cos\dfrac{x}{2}$ iii. $f(x) = \cos 3x$

    iv. $f(x) = \cos x$ v. $f(x) = \dfrac{1}{2}\sin\dfrac{x}{3}$ vi. $f(x) = 3\sin\dfrac{3x}{4}$

3. Find the y-intercepts of the following graphs:

    i. $y = \sin(x) + 1$ ii. $y = 2\cos x$ iii. $y = 2\sin(x) - 3$

LEVEL 3

1. Sketch the graphs of the following functions:

    i. $f(x) = 1 + \cos x, \; x \in [-360°, 360°]$

    ii. $f(x) = \cos(2x), \; x \in [-180°, 360°]$

    iii. $f(x) = 1 + 2\sin x, \; x \in [-360°, 360°]$

    iv. $f(x) = 1 - \dfrac{1}{2}\cos(2x), \; x \in [0°, 180°]$

    v. $f(x) = 3 + 2\sin(4x), \; x \in [0°, 90°]$

    vi. $f(x) = 2 - 3\cos\left(\dfrac{1}{2}x\right), \; x \in [0°, 360°]$

2. Find the smallest positive x-intercept of these graphs:

    i. $y = \cos 2x$ ii. $y = \sin 3x$ iii. $y = \cos\dfrac{x}{3}$

LEVEL QUESTIONS

1
2
3
4
ES
T
E
S
T

LEVEL 4

1. Give rules for the functions whose graphs are shown:

i.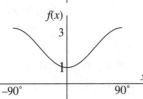

ii.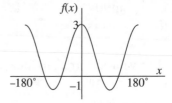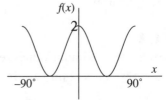

iii.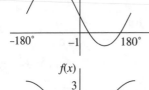

iv.

2. Solve the following equations giving all solutions in the intervals indicated. Where possible, give exact solutions. If exact solutions do not exist, give your answers correct to the nearest degree.

i. $2\sin x = 1, -360° \le x \le 360°$

ii. $2\cos x = \sqrt{3}, 0° \le x \le 360°$

iii. $\cos 2x = 0.3, 0° \le x \le 360°$

iv. $\cos 2x = 0.35, 0° \le x \le 180°$

v. $3\sin x + 1 = 0, 0° \le x \le 360°$

vi. $4\sin^2(2x) - 3 = 0, 0° \le x \le 180°$

3. The temperature (C°) over a 24 hour day in Montaville is modelled by the function:

$$C(t) = 18 - 6\cos(15t°), 0 \le t \le 24$$

where t is the time in hours after midnight.

i. What is the temperature at
    (a) midnight?
    (b) 2 pm?
ii. (a) What are the maximum and minimum temperatures reached?
    (b) When do the maximum and minimum temperatures occur?
iii. Sketch the graph of the function.
iv. At what times of the day is the temperature warmer than 20°C?
v. When is the temperature rising most rapidly. What is this largest rate of change?

QUESTIONS

EXAMINATION STYLE

1. A function is defined by: $f(x) = 3\sin(360x°)$ for $0 \le x \le 2$.

   i. What is the (a) period of the function?
             (b) amplitude of the function?

   ii. Sketch the graph of the function.

   iii. Find the average rate of change of the function over the interval $\left[\frac{1}{3}, \frac{1}{2}\right]$.

      Give your answer in exact form.

2. The height of the tide is h metres at time t hours, where $h = 5.5 + 1.5\sin(45t°)$.

   i. Copy and complete the table below.

t hours	0	1	2	3	4	5	6	7	8
h metres									

   ii. On a set of axes sketch the graph of $h = 5.5 + 1.5\sin(45t°)$, $0 \le t \le 24$.

   iii. Find the height of the tide at the following times
      (a) 12 hours. (b) 18 hours.

   iv. Find all the times in the first 24 hours when the height is 4.0 m.

3. A particle moves in a straight line according to the rule $x = 3 + 2\cos(120t°)$, where x metres is the distance from the origin O, t seconds after it started its motion.

   i. Find the
      (a) greatest distance reached by the particle from O.
      (b) least distance reached by the particle from O.

   ii. For $0 \le t \le 6$, find when the particle is 4 metres from O.

   iii. Sketch the graph of $x = 3 + 2\cos(120t°)$ for $0 \le t \le 6$.

   iv. For what percentage of the time is the particle at least 4 m from O during the first 6 seconds of its motion?

4. Florence is seated on one of the carriages at the local fair's Big Wheel. Her height, H metres above the ground after t seconds is given by the equation
$$H(t) = a\cos(kt°) + b, 0 \le t \le 12.$$

   i. The time it takes Florence to undergo one revolution is 12 seconds. Find the value of k.

   ii. When Florence steps into the carriage, she is 1 metre above the ground and six seconds later she is 21 metres above the ground. Find a and b.

   iii. Sketch the graph of H.

   iv. Find when Florence is 16 metres above the ground during one revolution.

   v. For what percentage of time is Florence at least 16 metres above the ground?

LEVEL QUESTIONS

1

2

3

4

ES

T
E
S
T

TEST

1. Give an exact value for   i. $\sin(-270°)$.   ii. $\cos(135°)$.

[2 marks]

2. State   i.   the amplitude
        ii.   the period
        iii.   the maximum value
of the function $f(x) = 5 - 2\sin(3x°)$.

[3 marks]

3. Find the smallest positive value of x such that $\sin 3x = \dfrac{1}{2}$. Give an exact answer.

[3 marks]

4. Sketch the graph of $y = 3 + 6\cos(60x°)$, $x \in [0, 6]$. Your sketch must include all intercepts with the axes.

[7 marks]

5. Find a function that has the graph shown:

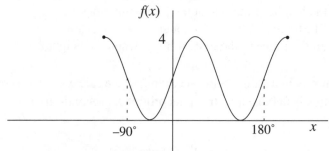

[4 marks]

6. The population, N, of a particular species of insect varies with time according to the model defined by the equation

$$N(t) = 2500\sin\left(\frac{90}{13}t°\right) + 4500,$$

where t is the time in weeks from the 1st of January 2000.

i.   State the period of $N(t)$.
ii.   State the largest and smallest population sizes reached by this species.
iii.   Sketch the graph of $y = N(t), 0 \le t \le 143$.
iv.   When will the species first reach
        (a)   its maximum size?
        (b)   6000?
v.   For the years 2000, during which months will the population be less than 3000?

[1 + 2 + 4 + 4 + 5 marks]
Total 35 marks

QUESTIONS

LEVEL 1

1. Sketch the following functions

    i. $f(x) = 2^x$ ii. $x \mapsto 0.3^x$ iii. $g(x) = 4^{-x}$

2. Evaluate the following for the given value of x:

    i. $y = 2 + 3 \times 5^{x-1}$ at $x = 2$.   ii. $y = 3 - \frac{1}{3} \times 2^{x+1}$ at $x = 1$

LEVEL 2

1. Solve, to one decimal place, the following equations using graph paper.

    i. $2^x = 12$ ii. $3^x = 15$ iii. $4^x = 12$

LEVEL 3

1. The graph with equation $f(x) = 2^{-x} + k$ passes through the point (1,1). Sketch the graph of $y = f(x)$. Hence, solve for x, where $f(x) = 2$.

2. The exponential function $y = k \times 3^x + c$ has an asymptote at $y = 2$ and passes through the point (1,0). Find the values of k and c.

3. Under laboratory conditions, the number of bacteria, N, in a particular culture doubles every 15 seconds. Initially there were 2 such bacteria in the culture.

    i.   Construct a table of values of N for the first minute of growth using 15 sec intervals.

    ii.   Sketch the graph of N against time t seconds for the first minute.

    iii.   Calculate the number of bacteria in the culture after 5 minutes.

LEVEL 4

1.   i.   On the same set of axes sketch the graphs of $f(x) = 2^x$ and

        $g(x) = 4 \times (0.5)^x$. Hence sketch the graph of $y = f(x) + g(x)$.

    ii.   Show that if $f(x) + g(x) = 5$, then $(2^x)^2 - 5 \times 2^x + 4 = 0$.

    iii.   Solve for x, if $f(x) + g(x) = 5$.

2. The rate R at which the drug enters the bloodstream t minutes after it was administered is approximated by the equation $R(t) = 5 \times (0.95)^t$ mg/min, while the amount A mg of the drug in the bloodstream t minutes after being administered is approximated by $A(t) = 98(1 - (0.95)^t)$.

    i.   What is the maximum rate at which the drug enters the bloodstream?

    ii.   Sketch, on separate axes, the graphs of   (a) $y = R(t)$.

                                                       (b) $y = A(t)$.

    iii.   How much of the drug is in the bloodstream when the drug is entering at a rate of 2.5 mg/min?

LEVEL   **QUESTIONS**

1

2

3

4

ES

T

E

S

T

EXAMINATION STYLE

1. The results from one annual reproduction of Pacific halibut provides that the number of halibut, $N(t)$ still alive after t years is approximated by the equation $N(t) = N_0 \times (0.82)^t$, where N_0 is the initial size of the Pacific halibut.

    i.   Sketch the graph of $y = N(t)$.

    ii.   Approximate the percentage of the original number still alive after 12 years.

    iii.   How long will it take for half of the halibut to disappear?

    The lengths, L cm, of the halibut from this cohort have lengths modelled by the equation $L(t) = a[1 - b \times (0.85)^t]$.

    iv.   Using $a = 250$ and $b = 0.95$, estimate the length of a 6 year old halibut.

    v.   A halibut measuring 20 cm is caught by the fisheries department. Estimate the age of this halibut.

    vi.   Sketch the graph of $y = L(t)$.

TEST

1. Sketch the graphs of $f(x) = 2 + 3^x, -1 \leq x \leq 2$. State its range.

                    [5 marks]

2. The exponential function $y = a - k \times b^{x+1}$ is shown in the diagram.
Find the values of a, k and b.

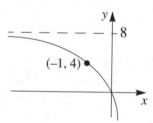

                    [5 marks]

3. Solve the equations   (a) $2^x + 3 = 12$ (b) $\dfrac{1}{2} - 4^x = \dfrac{1}{8}$.

    Give your answers correct to three decimal places.

                    [4 marks]

4. A radioactive substance decomposes in such a way that its mass, M gm, present t years after some initial time is given by $M = 200 \times a^t$. After 2 years, its mass is calculated to be 150 gm.

    i.   Find the value of a, giving your answer to three decimal places.

    ii.   Determine how long it takes for the mass to decompose by 60%.

    iii.   Sketch the graph of $y = M(t), 0 \leq t \leq 10$.

    iv.   Sketch the graph of the amount of radioactive substance that has decomposed.

                    [2 + 2 + 3 + 3 marks]

5. On the same set of axes, sketch the graphs of $g(x) = 3^x$ and $f(x) = 12 - 2^x$.

    Hence, find $\{x \mid 3^x + 2^x = 12\}$, giving your answer to one decimal place.

                    [4 marks]
                    Total 28 marks

QUESTIONS

LEVEL 1

1. The currency conversion rates between four countries are shown:

US $1.00   Aus $1.92   Sterling 0.58   Yen 152.35

Convert

i. $25 US to Yen.

ii.   £50 Sterling to $Australian.

iii.   ¥150 Yen to $Australian.

2. Tom invests $745 in an account paying 7% simple interest per annum for 5 years. How much interest has been paid over this period?

LEVEL 2

1. Sylvia receives a flat salary of $25,000 and a 6% commission on sales made. If she sells $30,000 worth of products a year, what is her income?

2. Find the interest charged for a loan of $4000 if it is levied at 6% compound interest over four years compounding annually.

LEVEL 3

1. Jack invests £650 at 5% annual interest compounded annually over a period of 15 years. Find the total interest paid, What simple interest rate would be needed to achieve the same result after 15 years?

2. Joanne invested GBP 25,000 in bonds, which return monthly interest at the simple rate of 12.0% per annum.

i.   What is the monthly interest rate?

ii.   How much does Joanne receive each (a) year? (b) month?

iii.   How long did it take for Joanne to receive $9000 interest?

3. Yuriko invested ¥1000 at 9% per annum compounded monthly. After t years, her return was ¥892.

i.   Show that $1.892 = 1.0075^{12t}$.

ii.   How long did Yuriko invest her money for?

LEVEL 4

1. On the same set of axes, plot a graph of the following investments:

i. $1000 at 9% simple interest over a 10 year period.

ii. $1000 at 7% compounded monthly for a period of 10 years.

Discuss the progress of the investment during the 10 year period.

2. A good way to compare investments is to determine their effective rates – that is the simple interest rates that would produce the same return in 1 year if the same principal had been invested at simple interest without compounding.

Bond A pays 16% compounded monthly, while bond B pays 16.2% compounded semiannually. Which is the better investment?

LEVEL ███████████████████████████ **QUESTIONS**

1
2
3
4

ES
T
E
S
T

EXAMINATION STYLE

1. The table below displays a currency conversion between GBP, USD and AUD.

	GBP	USD	AUD
GBP	1	1.42	x
USD	y	1	
AUD	0.38	z	1

Note: all answers are to be given to two decimal places.

(a) Find the values of   i. x ii. y iii. z

(b) Debbie decides to exchange GBP 500 at a money exchange outlet. How many AUD will Debbie receive if
  i.   there is no commission?
  ii. the money exchanger charges 2% commission?

(c) Debbie then decides to invest 50% of her AUD (from (b) ii.) in bonds, with an annual rate of return set at 6.5% compounded annually.
  i.   How much interest will she earn after 5 years?
  ii. She decides to cash in her bonds after she receives in interest, twice the initial amount she invested. How long will Debbie have to wait?

TEST

1. 1 Singapore dollar is worth US $0.70. Convert
  i.   50 Singapore dollars to US dollars.
  ii. $90 US into Singapore dollars.

[3 marks]

2. Find the interest on 2500 crowns if they are they invested at
  i.   4.8% p.a. simple interest for an eight year period.
  ii. 4.8% p.a. compounded monthly for an eight year period.

[4 marks]

3. A bank offers the following exchange rates for $1 Australian in relation to the French franc: 'We buy: 3.7979, we sell: 3.6848'. A customer wishes to exchange $1500 Australian for francs. How many francs will the customer receive? If the customer then immediately exchanges these francs for Australian dollars, how much will she receive? What is the effective commission? Round your answers to the nearest dollar.

[4 marks]

4. How long will it take for $12,000 to grow to $14,000 if it is invested at 8% p.a. compounded quarterly?

[3 marks]

5. Which is the better investment?
Option A: Buying notes paying 8% compounded monthly.
Option B: Buying notes paying 8.1% compounded semiannually.

[5 marks]
Total 19 marks

QUESTIONS
LEVEL

LEVEL 1
1. State the sets of inequations that represent the shaded regions shown below.

i. 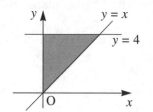 ii. 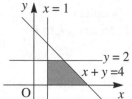 iii.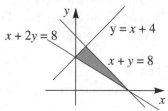

1
2
3
4

LEVEL 2

ES

1. Maximise the objective function $P(x, y) = 2x + 5y$ for each of the situations in question 1, Level 1.

T
E
S
T

2. In each of the following, represent the feasible region produced by the given constraints and find the coordinates of the boundary points in each case.

i. $x \geq 0, y \geq 0, x + y \leq 5, 2x + y \leq 6$.

ii. $y \geq 0, 3x + y \geq 6, 3x + 4y \leq 12$.

iii. $x \geq 0, 0 \leq y \leq 3, x + y \geq 2, x + y \leq 4$.

iv. $2 \leq x \leq 6, y - x \leq 4, x + y \geq 4, 0 \leq y \leq 6$.

LEVEL 3

1. Given the contraints $x \geq 0, y \geq 0, x + 2y \geq 6, 3x + y \geq 8$, find the minimum value of $p = 3x + 2y$. Does p have a maximum value?

2. A dietician suggests to her patient that his minimum daily intake of proteins, vitamins and carbohydrates are 25, 12 and 16 units respectively. The contents found in meat and vegetables(/kg) are shown below:

	protein	carbohydrates	vitamins
Meat	25	15	15
Vegetables	35	35	15

i. Let x kg and y kg be the amount of meat and vegetables used to satisfy the requirements. Set up the set of inequations satifying the constraints set by the dietician.

ii. On a set of axes, show the feasibility region satisfying the dieticians' recommendations.

iii. Meat costs $12.00 /kg and vegetables cost $8.00 /kg. Write an equation for the cost function involved in satisfying this diet.

iv. Find the minimum daily cost to the patient if he is to subscribe to this diet.

CHAPTER 17

1

2

3

4

ES

T
E
S
T

3. Aircraft carriers in the Australian Navy are one of type A or type B.
Type A carriers have 30 fighter planes and 20 helicopters.
Type B carriers have 35 fighter planes and 15 helicopters.
The Australian Navy requires to have at least 240 carrier-based fighter planes and at least 150 carrier-based helicopters.
What is the least number of carriers, including which type, required by the Navy?

LEVEL 4

1. Consider the set of points satisfying the following inequations:
$$x \geq 0,\ y \geq 0,\ y \leq 6x,\ x + y \geq 8,\ 6x + y \leq 24$$
    i.   On a set of axes, represent the region defined by these inequations.
    ii. Find the maximum value of the objective function $p = kx + 2y,\ k > 0$.

2. Packets of the Hot'n'spicy mix produced by Kadesh Foods come in two types.
The standard pack and the delux pack. Each packet contains the same three types of ingredients, but in a different ratio. In the standard pack, ingredients A, B and C are found in the ratio 3:2:1, whereas in the delux pack, they are in equal ratios. Each month, Kadesh Foods purchases 6 tonnes of ingredient A, 4.5 tonnes of ingredient B and 4 tonnes of ingredient C.

Each packet contains 1.5 kg of the Hot'n'spicy mix. Let a be the number of the standard packets produced each month and let b be the number of delux packets produced each month.

    i.   Find the set of inequalities that define the constraints described in producing the "Hot'n'spicy' mix.
    ii. On a set of axes, represent the region defined by these inequalities.

A profit of $6.00 is made on the standard packets while, a profit of $10.00 is made on the delux packets.

    iii. (a) Write down the objective function equation.
          (b) How many packets must be sold in order to maximise the monthly profit?

QUESTIONS

LEVEL

EXAMINATION STYLE

1. A petstore owner can sell two particular food mixes. Mix A at a profit of £ 0.20 per kg and mix B at a profit of £ 0.40 per kg. The nutrients, N1 (1000 units) and N2 (1000 units) present in each mix is tabulated below:

1
2
3
4

	Nutrients	
	N1	N2
Mix A	3	1
Mix B	4	4

The weekly requirements for his pet store are 36,000 units of N1 and 20,000 units of N2.

ES

Let x be the amount of Mix A and y the amount of Mix B used each week by the pet store owner.

T
E
S
T

(a) i.   Explain why two constraints imposed by the pet store owner are
$$x \geq 0, y \geq 0.$$

ii.   Show that the constraint relating to the amount of nutrient N1 used each week may be written as $3x + 4y \geq 36$.

iii. Write an inequality in x and y for the amount of nutrients N2 used each week.

(b) i.   Using graph paper, show the region defined by the constraints in (a).

ii.   Find the coordinates of the vertices of the feasible region.

(c) i.   Write down, in terms of x and y, the profit function for the total amount of food mix sold by the pet store owner.

ii.   How much of each mix should the owner purchase in order to maximise his profit? **?**

2. A feasibility region, **S**, is shown.

i.   Determine the set of inequalities that define this region.

ii. Find the maximum value of the objective function $p(x, y) = 5x + y$.

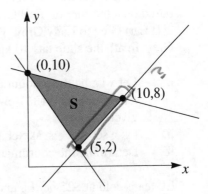

LEVEL

QUESTIONS

1
2
3
4

ES

T
E
S
T

TEST

1. The feasible region, **S**, based on a number of contraints is shown.
Find the minimum value of the objective funcion $z = 7x + 4y$.

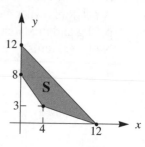

[2 marks]

2. i. On a set of axes, sketch the region defined by the following constraints:
$$x \le 6,\ y \le 7,\ x + y \ge 8.$$

ii. Find the maximum and minimum values of the objective function,
$p = x + 2y$ when subjected to the above constraints.

[5 marks]

3. Find the set of inequalities that satisfy the feasible region **S** in question 1.

[7 marks]

4. Find the maximum value of $5x + 9y$ subject to the constraints:
$$x \ge 0$$
$$y \ge 0$$
$$2x + 3y \le 24$$
$$2x + y \le 12$$

[4 marks]

5. 'The Tea Cup" store is famous for two types of tea it sells. The two types of tea are based on a mixture of Earl Grey tea and Lady Grey tea. The ratio for its EL tea is 2:1, Earl Grey to Lady Grey. The ratio for its LE tea is 1:2, Earl Grey to Lady Grey. In all, the shop has 10 kg of Earl Grey tea and 6 kg of Lady Grey tea.

i. Let x kg be the amount of EL tea produced and y kg be the amount of LE tea produced. Write down the set of inequalities that satisfy the constraints given.

ii. On a set of axes, sketch the feasible region defined by these inequalities.

iii. Determine the coordinates of the vertices of the feasible region.

EL tea is sold at \$25 per kg and LE tea is sold at \$30 per kg.

iv. (a) Write down the income equation from the sale of EL and LE tea.
   (b) Find the maximum income generated from the sale of EL and LE tea.

[5 + 3 + 3 + 1 + 2 marks]
Total 32 marks

QUESTIONS

LEVEL

LEVEL 1

1. If $A = \begin{bmatrix} 5 & -1 \\ 2 & -3 \end{bmatrix}$, $B = \begin{bmatrix} 0 & 2 \\ -1 & -3 \end{bmatrix}$ and $C = \begin{bmatrix} -4 & 1 \\ 2 & 0 \end{bmatrix}$, find:

i. $A + B$ ii. $A - B$ iii. $B + C$ iv. $2A - B$
v. $A - 2C$ vi. $A + B - C$ vii. $2C - 3A$ viii. $3A + 5C$

2. For each of the following paths, state
 i.   the number of vertices.
 ii.   the number of edges.
 iii.   the degree of the vertex with the least connections.

(a) 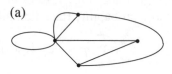   (b)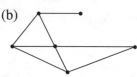

3. Draw a   i.   graph with 4 vertices and 5 edges.
 ii.   complete graph with 4 vertices.
 iii.   tree with 4 vertices.

4. Which of the following are connected graphs?
 i.   ii.   iii.

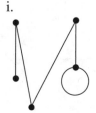   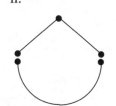   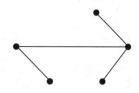

5. Use the following matrix to construct a directed graph
node   1 2 3 4

$$\begin{matrix} 1 \\ 2 \\ 3 \\ 4 \end{matrix} \begin{bmatrix} 0 & 1 & 1 & 1 \\ 0 & 0 & 0 & 0 \\ 0 & 0 & 0 & 1 \\ 0 & 0 & 0 & 0 \end{bmatrix}$$

6, Work out the maximum flow from A to B in each of the following

(a) 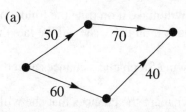   (b)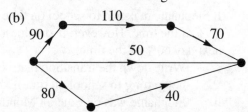

LEVEL
1 2 3 4 ES TEST

CHAPTER 18

LEVEL

1
2
3
4

ES

T
E
S
T

LEVEL 2

1. Find the following matrix products:

i. $\begin{bmatrix} 5 & 1 \\ 2 & -1 \end{bmatrix}\begin{bmatrix} 0 & 2 \\ -3 & 1 \end{bmatrix}$ ii. $\begin{bmatrix} 0 & 2 \\ -3 & 1 \end{bmatrix}\begin{bmatrix} 5 & 1 \\ 2 & -1 \end{bmatrix}$ iii. $\begin{bmatrix} 6 & 2 & 3 \\ -5 & 4 & -8 \\ 0 & 1 & 1 \end{bmatrix}\begin{bmatrix} -4 & 3 & -3 \\ 1 & 6 & -3 \\ 1 & 0 & 4 \end{bmatrix}$

iv. $\begin{bmatrix} 4 \\ 2 \\ 5 \end{bmatrix}\begin{bmatrix} 3 & -1 & -3 \end{bmatrix}$ v. $\begin{bmatrix} 3 & 1 & 2 \end{bmatrix}\begin{bmatrix} 4 & -6 & 0 \\ 0 & 2 & 3 \\ 0 & 1 & 0 \end{bmatrix}$

2. Express the following transition diagrams as a probability transition matrix.

i.

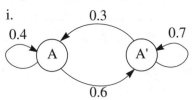

ii.

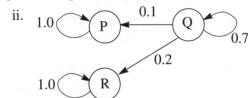

3. i. Write down the adjacency matrix for the network shown.
    ii. Calculate the two-stage route using the matrix in i.

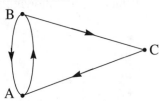

LEVEL 3

1. For the given matrices find (a) their determinant. (b) their inverses.

i. $\begin{bmatrix} 1 & 2 \\ -1 & 7 \end{bmatrix}$ ii. $\begin{bmatrix} 1 & 2 \\ 0 & 4 \end{bmatrix}$ iii. $\begin{bmatrix} 6 & 2 \\ -3 & 2 \end{bmatrix}$

2. Player A and player B each write the number 1 or the number 2 on a slip of paper. If they write the same numbers, B pays A $1, otherwise A pays B $1. Write down the payoff matrix.

3. If Stephanie makes it to school on time she will make it on time the following day 85% of the time. However, if she doesn't make it on time, she will be late the next day 60% of the time.
    i. Write down the transition matrix showing Stephanie's chances at getting (or not getting to school on time).
    ii. Stephanie was on time on Monday, what are the chances that she will
        (a) be on time on Wednesday?
        (b) be late on Thursday?

QUESTIONS
LEVEL

LEVEL 4

1. The following table gives the numbers of deliveries made between different stores from the same company:

From:→ To↓	A	B	C
A	0	4	5
B	2	0	4
C	2	3	0

The table indicates that there were two journeys made from depot A to depot B and three journeys made from B to C etc.

This second table gives the costs per delivery between the different stores.

Store	Cost
A	$60
B	$50
C	$55

It costs $60 for a delivery from store A etc.

i.   Write these two sets of information as matrices.
ii. Find the product of the two matrices.
iii. Explain the meaning of the entries in the product matrix.

2. Consider the two state Markov chain with states S = {0, 1}, with transition matrix

$$P = \begin{bmatrix} 1-\alpha & \alpha \\ \beta & 1-\beta \end{bmatrix}$$,where $0 < \alpha < 1, 0 < \beta < 1$. Find an expression for P^2 .

3. Find the value(s) of a for which the matrix $\begin{bmatrix} a & 2 \\ -1 & 2 \end{bmatrix}$ is singular. What does this tell

us about the solutions of the simultaneous equations $\begin{aligned} ax + 2y &= 3 \\ -x + 2y &= 1 \end{aligned}$?

EXAMINATION STYLE

1. The following table shows the sales of cars by a dealer over three months.

	Standard	De-Luxe	Luxury
January	5	3	2
February	7	9	1
March	11	3	2

The Standard sells for $16 500, the De-Luxe for $19 000 and the luxury for $23 500.

i.   Write the sales as an appropriate 3 by 3 matrix and the selling prices as a column matrix.
ii. Use a matrix method to find the total value of the sales for each month and for the whole period.

QUESTIONS

TEST

1. If $A = \begin{bmatrix} 3 & -1 & 4 \\ 3 & 0 & -2 \end{bmatrix}$, $B = \begin{bmatrix} -2 & 2 & -1 \\ 4 & 2 & -1 \end{bmatrix}$, find:

i. $A + B$ ii. AB iii. $3A - 4B$

[4 marks]

2. Harushee, Lizzie and Samuel are involved in producing decorative boxes. The process is made up of three steps:
Step A – Making the box.
Step B – Painting the box.
Step C – Packaging.
Harushee can do all three steps, Lizzie can make and paint the boxes and Samuel can make and package the boxes.
i. Draw a bipartite graph representing this situation.
The time it takes for Harushee to carry out steps A, B and C respectively are 4 minutes, 3 minutes and 2 minute. For Lizzie, steps A and B take 3 minutes and 4 minutes respectively. While for Samuel, steps A and C take 5 minutes and 4 minutes respectively.
ii. Represent this information in matrix form.
iii. Who is best allocated to each task?

[3 + 3 + 2 marks]

3. The weather in Towomba is represented by a Markov chain with the states {fine (F), cloudy (C), wet (W)}, with transition probability matrix given by

$$\begin{array}{c} \\ F \\ C \\ W \end{array} \begin{array}{ccc} F & C & W \\ \begin{bmatrix} 0.7 & 0.2 & 0.1 \\ 0.4 & 0.5 & 0.1 \\ 0.2 & 0.5 & 0.3 \end{bmatrix} \end{array}$$

If Wednesday is cloudy what is the probability that
i. Friday is fine?
ii. Saturday is fine?
iii. both Friday and Saturday are fine?

[2 + 2 + 3 marks]

4. A network for the travelling time (in minutes) on a road is shown in the diagram below. Find the shortest time taken to get from A to D.

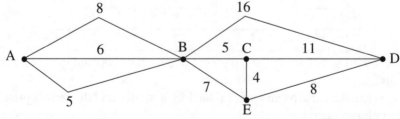

[6 marks]
Total 25 marks

QUESTIONS

LEVEL

LEVEL 1

1. If Z is a standard normal random variable, find

    i. $p(Z > 1)$ ii. $p(Z < 2)$ iii. $p(0 < Z < 1.5)$ iv. $p(|Z| \leq 0.5)$

2. Given that $Z \sim N(0, 1)$, find   i. $p(Z \geq 1)$ ii. $p(Z > 2|Z > 1)$

LEVEL 2

1. A random variable X is normally distributed with $\mu = 15$ and $\sigma = 3$.

    Find   i. $p(X \geq 12)$ ii. $p(0 \leq X < 12)$

2. Given that $X \sim N(9, 2)$ find   i. $p(X \leq 10)$ ii. $p(X > 8)$

3. The random variable X has a normal distribution with mean 25 and variance 4.

    Find   i. $p(|X - 26| \leq 2)$ ii. $p(X > 24|X < 28)$

LEVEL 3

1. A nationally administered test is scaled so that the mean score is 500 and the standard deviation is 125. Assuming that the distribution of scores is normal, what proportion of candidates throughout the nation scored between 650 and 700?

2. A large set of test grades was found to be approximately normally distributed with mean 145 and standard deviation 90. If a student scored 157 what was the student's ranking relative to the rest of the group?

3. If $X \sim N(50, 4)$, find the value of c such that $p(X \geq c) = 0.25$.

LEVEL 4

1. It has been found that the lengths of trout in a lake are normally distributed with mean 35.0 cm and variance 6.25. Assume that the trout are randomly distributed throughout the lake.

    (a)   What is the probability that a fisherman will catch a trout measuring at least 40.0 cm?

    (b)   Trout labelled '*For restaurants*' are those with lengths in the top 10% of lengths of trout in the lake. What is the minimum length that a trout must be in order to be labelled '*For restaurants*'?

2. $X \sim N(a, b^2)$. Find the values of a and b if $p(X > 4) = 0.15$ and $p(X \leq 3) = 0.70$.

LEVEL

1

2

3

4

ES

TEST

CHAPTER 19

LEVEL   QUESTIONS

EXAMINATION STYLE

1. **1.** The lifetime of "Long–Last" lightbulb has been found to be normally distributed with a mean of 2600 hours and a standard deviation of 450 hours.

2   (a) Find the percentage of light bulbs with lifetimes
            i.   in excess of 3000 hours.   ii.   less than 2000 hours.
3   (b) Given that a light bulb has lasted 2700, what are the chances that it will last
            at least 3000 hours?

4 **2.** The weights of crabs from a crab farm are found to be normally distributed with mean 3kg and standard deviation 0.5kg. The crabs fall into three categories:

ES

	Reject	Public	Gourmet
Weight	less than 2.5 kg	between 2.5 and 3.5 kg	greater than 3.5 kg

T   (a) Find the probability that a crab caught from the farm will be labelled
E   i.   as a Reject   ii.   as a Gourmet
S   (b) What is the probablity that a crab is mislabelled as being 'Public'?
T   (c) Restaurants are not satisfied with the Gourmet label. They require that a
            crab's weight is in the top 5% of weights from the crab farm in order to
            be labelled a Gourmet. What is the minimum weight for these crabs?
        (d) Three crabs have been randomly selected. What is the probability that
            i.   at least two of them will be labelled as 'Reject'.
            ii. all three are labelled as 'Public'.

TEST

1. Given that $X \sim N(5, 1.21)$, find $p(X > 7.5)$

[2 marks]

2. Find a and b, given that $X \sim N(a, b)$, $p(X > 2a) = 0.15$ and $p(X < 1) = 0.65$.

[4 marks]

3. The lengths of steel rods produced in a mill are known to be normally distributed with mean length 50cm and standard deviation 1.25cm. What percentage of these rods will have a length between 49cm and 52cm?

[3 marks]

4. The volume of drink in each 500ml bottle produced by Colar Drinks is known to be normally distributed with mean 497ml and variance 4.41ml.
    Find the probability that a randomly selected bottle will contain
    (a) i.   more than 500ml.   ii.   less than 495ml.
    (b) What is the probability that a randomly selected bottle will contain at least
        500ml given that it is known to contain at least 498ml?
    (c) Find the probability that from three randomly selected bottles, exactly two
        of them will contain at least 500ml.
    Adjustments are made to the machinery in order to improve consistency.
    (d) What value of σ will ensure that only 1% of bottles are under 495ml?

[4 + 3 + 3 + 2 marks]
Total 21 marks

QUESTIONS

LEVEL 1

1. (a) Draw a scatterplot for the data in the table below.

x	26	28	34	35	38	39	45	45	50	60
y	8	6	12	12	15	10	16	20	19	22

(b) Describe the direction, form and strength of the relationship between x & y.

2. For the set of data shown plot a scatter diagram.

x	5	6	8	8	6	9
y	8	6	1	3	6	0

Describe the direction, form and strength of the relationship.

LEVEL 2

1. For question 1, Level 1, determine the correlation coefficient.

2. Find the coefficient of correlation, r, for the set of data below.

x	12	14	15	17	19	20	21	25
y	5	6	8	8	9	11	12	13

LEVEL 3

1. Interprete the value of r and r^2 obtained in question 2, Level 2.

2. The grades obtained in two assessment tests in a small class studying Latin were:

Test 1 (x)	10	10	13	15	18	19	21	22
Test 2 (y)	15	16	13	13	9	10	11	9

(a) Plot these points on a scatter diagram.
(b) Determine the line of regression of y on x and draw it on your scatter diagram.
(c) Estimate the score on Test 2 if a score of 14 was obtained on Test 1.

3. Ten observations on, x and y, show a linear relationship with the following results:
$$\sum x = 900, \sum y = 140, \sum x^2 = 81956, \sum y^2 = 2214, \sum xy = 13054.$$
The least squares y on x regression line for this set of data is given by
$$y - \bar{y} = b(x - \bar{x})$$
(a) Find the value of b, and **use this** to find the product moment correlation coefficient.
(b) Estimate the value of y when x = 40.

4. What correlation between X and Y is required in order to assert that 90% of the variance of X depends on the variance of Y?

LEVEL QUESTIONS

1

2

3

4

ES

T
E
S
T

LEVEL 4

1. In a class of 5 students, an analysis of their final examination score (y) compared to their total test scores (x) revealed the following results.:

Test (x)	450	560	355	670	825	910	620	715
Exam (y)	52	60	45	75	90	99	65	80

(a) Plot a scatter diagram for this set of data.
(b) Is a straight line fit an appropriate model for this data set? Why?
(c) i. Find the least squares regression line of y on x.
      ii. Graph the regression line on the scatter diagram in part (a).
(d) Use the value of b, in the regression equation, $y = bx + c$, to determine the product moment correlation coefficient.
(e) Estimate the final exam score if a student obtains a total test score of 600.
(f) Is it possible to estimate the total test score based on a final exam score? How would you go about estimating a test score if a student's final exam score was 56?

2. A model to determine the population density, d, in relation to its radial distance, r, from the city centre, is thought to be of the form $d = k \times e^{-\alpha r}$. The following table displays a set of data taken at 8 different places.

r	0	2	4	6	8	10	12	14	20
d	150	54	20	40	16	6	2	7	1

(a) Plot a scatter diagram of d versus r.
In order to fit the model, a logarithmic transformation is used:
$$\log_e d = \log_e k - \alpha r$$

(b) Using the least squares $\log_e d$ on r regression line derive an estimate of k and α.
(c) i. Plot the fitted curve on the scatter diagram.
      ii. Estimate the population density at a radial distance of 16 km from the city centre.

QUESTIONS   LEVEL

EXAMINATION STYLE

1. The table shows the income (in thousands of dollars) and the annual expenditure, in hundreds of dollars for ten single male workers aged 30 – 40 yrs.

Income	42	34	36	38	40	39	36	38	39	38
Expenditure	55	39	47	49	55	53	42	44	50	51

(a) i. Plot the data on a scatter diagram.
    ii. Find the correlation coefficient.
(b) Calculate the proportion of the variance of *Expenditure* which can be explained by the variance of the *Income*.
(c) Find the least squares equation of the regression line.
(d) On the scatter diagram from (a), sketch the regression line.
(e) Estimate the expenditure by a single working person aged 30–40 yrs if their annual income is $37 000.

2. The relationship between the amount of chemical, x gm, in an item and the durability, y days of the item is thought to be linear. Samples were obtained from 35 randomly selected items. The results of this sample are:

$$\sum x = 154, \sum y = 492, \sum xy = 2235, \sum x^2 = 821, \sum y^2 = 7214$$

(a) Determine the mean and the standard deviation of
    i. the amount of chemical in the items.
    ii. the durability of the item.
The least squares y on x regression line for this set of data is given by
$$y - \bar{y} = b(x - \bar{x})$$
(b) Find the value of b, and **use this** to find the product moment correlation coefficient.
(c) Calculate the proportion of the variance of *durability* which can be explained by the variance of the *chemical content*.
(d) Estimate the durability of an item containing 3.5 units of the chemical.

3. A farmer is trying to establish a relationship between the final weight, x lbs and the carcass weight, y lbs, for a particular type of bull. From a pen of 10 such bulls, she obtained the following weights.

x	1030	1000	1060	980	995	1025	1055	1035	1380	1085
y	614	577	654	594	593	589	629	650	834	691

(a) i. Plot the data on a scatter diagram.
    ii. Find the correlation coefficient.
(b) Find the least squares equation of the regression line.
(c) On the scatter diagram from (a), sketch the regression line.
(d) Estimate the carcass weight of a bull if its final weight is known to be 1040 lbs.

LEVEL | **QUESTIONS**

1

2

3

4

ES

T
E
S
T

TEST

1. (a) Plot a scatter diagram of the data set tabulated below.

(b) Describe the type of relationship that exists between the variables a and b, including
 i. the direction
 ii. the form
 iii. strength of relationship

a	2	4	6	6	10	12
b	40.8	32.2	24.2	26.0	14.5	9.2

[6 marks]

2. The results of a set of 25 paired data (x, y) is summarised as follows:

$\sum x = 150$, $\sum x^2 = 1080$, $\sum y = 225$, $\sum y^2 = 2065$, $\sum xy = 1423$

(a) Determine the equation of the least squares regression line, $y = a + bx$.

(b) Predict the value of y when $x = 8$.

(c) Find the value of S_{xy}.

[5 marks]

3. What correlation between X and Y is required in order to assert that 80% of the variance of X depends on the variance of Y?

[2 marks]

4. The amount of potassium bromide, x gm, that would dissolve in 100ml of water was recorded for various temperatures, T °C, with the following results:

T	0	10	20	30	40	50
x	54	59	64	73	76	82

(a) Plot a scatter diagram of the data set.

The least squares regression line, $x = a + bT$ is obtained by solving the two simultaneous equations in a and b:

$$na + \left(\sum T\right)b = \sum x \quad \text{and} \quad \left(\sum T\right)a + \left(\sum T^2\right)b = \sum xT$$

(b) Find the least squares regression line of T on x using the simultaneous equations given above.

(c) On your scatter plot, draw the least squares regression line.

(d) How much potassium bromide do you predict will dissolve in 100ml of water at 25°C?

(e) i. What would you need to do in order to try and predict the temperature required in order to dissolve 70 gm of potassium bromide?

 ii. Predict the required temperature in (e) i.,.

[2 + 3 + 2 + 1 + 1 + 3 marks]
Total 25 marks

QUESTIONS

LEVEL

LEVEL 1

1. The contingency tables below show the observed 'Ai' and Bi' values obtained. For each table, find the expected frequencies (in table form).

(a)

	A1	A2
B1	35	15
B2	30	40

(b)

	A1	A2	A3
B1	19	20	11
B2	9	16	5

LEVEL 2

1. Use the χ^2 test at the 1% level of significance to investigate if there is any association between categories A and B based on the results of the contingency tables (a) and (b) in question 1, Level 1.

LEVEL 3

1. The table shows the absentee records of a sample of unskilled workers from two companies, A and B:

Absentee rocords

		Good	Poor
Company	A	14	16
	B	6	64

(a) Produce an expected frequency table corresponding to the given table.
(b) Use an appropriate test, at the 1% level of significance to determine if there is any significant difference in the absenteeism in the two companies.

LEVEL 4

1. The number of arrivals of antique tables per day at a customs office over a period of 11 weeks is given in the table below:

No. of arrivals	0	1	2	3	≥ 4
No. of days	12	19	11	8	5

Assume that each week has 5 working days.
It is thought that the number of deliveries conforms to a distribution known as a Poisson distribution, where, if the discrete random variable X denotes the number of arrivals per day, then $p(X = x) = \dfrac{e^{-\mu}\mu^x}{x!}$, $x = 0, 1, 2, \ldots$, where μ is the mean number of arrivals per day.

(a) i. Estimate the value of μ.

ii. Using μ in (a) i., display the theoretical probability distribution.

(b) Based on the probability distribution, set up a table showing the theoretical number of arrivals at the customs office for 1, 2, 3 and at least 4 days.

(c) Using the χ^2 test at a 5% level of significance, does the data actually conform to the Poisson distribution?

LEVEL ▓▓▓▓▓▓▓▓▓▓▓▓▓▓▓▓▓ QUESTIONS

1

2

3

4

ES

T
E
S
T

EXAMINATION STYLE

1. The self-esteem levels of non-smoking and smoking males were recorded as being High, Medium or Low. The results are tabulated below:

Table 1 Level of self-esteem

	High	Medium	Low
Smoker	25	22	22
Non–smoker	25	28	38

Table 2 Level of self-esteem

	High	Low
Smoker	36	33
Non–smoker	39	52

(a) Construct a table of expected frequencies using Table 1. What assumption have you made in constructing your table?

(b) Calculate the χ^2_{calc} – value for this set of data.

(c) Based on this data is there a significant difference between smokers and non–smokers and their level of self–esteem?

Because of the uncertainty in identifying a medium level of self esteem, the results were retabulated as shown in Table 2.

(d) Based on this new set of data is there a significant difference between smokers and non–smokers and their level of self–esteem?

TEST

1. In a statewide survey, "Best Bake', bread–chain outlet, wanted to determine if there was an association between the different types of cakes they produced and their customers opinions. The table gives the responses of a random sample of 400 customers from its various outlets:

		Type of bread			
		W	X	Y	Z
Opinion	**Satisfied**	82	66	56	56
	Dissatisfied	23	20	17	20

Use the χ^2 test at the 5% level of significance to investigate whether there is any significant difference between the different types of breads and the customers opinions. What initial assumption did you make in your calculations?

[6 marks]

2. The table below gives the wages of a sample of employees working at a large furniture manufacturer.

Weekly wage ($)	160–	200–	240–	280–	320–	360–400
No. of employees	20	35	55	20	15	15

(a) Find the sample mean and standard deviation of this sample.

It is thought that the wages are normally distributed.

(b) Construct a table of expected frequencies. State any assumption(s) made?

(c) Calculate the χ^2_{calc} – value for this set of data.

(d) Use a 5% level of significance to determine if the wages earned are in fact normally distributed.

[2 + 3 + 2 + 2 marks]

Total 15 marks

QUESTIONS

LEVEL

LEVEL 1

1. State the rate of change of y with respect to x if:

    i. $y = 2x - 1$ ii. $y = 3 - x$ iii. $2y = -x + 4$

2. Determine the average rate of change over the given interval, **I**, for the following:

(a)
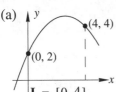
$\mathbf{I} = [0, 4]$

(b)
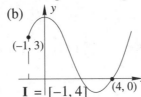
$\mathbf{I} = [-1, 4]$

(c)
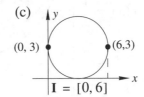
$\mathbf{I} = [0, 6]$

3. Over which section(s) of the graph shown below is the gradient

    i.   positive?
    ii.   negative?
    iii.   increasing?
    iv.   decreasing?

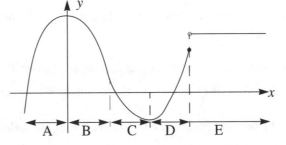

LEVEL 2

1. For each of the following, find the average rate of change over the domain **I**.

    (a) $f(x) = 5 - x^2, \mathbf{I} = [1,3]$ (b) $h(t) = \dfrac{20}{t} + 2, \mathbf{I} = [2,5]$

2. Given that $f(x) = \sqrt{x+1} - 1$, find the slope of the secant line through the points $(3, f(3))$ and $(8, f(8))$. What does this slope measure?

3. The temperature, $T\,°C$, of hot tea, t minutes after it has been poured into a cup is given by $T = 30 + \dfrac{60}{t+1}, t \geq 0$.

    Find the average rate of change in the temperature of the tea (after been poured)
    i.   over the first 9 minutes.
    ii.   over the last 10 minutes of the first hour.

4. If $f(x) = x^2$, find   i. $f(x+h) - f(x)$.   ii. $\dfrac{1}{h}(f(x+h) - f(x))$.

5. A vase is being filled with water at a constant rate. The cross section of the vase is shown alongside. Sketch a graph showing the variation in the height of the water level with respect to time.

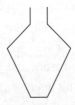

LEVEL   **QUESTIONS**

1

2

3

4

ES

TEST

LEVEL 3

1. Find the gradient of the secants passing through the points A and B:

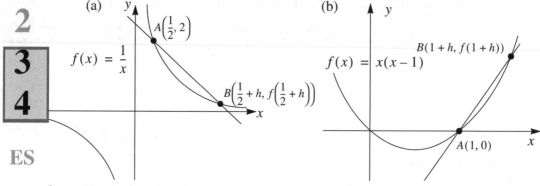

(a) $f(x) = \dfrac{1}{x}$, $A\left(\dfrac{1}{2}, 2\right)$, $B\left(\dfrac{1}{2} + h, f\left(\dfrac{1}{2} + h\right)\right)$

(b) $f(x) = x(x - 1)$, $B(1 + h, f(1 + h))$, $A(1, 0)$

2. For the functions in question 1., find the gradient of the curve at A using a limiting argument.

3. Find the gradient of the secant joining the points P at $x = a$ and Q at $x = a + h$, for the function $h(x) = a - x^3$. Hence, deduce the gradient of $h(x)$ at $x = a$.

4. Find from first principles, the derivative of the following:

(a) $f(x) = x^3$.

(b) $g(x) = \dfrac{1}{x} + 2$.

LEVEL 4

1. The revenue, $\$ R(x)$, from the sale of x wooden planter boxes is given by
$R(x) = 30x - 0.03x^2$.

    (a)   i.   For what value(s) of x will the revenue remain positive?

           ii.   Sketch the graph of the revenue function.

    (b)   Find the change in revenue when production increases from

           i.   100 to 400 planters.   ii.   100 to 900 planters.

    (c)   The initial production is set at 200 planters. What is the largest increase in production allowed if the average rate of change in revenue must remain positive?

    (d)   Using the points P, $x = 200$ and Q, $x = 200 + h$, where h is small, find the rate of change in revenue when 200 wooden boxes are manufactured.

2. The x–coordinate of a particle after t seconds is given by $x(t) = 10t - 2t^2, t \geq 0$.

    (a)   i.   Find an expression for $x(t + h) - x(t)$.

           ii.   Hence find the velocity of the particle 2 seconds into its motion.

    (b)   Find the particle's acceleration when it comes to a stop.

3. Find from first principles, the derivative of $f(x) = 2^x$ when $x = 1.4$. Verify this result using a graphics calculator.

QUESTIONS

LEVEL

EXAMINATION STYLE

1. The temperature, $T\,°C$, of a kettle t minutes after it is switched off is modelled by the function $T(t) = 30 + \dfrac{60}{t+1}, t \geq 0$.

1
2
3
4

(a) Construct a table of values showing the trend in the kettle's temperature during the first 10 minutes after it is switched off .

(b) Find the average rate of change in its temperature during the first 2 minutes after it was switched off.

(c) i. Find an expression in terms of h, for the average rate of change in temperature after it is switched off, in the time interval $[2, 2 + h]$.

ii. Hence, find the rate of change in temperature 2 minutes after it was switched off.

ES

(d) i. Sketch the graph of the kettle's temperature t minutes after it is switched off.

ii. From your graph deduce the kettle's temperature over the long term.

T
E
S
T

TEST

1. A vase is being filled with water at a constant rate.
The profile of the vase is shown alongside.
Sketch a graph of how the water level changes with height.

[4 marks]

2. Use a limiting process to find the gradient of $g(t) = 2^t$ at $t = 2$ (ans to 2 dec.pl).

[4 marks]

3. A particle's position along the x–axis is given by $x(t) = 2t^2 - 4t, t \geq 0$. Find its average velocity during the first 2 seconds of motion.

[3 marks]

4. The number, N, of infant deaths per 100,000 births in a particular country since 1960 has been tabulated below:

t (years)	0	10	20	30	40
N	52.4	38.2	26.6	17.6	11.2

(a) Plot and sketch a graph of the above data on an appropriate set of axes.

(b) Find the average rate of change in the number of infant deaths per 100,000 during the period 1970 to 1990.

(c) During which decade is the rate of change least?

It is suggested that a model for the data has the form $N(t) = at^2 - bt + c, t \geq 0$.

(d) i. Show that $a = 0.013$, $b = 1.55$ and $c = 52.4$.

ii. Based on this model, how many deaths can be expected in 2010?

(e) i. Find an expression for $N(t + h) - N(t)$.

ii. Hence, find the rate of change in the number of deaths per 100,000 in 1995.

[2 + 2 + 2 + 3 + 2 + 2 + 3 marks]
Total 27 marks

QUESTIONS

LEVEL

1
2
3
4
ES
T
E
S
T

CHAPTER 23

LEVEL 1

1. Find the derivative of:

i. x^7 ii. $6x^2 + 1$ iii. $12 - x$

2. Find the derived functions of the following.

i. $(x+1)(x-1)$ ii. $(2x+1)(3x-2)$ iii. $x\left(x - \dfrac{1}{x}\right)$

3. Differentiate the following.

i. $x^2(x-1)$ ii. $2\sqrt{x} - x$ iii. $x^2(\sqrt{x}) - 3(\sqrt[3]{x})$

iv. $\dfrac{(x+1)^2}{x}$ v. $\sqrt{x}(9 - \sqrt{x})^2$ vi. $\dfrac{x}{\sqrt{x}} - \dfrac{\sqrt{x}}{x} + x\sqrt{x}$

LEVEL 2

1. Find the gradient of the function at the point indicated.

(a) $y = x - \dfrac{1}{x^2} + 1$ at $(1,1)$ (b) $f(x) = 27 - x^3$ at $(3,0)$

2. Find the coordinate(s) on the curve $y = x^4 - 4x^2$ where the gradient is zero.

3. An object's displacement function, x m after being in motion for t seconds, is given by $x(t) = t^3 - 4t^2 + t$, $t \geq 0$.

(a) Find its velocity when $t = 1$.
(b) Find its acceleration after 2 seconds.

4. Find the slope of the curve $y = x^3 - x + 2$ at $x = -1$.

5. Sketch the graph of the gradient function corresponding to each of the folowing.

(a) 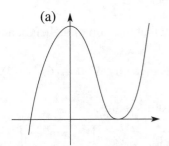   (b) 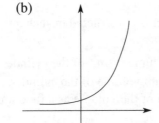   (c)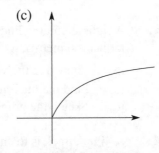

6. The revenue, R, from the sale of x items is given by $R(x) = x\left(8 + \dfrac{16}{\sqrt{x}}\right)$. Find the rate of change of the revenue (i.e., its marginal revenue) if 25 items are sold.

LEVEL QUESTIONS

1

2

3

4

ES

T
E
S
T

LEVEL 3

1. For the curve with equation $y = x^3 - 3x$, find

(a) $\dfrac{dy}{dx}$. (b) its gradient at the origin.

(c) the coordinates where the gradient is zero.

2. The displacement equation of a particle from an origin O is given by
$s = 4t - 2t^2$, where s is measured in metres and t in seconds.
Find the greatest positive displacement from O for this particle

3. Use first principles to find $f'(x)$, where $f(x) = 2 - 3x^{-2}$.

4. Find a and b, given that $f(x) = ax^2 + 2bx + 4$ and $f(1) = 10$ and $f'(2) = 0$.

5. Given that $f(x) = x^2(x - 3)$, find the value(s) of x for which $f'(x) = 0$.

6. The running cost, \$ C, of an engine is given by $C = v^2 - 6v + 15$, where v is the propagating speed of the engine. Find the most economical running speed.

LEVEL 4

1. A rectangular paddock is fenced off using one side of an exsisting wall so that the enclosed area, A m^2, is given by $A = 2x(100 - x)$. Determine the value of x for which the paddock will have the largest area. Find the largest area possible.

2. A triangular prism with an equilateral triangle as its cross section and having a fixed volume of 128 cm^3,

has a total surface, in cm^2, given by $S = 3xy + \dfrac{\sqrt{3}}{2}x^2$.

Its volume, V cm^3, is given by $V = \dfrac{\sqrt{3}}{4}x^2y$.

Find the minimum surface area.

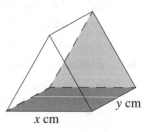

y cm

x cm

3. A right circular cylinder is constructed in such a way that the sum of its height and radius is 6 metres.

i. Show that the volume, V m^3 of the cylinder is given by, $V = \pi(6r^2 - r^3)$.
ii. Find the maximum volume of the cylinder.
iii. Sketch the graph of the volume as a function of its radius.

4. A 400 m track is to enclose a rectangular playing field. Given that the curved portions of the track are semicircles find the largest possible area contained by the track.

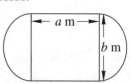

a m

b m

QUESTIONS

EXAMINATION STYLE

1. **i.** Consider the graph of $y = f(x)$ as shown below.

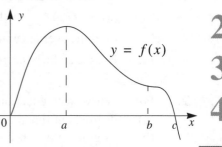

    (a) Identify the nature of the turning point for $x = a$.

    (b) Identify those regions for which the gradient is positive.

    (c) Sketch the graph of the gradient function, $y = f'(x)$.

ii. Part of the graph in i., is shown again. For $a < x < b$, the curve can be approximated by the equation, $y = 1 - (x - 2)^3$.

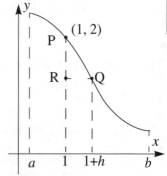

    (a) Copy and complete the table below.

h	0.1	0.01	0.001
PR			

    (b) Using your table, deduce the gradient of the curve with equation $y = 1 - (x - 2)^3$ at the point (1, 2).

    (c) Verify your result in (b).

iii. A cylindrical can without a top is to have a surface area of 400π cm^2. The cylinder has a base radius of r cm and a height of h cm.

    (a) Show that $h = \left(\dfrac{200}{r} - \dfrac{r}{2}\right)$.

    (b) Show that the volume measure of the cylinder, V cm^3 is given by

$$V = \left(200r - \frac{1}{2}r^3\right)\pi$$

    (c) Calculate the greatest volume, giving your answer in exact form.

    (d) Sketch the graph of the volume function.

2. A particle moves in a straight line such that its displacement, s m, from a fixed point O at time t seconds is given by the equation $s(t) = 10 + 2t - t^2, t \geq 0$.

    i. Find

        (a) its initial position.

        (b) its initial velocity and acceleration.

        (c) when the particle reverses its direction of motion.

    ii. Sketch the graph of the particle's motion.

    iii. Find the distance travelled by the particle after the first 4 seconds of motion.

LEVEL **QUESTIONS**

1
2
3
4
ES

TEST

T
E
S
T

1. i. For the function $f(x) = 2x^2 + 1$ find
   (a) $f(2)$ (b) $f(2+h)$
   ii. Find the average gradient of $f(x)$ from $x = 2$ to $x = 2 + h$.
   iii. Hence, deduce the gradient at $x = 2$.

   [6 marks]

2. For the curve with equation $y = -2x^3 + 24x - 32$ find:
   (a) its gradient function.
   (b) its gradient when $x = a$.
   (c) the coordinates where its gradient is 18.

   [1 + 1 + 2 marks]

3. The curve with equation $f(x) = x^3 - bx^2 - 5x + 1$ has a local maximum when $x = -1$. Find b.

   [3 marks]

4. i. Sketch the graph of the curve with equation $y = \frac{1}{4}x^2(3 - x)$, clearly

   showing all points of intersection with the axes and the coordinates of its turning point(s).
   ii. Hence, state the maximum value of $kx^2(3 - x)$, for $x > 0$.

   [7 marks]

5. A farmer wishes to enclose his sheep in a rectangular pen using the existing wall as shown. He has 100 m of fencing available to him.
   i. Express y in terms of x.
   ii. Show that the enclosure has an area A m^2, where $A = 196 + 94x - 2x^2$.
   iii. Show that the domain of A is [39, 49].
   iv. Find the rate of change of the area A with respect to x.
   v. Find the maximum area the pen can have.

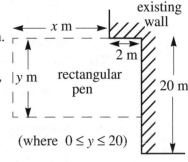

(where $0 \le y \le 20$)

   [2 + 2 + 4 + 2 + 4 marks]

6. A particle moves in a straight line such that its position, s m from a fixed point O at time t seconds is given by $s = t^3 - 27t + 20, t \ge 0$.
   i. Find (a) its velocity after 2 seconds.
            (b) its acceleration after 2 seconds.
   ii. Find when its velocity is zero.
   iii. Sketch its displacement-time graph.
   iv. How far has the particle travelled by the time it passes O a second time?

   [2 + 2 + 2 + 4 + 3 marks]
   Total 47 marks

QUESTIONS
LEVEL

LEVEL 1

1. Find the indefinite integral in the following.

i. $3x^3 + 2x$ ii. $\frac{1}{2}t^2 + 4$ iii. $\frac{3}{2}t - 6t^4$ iv. $5 - \frac{2}{x^2}$

2. Find

i. $\int (9 - x^3)\,dx$ ii. $\int (8 - \sqrt{x})\,dx$ iii. $\int t(1 - t)\,dt$

LEVEL 2

1. Find

i. $\int \frac{x^3 + 2x^2}{x}\,dx$ ii. $\int \left(\frac{t-1}{t^3}\right)\,dt$ iii. $\int (x^2 - 3x)(2x - 3)\,dx$

iv. $\int \sqrt{x}(1 - \sqrt{x})^2\,dx$ v. $\int (ax - 1)^2\,dx$ vi. $\int \frac{2t - 4t^3 + 1}{t^3}\,dt$

2. If $\frac{dy}{dx} = 2x - \sqrt{x}$, find an expression for y.

LEVEL 3

1. Given that $f'(x) = 4 - x^2$ and $f(1) = 8$, find $f(x)$.

2. A curve passing through the point (2, –4) has a gradient function defined by $(x - 2)^2$. Find the equation of this function.

3. Given that $\frac{dR}{dt} = \frac{100}{t^2}$, $R(1) = 500$, find $R(2)$.

4. The marginal cost of producing x electrical units is given by $C'(x) = 0.4x^2 + 2x$ with a fixed cost of $1500.
   i.   Find the cost function, $C(x)$.
   ii. What cost is involved in producing 10 electrical units?

LEVEL 4

1. The velocity, V m/s, of a particle at time t seconds is given by the equation $V = 12t - 3$. Find its displacement after 5 seconds if it started at the origin.

2. The rate growth of the population $N(t)$, of a newly established housing estate, t years after being incorporated is approximated by the model

$$\frac{dN}{dt} = 300 + 500\sqrt{t},\ 0 \le t \le 16$$

At the time of incorporation, the population numbered 4000.
Find the population after 16 years.

LEVEL

QUESTIONS

1
2
3
4

3. A particle moving in a straight line passes a fixed point O with a velocity of 2 m/s. It has an acceleration, a m/s^2, given by $a = 12 - 6t$, where t seconds is the time after the particle passes the origin, O.
   (a) Determine its velocity at time t seconds after passing O.
   (b) Find its displacement equation.
   (c) Find the particle's position 5 seconds after passing point O.

4. The function $f(x)$ has a turning point at $(4, 6)$ and passes through the point $(0, 2)$. Find the values of a and b, given that $f'(x) = a\sqrt{x} - bx$.

ES

EXAMINATION STYLE

1. The graph of the marginal cost funcion from the manufacturing of x thousand electrical devices per month is shown below.
The equation of the marginal cost is given by

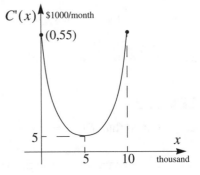

$$C'(x) = ax^2 + bx + c, 0 \le x \le 10.$$
   i. Using simultaneous equations, show that $a = 2$, $b = -20$ and $c = 55$.
The fixed costs has been set at \$25,000.
   ii. Find the cost function.
   iii. What is the cost involved in producing 5000 devices?
   iv. Sketch the graph of the cost function for $0 \le x \le 10$.

T
E
S
T

TEST

1. Find the antiderivative of the following

   i. $9x^8 - \sqrt{x}$ ii. $\dfrac{1}{x^2} + 2x$ iii. $(x-3)^2$

   [6 marks]

2. $\dfrac{dV}{dt} = 0.2t\sqrt{t}$, $V(4) = 5$. Find $V(t)$.

   [4 marks]

3. A particle moves in a straight line from a fixed origin O. After t seconds of motion the particle has an acceleration of $8 - 2t$ m/s^2. The particle starts at rest from O.
   (a) Find its   i. velocity equation, $v(t)$ m/s.
                   ii. displacement equation, $x(t)$ m.
   (b) Find when the particle comes to rest.   [7 marks]

4. The graph of $y = f'(x)$ is shown alongside. Sketch the graph of $y = f(x)$.

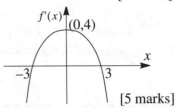

   [5 marks]

   Total 22 marks

CHAPTER 2
LEVEL 1
1. i., ii., iii., v., viii. & ix.

2. i. 3.4×10^1 ii. 5.67×10^4 iii. 6.00056×10^5 iv. 4×10^{-1} v. 4.38×10^{-3} vi. 4.0456×10^0

vii. 2.0×10^{-3} viii. 7.5×10^{-1} ix. 5.4×10^{-6} x. 1×10^4 xi. 6×10^{-2} xii. 7.5×10^{-2}

xiii. 6.25×10^{-4} xiv. 1×10^{-2} xv. 8.1×10^{-7}

LEVEL 2
1. i. 7.92×10^3 ii. 1.96×10^2 iii. 3.15×10^{-2} iv. 4.83×10^1 v. 2.45×10^{-6} vi. 1.39×10^0

vii. 1.96×10^2 viii 2.48×10^{-2} ix -6.27×10^7 x. 9.85×10^{-1}

2. i. 3.3% ii. 11% iii. 6.9% iv. 11% v. 11% vi. 14%

3. i. $\dfrac{13}{10}$ ii. $\dfrac{1}{4}$ iii. $\dfrac{1}{3}$ iv. $\dfrac{5}{9}$ v. $\dfrac{5}{6}$ vi. $\dfrac{83}{99}$ vii. $\dfrac{3}{7}$

LEVEL 3

1. i. $\dfrac{1}{u} + \dfrac{1}{v} = \dfrac{1}{f} \Rightarrow \dfrac{1}{v} = \dfrac{1}{f} - \dfrac{1}{u} = \dfrac{u-f}{uf} \Rightarrow v = \dfrac{uf}{u-f}$

ii. Smallest value $= \dfrac{(1.9 - 0.06)(0.4 - 0.003)}{(1.9 + 0.06) - (0.4 - 0.003)} = 0.46735765$

Largest value $= \dfrac{(1.9 + 0.06)(0.4 + 0.003)}{(1.9 - 0.06) - (0.4 + 0.003)} = 0.54967293$

iii. Nominal value $= \dfrac{1.9(0.4)}{1.9 - 0.4} = 0.50666667$.

Error range $= 0.54967293 - 0.46735765 = 0.08231528$

An estimate of the absolute error is $\dfrac{0.08231528}{2} = 0.04115764$ since the error range is not

symmetric about the nominal value. Relative error $= \dfrac{0.04115764}{0.50666667} = 0.08123219$

Percentage error $= 0.08123219(100) = 8.12\,\%$

2. i. $E = 0.2((3)(10^8))^2 = 1.8 \times 10^{16}$ The units are kg m^2 sec^{-2} or Joules.

ii. Mass destroyed $= 5(10^6)(1.67(10^{-27})) = 0.835 \times 10^{-20}$ kg.

Energy released $= 0.835 \times 10^{-20}((3)(10^8))^2 = 0.0007515$ J

3. $A = 4.3^2 \therefore V = \dfrac{1}{3} \times 4.3^2 \times 12.4 = 76.4253$. i. 76.4 cm^3 ii. 76.43 cm^3 iii. 76 cm^3.

LEVEL 4

1. $kx - 2 = \sqrt{2} \Leftrightarrow kx = 2 + \sqrt{2} \Leftrightarrow x = \dfrac{2 + \sqrt{2}}{k}$. For $\dfrac{2 + \sqrt{2}}{k} \in \mathbb{Q}$, $k = m(2 + \sqrt{2}), m \in \mathbb{Q}$.

2. The error in $f(0)$ is zero. The largest errors will be found when $x = 20$.

Nominally, $f(20) = 3(20) + 6 = 66$ and the maximum allowed error is 6% so the smallest and largest function values are $66(0.94) = 62.04$ and $66(1.06) = 69.96$. If the two values of the required coefficient are a_{min}, a_{max}, then:

$$a_{min}(20) + 6 = 62.04 \qquad a_{max}(20) + 6 = 69.96$$

$$a_{min} = \frac{62.04 - 6}{20} \text{ and } \qquad a_{max} = \frac{69.96 - 6}{20}$$

$$= 2.802 \qquad\qquad = 3.198$$

The two absolute errors in the coefficient are: $3 - 2.802 = 0.198$ and $3.198 - 3 = 0.198$

The relative error is: $\dfrac{0.198}{3} = 0.066$ and the percentage error $(0.066)(100) = 6.6\,\%$.

3. Nominal volume $= 180(245)(567) - 2\pi\left(\dfrac{190}{2}\right)^2 180 = 14797665\,mm^3$.

The largest dimensions of the cuboid are:
$180(1.002) = 180.36$, $245(1.002) = 245.49$, $567(1.002) = 568.134$ mm
The smallest dimensions of the cuboid are:
$180(0.998) = 179.64$, $245(0.998) = 244.51$, $567(0.998) = 565.866$ mm
The smallest and largest values of the diameters of the holes are $190(0.999) = 189.81$ mm and

$190(1.001) = 190.19$ mm and for the radii, these figures are $\dfrac{189.81}{2} = 94.905$ mm and

$\dfrac{190.19}{2} = 95.095$ mm. The smallest block with the largest hole gives the smallest volume of

metal. This is: $179.64(244.51)(565.866) - 2\pi(95.095)^2(179.64) = 14647968\,mm^3$

The largest is $180.36(245.49)(568.134) - 2\pi(94.905)^2(180.36) = 14948025\,mm^3$.

The two values of the absolute error are: $14797665 - 14647968 = 149697\,mm^3$ and

$14948025 - 14797665 = 150359\,mm^3$ which is not a symmetric error band.

The absolute error is about $\dfrac{14948025 - 14647968}{2} = 150028\,mm^3$.

The percentage error is $\dfrac{150028}{14797665}(100) = 1.0138626$ or about 1%.

EXAMINATION STYLE QUESTIONS

1. i.

t	0	10	20	30	40	50
O	2.5×10^1	6.0×10^2	9.9×10^2	1.0×10^3	1.2×10^3	1.1×10^3

ii.

iii. $O(20) = -0.9(20)^2 + 66(20) + 25 = 985$, $O(30) = -0.9(30)^2 + 66(30) + 25 = 1195$

The average rate of change $= \dfrac{1195 - 985}{30 - 20} = 21$ °C per hour.

iv. The two possible coefficients are: $66(1.1) = 72.6$ and $66(0.9) = 59.4$.

Two rules are: $O = -0.9t^2 + 72.6t + 25, 0 \le t \le 50$ & $O = -0.9t^2 + 59.4t + 25, 0 \le t \le 50$.

$O_{max}(20) = -0.9(20)^2 + 72.6(20) + 25 = 1117$

$O_{max}(30) = -0.9(30)^2 + 72.6(30) + 25 = 1393$

$O_{min}(20) = -0.9(20)^2 + 59.4(20) + 25 = 853$

$O_{min}(30) = -0.9(30)^2 + 59.4(30) + 25 = 997$

The minmum average rate of change $= \dfrac{997 - 1117}{30 - 20} = -12$ °C per hour.

The maximum average rate of change $= \dfrac{1393 - 853}{30 - 20} = 54$ °C per hour.

the percentage error $(0.066)(100) = 6.6\%$.

2. We have that $5.5 \le R \le 6.5$ & $3.5 \le I \le 4.5$.

So, $V_{min} = 5.5 \times 3.5 = 19.25$ and $V_{max} = 6.5 \times 4.5 = 29.25 . \therefore 19.25 \le V \le 29.25$.

3. i. No calculation is necessary as the error is also 5%.

ii. The largest angle is opposite the longest side. The nominal value is found using the cosine rule:

$63^2 = 47^2 + 34^2 - 2(47)(34)\cos\theta \therefore \cos\theta = \dfrac{47^2 + 34^2 - 63^2}{2(47)(34)} = -0.18898623$

$$\therefore \theta = arccos(-0.18898623)$$

$$= 1.760926^c$$

$$= 100.89363°$$

The range of values possible for the sides are: $34(0.95) = 32.3 \to 34(1.05) = 35.7$,

$47(0.95) = 44.65 \to 47(1.05) = 49.35$ and $63(0.95) = 59.85 \to 63(1.05) = 66.15$.

The smallest value for the angle comes from this triangle:

$59.85^2 = 49.35^2 + 35.7^2 - 2(49.35)(35.7)\cos\theta$

$\cos\theta = \dfrac{49.35^2 + 35.7^2 - 59.85^2}{2(49.35)(35.7)}$

$\therefore \theta = 87.919972°$

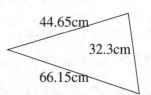

49.35cm

35.7cm

59.85cm

The largest value for the angle comes from this triangle:

$66.15^2 = 44.65^2 + (32.3)^2 - 2(44.65)(32.3)\cos\theta$

$\cos\theta = \dfrac{44.65^2 + (32.3)^2 - 66.15^2}{2(44.65)(32.3)}$

$\therefore \theta = 117.65793°$

44.65cm

32.3cm

66.15cm

The absolute errors are: $1.760926 - 1.534493 = 0.22643302$

and $2.0535182 - 1.760926 = 0.29259218$ which is non-symmetrical. Taking the absolute error

as $\dfrac{2.0535182 - 1.534493}{2} = 0.2595126$ or $\dfrac{0.22643302 + 0.29259218}{2} = 0.2595126$ gives a

percentage error of $\dfrac{0.2595126}{1.760926}(100) = 14.73728$ or about 14.7%.

iii. Nominal area $\left(\text{using Area} = \dfrac{1}{2}bc\sin A\right)$ is $\dfrac{1}{2}(47)(34)\sin(1.760926) = 784.60181\text{cm}^2$

The smallest area results from taking the three smallest sides:
The angles of this triangle have not been calculated. This is not necessary as this smaller triangle is similar to the 'no error' triangle and so has the same angles.

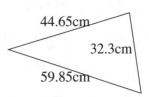

$A = \dfrac{1}{2}(44.65)(32.3)\sin 1.760926 = 708.10313\text{cm}^2$

Similarly, the largest possible area is:

$A = \dfrac{1}{2}(49.35)(35.7)\sin 1.760926 = 865.0235\text{cm}^2$

Absolute error $= \dfrac{865.0235 - 708.10313}{2} = 78.460181\text{cm}^2$

Percentage error $= \dfrac{78.460181}{784.60181}(100) = 10\,\%$

4. i. $f(1) = 35 - a$ ∴ nominal value is $35 - 3.6 = 31.4$.

Now, $f_{\min}(1) = 35 - 3.8 = 31.2$ and $f_{\max}(1) = 35 - 3.4 = 31.6$.

Abs. error $= 31.4 - 31.2 = 0.2$ [or $31.6 - 31.4 = 0.2$]. ∴ % error $= \dfrac{0.2}{31.4} \times 100 = 0.6369\,\%$.

That is, it is approx. 0.64 %.

ii. $f'(x) = -3ax^2$ ∴ $f'(1) = -3a$, so nominal value is -10.8. $f'_{\max}(1) = -3 \times 3.4 = -10.2$

and $f'_{\min}(1) = -3 \times 3.8 = -11.4$. Abs. error $= -10.2 - (-10.8) = 0.6$ [or $-10.8 - (-11.4) = 0.6$].

Therefore, % error $= \dfrac{0.6}{10.8} \times 100\% = 5.55\%$. i.e., 5.6%

TEST

1. i. $\dfrac{c}{ab} = \dfrac{6.2(10^4)}{4.7(10^3)9.1(10^{-2})} = 144.96142 = 1.45 \times 10^2$ [1].

ii. $a^3 + c^2 = (4.7(10^3))^3 + (6.2(10^4))^2 = 1.07667 \times 10^{11} = 1.08 \times 10^{11}$ [1].

iii. $\dfrac{b}{c-a} = \dfrac{9.1(10^{-2})}{6.2(10^4) - 4.7(10^3)} = 1.59 \times 10^{-6}$ [1]. All answers correctly rounded [1].

All answers in scientific form [1].

2. i. 4010 [1] ii. 0.00506 [1] iii. 109000 [1]

3. Nominal mass $= 1.50$ kg, abs. error is 0.005 [1] ∴ % error $= \dfrac{0.005}{1.50} \times 100 = \dfrac{1}{3}\% \approx 0.33\%$.[2]

4. (a) $a(c^2 - b) = 3.14 \times (1.04^2 - 0.98) = 0.319024$ [2] (b) 0.319 [1] (c) 0.32 [1]

(d) 3.19024×10^{-1} .[1] (Accept 3.19×10^{-1})

5. $2.\dot{2}\dot{3} = 2.23232323... = 2 + 0.23232323....$ Let $x = 0.232323......2.\dot{2}\dot{3} = 2 + x$

From $x = 0.232323...$ we have that $100x = 23.232323... \Leftrightarrow 100x = 23 + 0.232323...$ [1]

$$\Leftrightarrow 100x = 23 + x$$
$$\Leftrightarrow 99x = 23 \quad [1]$$
$$\therefore x = \frac{23}{99}$$

So, $2.\dot{2}\dot{3} = 2 + \frac{23}{99} = \frac{221}{99}$. Therefore, $2.\dot{2}\dot{3} \in Q$ [1]

6. i. $10.15 \le x \le 10.25, 3.55 \le y \le 3.65, 31.5° \le \theta \le 32.5°$.

$A_{max} = \frac{1}{2} \times 10.25 \times 3.65 \times \sin 32.5° = 10.05086$ [1]

$A_{min} = \frac{1}{2} \times 10.15 \times 3.55 \times \sin 31.5° = 9.41346$. [1] Therefore, $9.41 \le A \le 10.05$ [1]

ii. Nominal value $= \frac{1}{2} \times 10.2 \times 3.6 \times \sin 32° = 9.72931$.[1]

Therefore, % error $= \dfrac{\left(\frac{1}{2}\right)(10.05086 - 9.41346)}{9.72931} \times 100 = \dfrac{0.3187}{9.72931} \times 100 = 3.275\% \approx 3.3\%$ [2]

CHAPTER 3
LEVEL 1

1. i A.P ii. A.P iii. Neither iv. G.P **2.** i. 13 ii. -19 iii. 6 iv. 16 **3.** i. $u_1 = 8 + (1-1) \times 10 = 8$

ii. $u_5 = 8 + (5-1) \times 10 = 8 + 4 \times 10 = 48$. **4.** For an A.P use $u_n = a + (n-1)d$ and for a

G.P use $u_n = a \times r^{n-1}$: i. $a = 2, d = -3$, so, $u_{15} = 2 + (15-1) \times -3 = 2 - 14 \times 3 = -40$.

ii. $a = \frac{1}{8}, d = \frac{1}{8} \therefore u_{15} = \frac{1}{8} + (15-1) \times \frac{1}{8} = \frac{15}{8} = 1.875$

iv. $a = 3, r = -2 \therefore u_{15} = 3 \times (-2)^{14} = 49152$ 5. i. $s_{15} = \frac{15}{2}[2 \times 2 + 14 \times -3] = -285$

ii. $s_{15} = \frac{15}{2}\left[2 \times \frac{1}{8} + 14 \times \frac{1}{8}\right] = 15$ iv. $s_{15} = \dfrac{3[(-2)^{15}-1]}{-2-1} = 32769$

LEVEL 2

1. $a = -12, d = 5$ & $u_n = 208 \therefore 208 = -12 + (n-1) \times 5 \Leftrightarrow 5(n-1) = 220 \Leftrightarrow n = 45$.

2. $a = 1, r = -5 \therefore 15625 = 1 \times r^{n-1} \Leftrightarrow (-5)^{n-1} = (5)^6 \therefore (n-1) = 6 \Leftrightarrow n = 7$.

Note: $(5)^6 = (-5)^6$ **3.** 4782968 **4.** 22 years

5. $b = \frac{a+c}{2}$ **6.** Using $S_n = \frac{n}{2}[2a + (n-1)d]$ with $a = 60,000, d = 6000$ and $n = 5$, we have

$S_5 = \frac{5}{2}[2 \times 60000 + 4 \times 6000] = 360,000$. i.e, \$360,000.

7. We have $a = 126, ar = x, ar^2 = 56$. So that $126r = x$ and $xr = 56 \therefore 126r^2 = 56$.

That is, $r^2 = \frac{56}{126} = \frac{4}{9} \therefore r = \pm\frac{2}{3}$. Substitute into $ar = x \Rightarrow x = 126 \times \pm\frac{2}{3} = \pm84$.

8. $a = 9, r = \frac{1}{3}, S_5 = \dfrac{9\left[1 - \left(\frac{1}{3}\right)^5\right]}{1 - 1/3} = \dfrac{27}{2}\left[1 - \dfrac{1}{243}\right] = \dfrac{121}{9}(= 13.\dot{4})$

9. $a = 3, r = 2, \therefore S_N = \dfrac{3[2^N - 1]}{2 - 1} = 1533 \Leftrightarrow 2^N - 1 = 511 \Leftrightarrow 2^N = 512 \therefore N = 9$

LEVEL 3

1. (a) 9 (b) 93 (c) 48 **2.** (a) 313 (b) 1738 (c) 2 (d) 6141 **3.** 58

4. $b = a + x \Rightarrow x = (b - a)$ and $d = a + 3x = a + 3(b - a) \therefore d = 3b - 2a$.

So, $3b = d + 2a \Leftrightarrow b = \frac{1}{3}(d + 2a)$.

LEVEL 4

1. 21 **2.** 21 months. **3.** 15% **4.** (a) 4950 (b) 24th day (c) 130 150

5. (c) The series is: $100 \times 1.005^{50} + 100 \times 1.005^{49} + \ldots + 100 \times 1.005^1$

or $100 \times 1.005^1 + 100 \times 1.005^2 + \ldots + 100 \times 1.005^{49} + 100 \times 1.005^{50}$. This is a G.P with

$a = 100 \times 1.005^1 = 100.5, r = 1.005, n = 50. S_{50} = \dfrac{100.5(1.005^{50} - 1)}{1.005 - 1} = 5692.8389$ or

$5,692.84

EXAMINATION STYLE

1. (a) Amount of Zylacan = 500×3 = 1500 mg (or 1.5 gm) (b) In the first hour there are 12 drips per minute which means that there will be 12×60=720 drips during the entire hour. This means that the amount of solution received by the patient is 720×0.06=43.2ml in the first hour.
The three results are:

Hour	drips/min	drips/hour	volume (ml)
1	12.0	720	43.2
2	11.5	690	41.4
3	11.0	660	39.6

(c) The volumes form an AP: 43.2, 41.4, 39.6, ...
The six terms can be added directly or the S_n formula can be used to get a value of 235.2ml after 6 hours. The volume remaining is 267.8ml.
(d) The amounts are 3×43.2 = 129.6 mg, 3×41.4 = 124.2 mg & 3×39.6 = 118.8 mg.
(e) The amounts of drug delivered in each hour are an AP: 129.6, 124.2, 118.8,...
$a = 129.6$ and $d = -5.4$ and we need to solve $a + (n - 1)d = 65$: $129.6 - 5.4(n - 1) = 65$ giving $n = 11.96$ so the drip should be replaced after 12 hours or at the beginning of the 13th hour.

(f) $S_n = \frac{n}{2}[2a + (n - 1)d]$ with $a = 43.2, d = -1.8$ $S_n = 500$ (because the contents of the bottle are

completely used) and n is unknown. $500 = \frac{n}{2}[2 \times 43.2 + (n - 1)(-1.8)]$

$$500 = \frac{n}{2}[86.4 + (n - 1)(-1.8)]$$

$$-\frac{1.8n^2}{2} + \frac{88.2n}{2} - 500 = 0$$

$$-1.8n^2 + 88.2n - 1000 = 0$$

$$n = \dfrac{-88.2 \pm \sqrt{88.2^2 - 4(-1.8)(-1000)}}{2(-1.8)}$$

That is, $n = 17.81461$ or $31.18539 \approx 17.81$ hours or (31.18 - discard).

2. (a) $P_{10} = 7 + 2 \times 9 = 25$ hours. (b) $P_t = 7 + (t-1)2 = 2t + 5$.

$C_t = 180(2t + 5) = 360t + 900$ ($/hr)

(c) $S_n = \frac{n}{2}[2a + (n-1)d] \therefore S_{20} = \frac{20}{2}[2 \times 7 + (20-1)2] = 520$ (hrs)

(d)The money allows 1000 hours of preparation.

$S_n = \frac{n}{2}[14 + (n-1)2] \therefore \frac{n}{2}(2n + 12) = 1000 \Leftrightarrow n^2 + 6n - 1000 = 0$, so $n \approx 28.76$

So the money will last about 29 years. (e) Cost $= 6000 \times (1.07)^{n-1}$

TEST

1. The sequence is arithmetic with $a = -12$, $d = 5$ [1]

$t_n = a + (n-1)d \therefore 123 = -12 + (n-1)5 \Leftrightarrow 123 = 5n - 17 \therefore n = 28$ [1]

2. The series is geometric with $a = -5$ & $r = -2$. [1]

$t_n = ar^{n-1} \Rightarrow 640 = (-5)(-2)^{n-1} \Rightarrow n = 8$ [1] $S_8 = \frac{(-5)((-2)^8 - 1)}{-2 - 1} = 425$ [1]

3. (a) $a = 30{,}000$, $r = 0.935$. $t_3 = 30000 \times (0.935)^2 = 26226.75$ i.e., \$26,226.75 [2]

(b) $t = 1$, $V = 28050$; $t = 2$, $V = 26226.75$; $t = 3$, $V = 24522.01$; $t = 4$, $V = 22928.08$ [2]

Years since purchase (t)	1	2	3	4
Value of car ($ V$)	28050	26226.75	24522.01	22928.08

(c) $V_t = 30000 \times (0.935)^t$, $t = 0, 1, 2, \ldots$ [2]

4. (a) Number $= 1 + 2 + 3 + 4 = 10$ [1] (b) The series is arithmetic with $a = d = 1$ [1].

$S_n = \frac{n}{2}[2(1) + (n-1)1] = \frac{n^2}{2} + \frac{n}{2}$ [1].

$\frac{n^2}{2} + \frac{n}{2} = 55$ [1] $\therefore n^2 + n - 110 = 0 \Leftrightarrow (n - 10)(n + 11) = 0 \Leftrightarrow n = 10, -11$ i.e., 10 rows [1].

5. (a) $t_5 = 12000(1.08^4) = 16325.868$ or 16326 ratchets [1].

(b) $S_5 = \frac{12000(1.08^5 - 1)}{1.08 - 1} = 70399.212$ or 70399 ratchets [1].

(c) Solving $24000 = 12000[1.08^{(n-1)}]$ [1].

$1.08^{(n-1)} = 2 \Rightarrow (n-1)\log 1.08 = \log 2 \Rightarrow n = \frac{\log 2}{\log 1.08} + 1 = 10.006468$ [1].

(d) Solving $\frac{12000(1.08^n - 1)}{1.08 - 1} = 10^6$ [1].

$1.08^n = \frac{0.08(10^6)}{12000} + 1 \Rightarrow n = \frac{\log\left(\frac{0.08(10^6)}{12000}\right)}{\log 1.08} + 1 = 25.6503$. That is, the 26th year[1].

CHAPTER 4
LEVEL 1

1. (a) i. $\{x | 4 \le x \le 9\}$ ii. [4, 9] (b) i. $\{x | x > 6\}$ ii. (6, ∞) (c) i. $\{x | x < -3\}$ ii. ($-\infty$, -3)

2. i.   ii.   iii.

LEVEL 2

1. i. $x = 4$ **ii.** $3s = 9 \Leftrightarrow s = 3$ **iii.** $-7x = -7 \Leftrightarrow x = 1$ **iv.** $-\dfrac{1}{2}t = -2 \Leftrightarrow t = 4$

v. $2x - 2 = 7 \Leftrightarrow 2x = 9 \Leftrightarrow x = 4.5$ **vi.** $-3y - 6 = 4 \Leftrightarrow -3y = 10 \Leftrightarrow y = -\dfrac{10}{3}$

2. i. $x > -1$ **ii.** $-x \le 4 \Leftrightarrow x \ge -4$ **iii.** $\dfrac{1}{2}y < -3 \Leftrightarrow y < -6$ **iv.** $-3 + 3x > 3 \Leftrightarrow 3x > 6 \Leftrightarrow x > 2$.

v. $\dfrac{2}{3}(x-4) < 2 \Leftrightarrow x - 4 < 3 \Leftrightarrow x < 7$ **vi.** $-2\left(1 + \dfrac{2}{5}x\right) < -2 \Leftrightarrow 1 + \dfrac{2}{5}x > 1 \Leftrightarrow \dfrac{2}{5}x > 0 \Leftrightarrow x > 0$.

LEVEL 3

1. i. $(\times 6) \Rightarrow 2(x - 1) + 6 = 3x \Leftrightarrow x = 4$

ii $(\times 20) \Rightarrow 80 - 8(2 - x) = 5(2x + 3) \Leftrightarrow 80 - 16 + 8x = 10x + 15 \Leftrightarrow 49 = 2x \Leftrightarrow x = 24.5$

iii. $(\times 6) \Rightarrow 2(5 - 2s) - 6 < s \Leftrightarrow 10 - 4s - 6 < s \Leftrightarrow 4 < 5s \Leftrightarrow s > 0.8$

iv. $(\times 6) \Rightarrow 3(3y - 1) > 2(y + 4) + 6 \Leftrightarrow 9y - 3 > 2y + 8 + 6 \Leftrightarrow 7y > 17 \Leftrightarrow y > \dfrac{17}{7}$

v. $(\times (1 - x)) \Rightarrow 2 + (1 - x) = x \Leftrightarrow 3 = 2x \Leftrightarrow x = \dfrac{3}{2}$

vi. $(91 \times 10) \Rightarrow 2(5 - 2a) \ge 20 - 15(1 + a) \Leftrightarrow 10 - 4a \ge 20 - 15 - 15a \Leftrightarrow a \ge -\dfrac{5}{11}$

2. Let Joseph be x years old. Therefore, mother is $3x$ years old. So, $x + 3x = 88$, i.e., $4x = 88$. Therefore $x = 22$. i.e., Joseph is 22 years old.

LEVEL 4

1. i. $ax = ba - a \Leftrightarrow ax = a(b - 1) \Leftrightarrow x = b - 1$

ii. $\dfrac{a}{b}x + \dfrac{b}{a}x > a + b \Leftrightarrow \dfrac{a^2 + b^2}{ab}x > a - b$. If $ab > 0 \Rightarrow x > \dfrac{ab(a + b)}{a^2 + b^2}$, if $ab < 0 \Rightarrow x < \dfrac{ab(a + b)}{a^2 + b^2}$.

2. Let the speed of the train be $v_T = 80$ after travelling for $t = T$ hr and let the speed of the plane be $v_p = 200$ after it has travelled $T - 3$ hr. Therefore, when they have travelled the same distance we have that $80T = 200(T - 3) \Leftrightarrow T = 5$, so that the plane travels $200 \times 2 = 400$ km. We have assumed that they travel in the same direction. i.e., in a straight collinear line.

EXAMINATION STYLE QUESTIONS

1. Let the speed of the train be V_T so that $V_T = \begin{cases} s & 0 \le t \le 3 \\ s + 10 & 3 < t \le 7 \end{cases}$.

i. Therefore, during the next four hours, the distance travelled $= 4(s + 10)$ km

ii. $3s + 4(s + 10) = 650 \Leftrightarrow 7s = 610 \Leftrightarrow s = \dfrac{610}{7}$.

2. $(x + 2)^2 = x^2 + (x + 3)^2 - 2 \cdot x \cdot (x + 3) \cdot \cos 60°$ (using cosine rule).

$\Leftrightarrow x^2 + 4x + 4 = x^2 + x^2 + 6x + 9 - x^2 - 3x$

$\Leftrightarrow 4x + 4 = 3x + 9$

$\Leftrightarrow x = 5$

Therefore, the perimeter is $(5) + (5+2) + (5+3) = 5 + 7 + 8 = 20$ units

3. i. $50x + 10y > 450$ ii. $y = 26 - x$ iii. $50x + 10(26 - x) > 45 \Leftrightarrow 40x > 190 \Leftrightarrow x > 4.75$

Therefore, $x_{min} = 5$.

TEST

1.   **2.**   i. $8h = 16 \Leftrightarrow h = 2$ [2] ii. $3y = 15 \Leftrightarrow y = 5$ [2]

$\rightarrow x$ [2]   iii. $2x - 1 = 7 \Leftrightarrow 2x = 8 \Leftrightarrow x = 4$ [2]

3. i $(a - 1) - 4 = 2a + 8 \Leftrightarrow a = -13$ [2] [1]

ii. $5(4x + 1) \leq 3(2 - x) \Leftrightarrow 20x + 5 \leq 6 - 3x \Leftrightarrow x \leq \dfrac{1}{23}$ [2] [1]

4. i. $10 - x$ [1] ii. $\dfrac{10 - x}{x} = \dfrac{x}{5 - x} \Leftrightarrow (10 - x)(5 - x) = x^2 \Leftrightarrow 15x = 50 \Leftrightarrow x = \dfrac{10}{3}$. [2] [1]

5. i. Let the stock be worth x. Therefore: $x\left(1 + \dfrac{y}{100}\right) = 6400 - (1)$ & $x\left(1 - \dfrac{y}{100}\right) = 6000 - (2)$

Dividing (1) by (2): $\dfrac{x\left(1 + \dfrac{y}{100}\right)}{x\left(1 - \dfrac{y}{100}\right)} = \dfrac{6400}{6000} \Leftrightarrow \dfrac{\left(\dfrac{100 + y}{100}\right)}{\left(\dfrac{100 - y}{100}\right)} = \dfrac{64}{60} \Leftrightarrow \dfrac{100 + y}{100 - y} = \dfrac{16}{15}$. [2] [2]

ii. $\dfrac{100 + y}{100 - y} = \dfrac{16}{15} \Leftrightarrow 1500 + 15y = 1600 - 16y \Leftrightarrow 31y = 100 \Leftrightarrow y = \dfrac{100}{31}$. [1] [1]

iii. $x\left(1 + \dfrac{\left(\dfrac{100}{31}\right)}{100}\right) = 6400 \Leftrightarrow \dfrac{32}{31}x = 6400 \Leftrightarrow x = 6200$ [1]

CHAPTER 5
LEVEL 1

1. (a) No (b) Yes (c) Yes **2.** (a) $x(x + 1)$ (b) $x(2 - x)$ (c) $ax(4 + x)$ (d) $6y(y + 2)$
(e) $3b(3b - 1)$ (f) $4ay(3y + 1)$ **3.** (a) $(2 + a)(a + b)$ (b) $(z - 3)(z - 1)$ (c) $(x - 2)(x + 1)$
(d) $(y + x)(x - y)$

LEVEL 2

1. (a) $(x + 4)(x - 1)$ (b) $(y - 5)(y - 1)$ (c) $(x + 7)(x - 2)$ (d) $(a - 1)^2$ (e) $(a - 3)(a + 1)$
(f) $(y - 9)(y - 7)$ **2.** (a) $(2x - 1)(x + 3)$ (b) $(3x + 1)(x + 1)$ (c) $(2y + 3)(y - 1)$
(d) $(3z + 1)(2z + 1)$ (e) $(4x + 3)(3x + 4)$ (f) $(5x + 1)(x - 3)$

3. i. $-4, 1$ ii. $1, 5$ iii. $-3, -2$ iv. 1 v. $-7, 2$ vi. $7, 9$ **4.** i. $\dfrac{-1 \pm \sqrt{29}}{2}$ ii. $\dfrac{-3 \pm \sqrt{41}}{4}$ iii. $-2 \pm \sqrt{13}$

iv. $\dfrac{3 \pm \sqrt{89}}{10}$ v. none vi. $\dfrac{-5 \pm \sqrt{133}}{6}$

LEVEL 3

1. i. To find the turning point we complete the square:

$y = x^2 - 6x + 13 = x^2 - 6x + \left(\dfrac{6}{2}\right)^2 - \left(\dfrac{6}{2}\right)^2 + 13 = (x - 3)^2 + 4$. Turning point occurs at $(3,4)$

ii. $(-1,3)$ iii. $(1,-3)$ iv. In this instance, we need to first factorise the leading coefficient:

$$y = 3x^2 - 6x + 4 = 3\left(x^2 - 2x + \frac{4}{3}\right) = 3\left(\left(x^2 - 2x + \left(\frac{2}{2}\right)^2\right) - \left(\frac{2}{2}\right)^2 + \frac{4}{3}\right)$$

$$= 3(x-1)^2 - 3 + 4$$

$$= 3(x-1)^2 + 1$$

So, turning point occurs at (1,1) v. (0.5,3) vi. (1,0)

2. i. $y = x^2 - x - 2$ ii. $y = 4 - x^2$ iii. $y = x^2 - 2x - 1$ iv. $y = x^2 - 4x + 4$

3. (a) $x^2 + x - 4 = 0 \Leftrightarrow x^2 + x + \left(\frac{1}{2}\right)^2 - \left(\frac{1}{2}\right)^2 - 4 = 0 \Leftrightarrow \left(x + \frac{1}{2}\right)^2 - \frac{17}{4} = 0$

$$\Leftrightarrow \left(x + \frac{1}{2} + \frac{\sqrt{17}}{2}\right)\left(x + \frac{1}{2} - \frac{\sqrt{17}}{2}\right) = 0$$

$$\Leftrightarrow x = \frac{-1 \pm \sqrt{17}}{2}$$

(b) $2x^2 - 2x - 7 = 0 \Leftrightarrow 2\left(x^2 - x - \frac{7}{2}\right) = 0 \Leftrightarrow \left(x^2 - x + \left(\frac{1}{2}\right)^2\right) - \left(\frac{1}{2}\right)^2 - \frac{7}{2} = 0$

$$\Leftrightarrow \left(x - \frac{1}{2}\right)^2 - \frac{15}{4} = 0$$

$$\Leftrightarrow \left(x - \frac{1}{2} - \frac{\sqrt{15}}{2}\right)\left(x - \frac{1}{2} + \frac{\sqrt{15}}{2}\right) = 0$$

$$\Leftrightarrow x = \frac{1 \pm \sqrt{15}}{2}$$

(c) $x^2 - 6x - 1 = 0 \Leftrightarrow (x^2 - 6x + 9) - 9 - 1 = 0 \Leftrightarrow (x - 3)^2 - 10 = 0$

$$\Leftrightarrow (x - 3 - \sqrt{10})(x - 3 + \sqrt{10}) = 0$$

$$\Leftrightarrow x = 3 \pm \sqrt{10}$$

(d) $3(x^2 - 4x + 1) = 0 \Leftrightarrow (x^2 - 4x + 4) - 4 + 1 = 0 \Leftrightarrow (x - 2)^2 - 3 = 0$

$$\Leftrightarrow (x - 2 - \sqrt{3})(x - 2 + \sqrt{3}) = 0$$

$$\Leftrightarrow x = 2 \pm \sqrt{3}$$

(e) $2\left(x^2 - \frac{1}{2}x - 1\right) = 0 \Leftrightarrow \left(x^2 - \frac{1}{2}x + \left(\frac{1}{4}\right)^2\right) - \left(\frac{1}{4}\right)^2 - 1 = 0 \Leftrightarrow \left(x - \frac{1}{4}\right)^2 - \frac{17}{16} = 0$

$$\Leftrightarrow \left(x - \frac{1}{4} - \frac{\sqrt{17}}{4}\right)\left(x - \frac{1}{4} + \frac{\sqrt{17}}{4}\right) = 0$$

$$\Leftrightarrow x = \frac{1 \pm \sqrt{17}}{4}$$

(f) $(x^2 - 6x + 9) - 9 + 2 = 0 \Leftrightarrow (x - 3)^2 - 7 = 0 \Leftrightarrow x = 3 \pm \sqrt{7}$

4. (a)   (b)   (c)

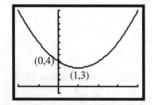

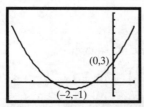

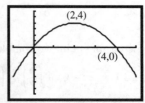

(d)

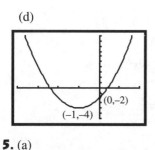

$(0,-2)$
$(-1,-4)$

(e)

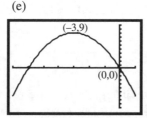

$(-3,9)$

$(0,0)$

(f)

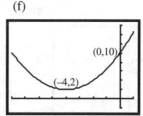

$(0,10)$

$(-4,2)$

5. (a)

0   2

(b)

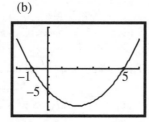

-1 5

-5

(c)

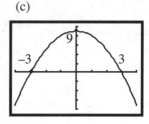

9

-3 3

(d)

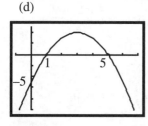

1   5

-5

(e)

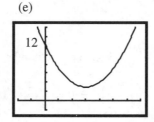

12

(f)

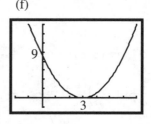

9

3

LEVEL 4

1. Completing the square: $y = x^2 + kx + 4 \Rightarrow y = \left(x + \dfrac{k}{2}\right)^2 - \dfrac{k^2}{4} + 4$, so t.pt at $\left(-\dfrac{k}{2}, -\dfrac{k^2}{4} + 4\right)$.

2. (a) $N = a^2 - 3a + 3 = \left(a^2 - 3a + \left(\dfrac{3}{2}\right)^2\right) - \left(\dfrac{3}{2}\right)^2 + 3 = \left(a - \dfrac{3}{2}\right)^2 + \dfrac{3}{4}$, As $\left(a - \dfrac{3}{2}\right)^2 \geq 0$ for

all real values of a, then $N \geq \dfrac{3}{4}$. Therefore, N will always be positive. (b) $N_{min} = \dfrac{3}{4}$.

3. (a) $h = 0 \Leftrightarrow 1.5 + 10t - 5t^2 = 0 \Leftrightarrow t = \dfrac{-10 \pm \sqrt{10^2 - 4 \times 1.5 \times -5}}{-10} = 1 \mp 1.14$

$$\therefore t = 2.14, -0.14$$

As $t > 0$, $t = 2.14$

(b) Maximum occurs at midpoint. i.e., $t = \dfrac{2.14 + (-0.14)}{2} = 1 \therefore h(1) = 1.5 + 10 - 5 = 6.5$ m.

(c) $h = 5 \Rightarrow -5t^2 + 10t + 1.5 = 5 \Leftrightarrow -5t^2 + 10t - 3.5 = 0 \Leftrightarrow t^2 - 2t + 0.7 = 0$

$$\Leftrightarrow (t-1)^2 - 0.3 = 0 \Leftrightarrow t = 1 \pm \sqrt{0.3}$$

So, we have that $t_1 = 1 - \sqrt{0.3}$, $t_2 = 1 + \sqrt{0.3} \therefore (t_2 - t_1) = 2\sqrt{0.3} \approx 1.095$ (i.e., ~ 1.1).

(d)

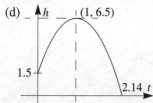

h $(1, 6.5)$

1.5

2.14 t

4. (a)

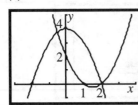

(b) $2x^2 - 3x - 2 = 0 \Leftrightarrow (2x + 1)(x - 2) = 0$

$$\Leftrightarrow x = -0.5 \ \text{or} \ x = 2$$

(c) $2x^2 - 3x - 2 = 0 \Leftrightarrow x^2 - 3x + 2 + x^2 - 4 = 0$

$$\Leftrightarrow x^2 - 3x + 2 = 4 - x^2$$

i.e., curves intersect at $x = -0.5$ & $x = 2$.

Therefore, points are: $(-0.5, 3.75)$ & $(2, 0)$

5. Let the number be x, so that: $x + \dfrac{1}{x} = 5 \Leftrightarrow x^2 + 1 = 5x \Leftrightarrow x^2 - 5x + 1 = 0 \Leftrightarrow x = \dfrac{5 \pm \sqrt{21}}{2}$.

6. Let Pablo's speed be v km/h, so that: Time taken, $t = \dfrac{17}{v}$ hence, $t - 1 = \dfrac{17}{v + 1}$.

Therefore, $\dfrac{17}{v} - 1 = \dfrac{17}{v + 1} \Leftrightarrow 17(v + 1) - v(v + 1) = 17v \Leftrightarrow v^2 + v - 17 = 0$

$$\Leftrightarrow v = \dfrac{-1 \pm \sqrt{69}}{2}$$

Then, as $v > 0$, we have that $v = \dfrac{-1 + \sqrt{69}}{2} \approx 3.65$. i.e., 3.65km/hr

7. (a) $\dfrac{x}{a} + \dfrac{1}{a} + \left(1 + \dfrac{1}{a}\right) = 0 \Leftrightarrow \dfrac{1}{a}x^2 + 1 + \left(1 + \dfrac{1}{a}\right)x = 0 \Leftrightarrow \dfrac{1}{a}x^2 + \left(1 + \dfrac{1}{a}\right)x + 1 = 0$

$$\Leftrightarrow \left(\dfrac{1}{a}x + 1\right)(x + 1) = 0$$

$$\Leftrightarrow x = -a \ \text{or} \ x = -1$$

(b) $0.5x^2 + 1 + 1.5x = 0 \Leftrightarrow 0.5x + \dfrac{1}{x} + 1.5 = 0 \Leftrightarrow \dfrac{1}{2}x + \dfrac{1}{x} + \left(1 + \dfrac{1}{2}\right) = 0$. i.e., $a = 2$.

Therefore, $x = -2$ or $x = -1$.

8. Interest for schemes $A = a\left(1 + \dfrac{x}{100}\right)^2 - a$; $B = 2(a + 100)\left(\dfrac{x - 1}{100}\right)$; $C = 2(a + 50)\left(\dfrac{x}{100}\right)$

We have: $a\left(1 + \dfrac{x}{100}\right)^2 - a = 2(a + 50)\left(\dfrac{x}{100}\right) \Leftrightarrow a\left(1 + \dfrac{2x}{100} + \dfrac{x^2}{10000}\right) - a = \dfrac{2x(a + 50)}{100}$

$$(\times \text{by } 100) \qquad \Leftrightarrow \dfrac{ax^2}{100} + 2xa = 2xa + 100x$$

$$\Leftrightarrow \dfrac{ax^2}{100} = 100x$$

$$\therefore x = \dfrac{10000}{a} \ (\text{as } x \neq 0)$$

Also, $2(a + 100)\left(\dfrac{x - 1}{100}\right) + 40 = 2(a + 50)\left(\dfrac{x}{100}\right) \Leftrightarrow 2(a + 100)(x - 1) + 4000 = 2(a + 50)(x)$

Therefore, $100x - 2a + 3800 = 0 \Leftrightarrow x = \dfrac{2a - 3800}{100}$.

This means that $\dfrac{10000}{a} = \dfrac{2a - 3800}{100} \Leftrightarrow 2a^2 - 3800a = 1000000$.

Using a graphics calculator, we have $a = 2134.27$ and so, $x \approx 4.685$.

for a question such as this, once you have equated the two equations in 'a', there is no need ...plify the result into a quadratic, simply use your graphics calculator.

...MINATION STYLE QUESTIONS

$ = -5t^2 + 12t \Rightarrow h(2) = -5(2)^2 + 12(2) = 4$ metres.

$= -5t^2 + 12t = -5\left(t^2 - \frac{12}{5}t\right) = -5\left(\left(t - \frac{6}{5}\right)^2 - \frac{36}{25}\right) = -5\left(t - \frac{6}{5}\right)^2 + \frac{36}{5}$. Therefore, the

maximum occurs at $t = \frac{6}{5}, h = \frac{36}{5}$.

iii. $-5t^2 + 12t = 5 \Rightarrow 5t^2 - 12t + 5 = 0 \Rightarrow t = \dfrac{12 \pm \sqrt{(-12)^2 - 4(5)(5)}}{2(5)} \approx 0.537, 1.86$ sec.

iv. $-5t^2 + 12t = 0 \Rightarrow t(-5t + 12) = 0 \Rightarrow t = 0, \frac{12}{5}$ so the ball is in the air for $\frac{12}{5} = 2.4$ sec.

2. (a) For $\Delta CYD: A = \frac{1}{2} \cdot x \cdot 5 = \frac{5}{2}x$; For $\Delta XBY: A = \frac{1}{2} \cdot x \cdot (5 - x)$

Therefore, total area, $A = \frac{5}{2}x + \frac{5}{2}x - \frac{1}{2}x^2 = 5x - \frac{1}{2}x^2$

(b) $\dfrac{\frac{5}{2}x}{\frac{x(5-x)}{2}} = \frac{4}{3} \Leftrightarrow 4(5 - x) = 15 \Leftrightarrow 4x = 5 \therefore x = \frac{5}{4}$.

3. (a) From the graph, $b = 27$. Therefore, $y = x^2 + ax + 27$. The factors are $(x + 9)$ & $(x + 3)$.
So that $y = k(x + 9)(x + 3) = k(x^2 + 12x + 27) = kx^2 + 12kx + 27k \Rightarrow k = 1 \therefore a = 12$.
(b) $y = x^2 + 12x + 27 = (x^2 + 12x + 36) - 9 = (x + 6)^2 - 9 \therefore y_{min} = -9$ (when $x = -6$).

TEST

1. $x^2 - 6x - 7 = 0 \Leftrightarrow (x - 7)(x + 1) = 0 \Leftrightarrow x = 7$ or $x = -1$.[2]
This means that the x–intercepts occur at $x = 7$ and $x = -1$.
Graph [2]

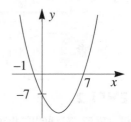

2. (a) $(x - 8)(x - 4)$ [2] (b) $(x - 6)^2$ [1]
(c) $x^2 - 12x + 36 - 6 = (x - 6)^2 - 6 = (x - 6 - \sqrt{6})(x - 6 + \sqrt{6})$ [3]

3. $5 - 3x - 3x^2 = 0 \Rightarrow x = \dfrac{-(-3) \pm \sqrt{(-3)^2 - 4(-3)(5)}}{2(3)} = 0.88443731, -1.8844373$ [1]

corrct to 3 sig.figs, x is equal to 0.884, −1.88 [1]
4. The intercept suggests factors of $x + 1$ and $x - 3$. [1]. The parabola is 'vertex up' and so we will need to consider either $y = (x + 1)(3 - x)$ or $y = -(x - 3)(x + 1)$ (there are a few other variants) [1]. We also need to check the y-intercept. This 3 and the functions multiply out to:
$y = -x^2 + 2x + 3$ which is correct [1]. If it had not been, we would have had to find the value of k in $y = k(x + 1)(3 - x)$ that gives the correct intercept. By symmetry, the maximum point occurs midway between the intercepts (at $x = 1$) [1] $y = (1 + 1)(3 - 1) = 4$ [1] (Maximum occurs at (1,4)).

5. $x = 1 + \dfrac{6}{x} \Rightarrow x^2 = x^2 - x - 6 = 0 \Rightarrow (x-3)(x+2) = 0$. [2], $-2, 3$ [1].

6. (a) Let y m be the length of the side parallel to the wall. $\therefore y + 2x = 100 \Leftrightarrow y = 100 - 2x$ [1]

(b) Let A m^2 be the enclosed area. $\therefore A = xy = x(100 - 2x), 0 \le x \le 50$ [2]

(c) Using the graph of $A(x)$: [1]

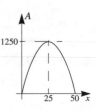

　　We have that at $x = 25$, $A = 25 \times (100 - 50) = 1250$.

　　That is, the maximum area is 1250 m^2. [1]

7. (a) i. $-x^2 + 14x - 40 = -(x^2 - 14x + 40) = -(x - 10)(x - 4)$ [2]

　　ii. $8x - x^2 = x(8 - x)$ [1]. Hence, $A \equiv (4, 0), B \equiv (8, 0)$ and $C \equiv (10, 0)$ [2]

(b) $8x - x^2 = -x^2 + 14x - 40 \Leftrightarrow 40 = 6x \Leftrightarrow x = \dfrac{20}{3}$ [3]

(c) We first need to find h: when $x = \dfrac{20}{3}, y = 8 \times \dfrac{20}{3} - \left(\dfrac{20}{3}\right)^2 = \dfrac{80}{9}$

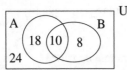

$\therefore$ Area $= \dfrac{1}{2} \times (BC) \times h = \dfrac{1}{2} \times 2 \times \dfrac{80}{9} = \dfrac{80}{9}$ sq. units [2]

CHAPTER 6
LEVEL 1

1. $\{3, 4, 5, 6, 7\}$ **2.** "I will not go swimming." is given by $\neg q$. "If it is hot, then I will not go swimming." is the implication. Therefore, p implies the negative of q. i.e., $p \Rightarrow \neg q$.

3. i.　　　　　　　　　ii.　　　　　　　　　iii.

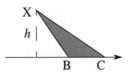　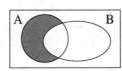　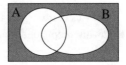

LEVEL 2

1. i. $\neg p \Rightarrow q$ is an implication, stating the negative of p implies q. $\therefore$ the converse is $p \Rightarrow \neg q$

ii. "She is not tall" is represented by $\neg x$. "She is not tall and she is beautiful" is the conjunction of $\neg x$ and y. i.e., $\neg x \wedge y$.

2.

LEVEL 3

1. i.

p	q	$\neg p$	$\neg p \Rightarrow q$	$p \vee q$	$(\neg p \Rightarrow q) \Leftrightarrow (p \vee q)$
T	T	F	T	T	T
T	F	F	T	T	T
F	T	T	T	T	T
F	F	T	F	F	T

ii. Regardless of the truth value of p and q, the result is always true. So, $(\neg p \Rightarrow q) \Leftrightarrow (p \vee q)$ is a tautology. iii. If I do not train, I will get into trouble. $p \vee q$ is the disjunction of p and q, that is, "I train or I get into trouble". So, either p and q are both true, or at least one of them is true.

2. i. $x + xy = x(1 + y) = x(1) = x$ ii. $xy' + x'y + xy = x + y$ (Use a Venn diagram).

LEVEL 4

1. Consider the contrapositive approach:

$\neg q$ i.e., the triangle is equilateral

$\neg p$ i.e., the line drawn from the vertex of a triangle to the midpoint of the opposite side does intersect this side at a right angle.

Therefore, we must prove that $\neg q \Rightarrow \neg p$.

Consider the $\triangle ABC$ as shown in the diagram: Given that $AB = AC$ & $BX = CX$

then, as AX is common

we have $\triangle ABX \cong \triangle ACX$ (SSS)

$\therefore \angle AXB = \angle AXC$

$\therefore \angle AXB = 90°$ (straight line)

Hence, $\neg q \Rightarrow \neg p$ which is equivalent to $p \Rightarrow q$ (as required).

Or very simply: $\neg q \Rightarrow \neg p$ so $\neg(\neg q) \Rightarrow \neg(\neg p)$ or $p \Rightarrow q$

2. $A' \cup B' \cup (A \cap B \cap C') = (A' \cup B') \cup (A \cap B \cap C')$

$= (A \cap B)' \cup (A \cap B \cap C')$

$= (A \cap B)' \cup ((A \cap B) \cap C')$

$= \{(A \cap B)' \cup (A \cap B)\} \cap \{(A \cap B)' \cup C'\}$

$= U \cap \{(A \cap B)' \cup C'\}$

$= (A \cap B)' \cup C'$

$= ((A \cap B) \cap C)'$

$= (A \cap B \cap C)'$

EXAMINATION STYLE QUESTIONS

1. i. $n(U) = 62$, $n(I) = 40$, $n(S) = 25$, $n(I \cap S) = 17$

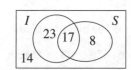

ii. $n(I \cap S') = 23$ iii. $p(I \cap S) = \dfrac{17}{62}$ iv. $p(I \cap S') = \dfrac{23}{62}$

v. $p(S|I) = \dfrac{p(S \cap I)}{p(I)} = \dfrac{17}{40}$

TEST

1. i. [2] ii. [2]

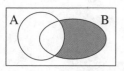 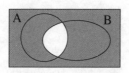

2. A: $x \wedge y$ is the conjunction of x and y. It is true only if both x and y are true. Since y is false, then $x \wedge y$ is false. [2]

B: $x \vee y$ is the disjunction of x and y. It is true if either x or y is true. If x is true then $x \vee y$ is true.[1]

C: The statement y is false because $3 \times 4 = 12$ ($\neq 18$). [1]

D: $x \Rightarrow y$ is the implication, if x is true then y is true. However, x is true but y is false. [1]

3. [3]

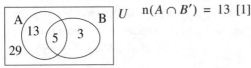

U $n(A \cap B') = 13$ [1]

4. i.

p	q	$p \Rightarrow q$	$\neg q$	$p \wedge \neg q$	$\neg(p \wedge \neg q)$	$(p \Rightarrow q) \Leftrightarrow \neg(p \wedge \neg q)$
T	T	T	F	F	T	T
T	F	F	T	T	F	T
F	T	T	F	F	T	T
F	F	T	T	F	T	T

[2] marks for each row.

ii. The statement "If Nora lives in Sydney, then Nora lives in N.S.W" is represented by $p \Rightarrow q$. However, the statement "It is false that Nora lives in Sydney and Nora does not live in N.S.W" is given by $\neg(p \wedge \neg q)$. [2]

5. i. $n(V) = 20$, $n(B) = 22$ and $n(V \cup B) = 25$. Venn diagram: $y = 37 - 25 = 12$.[1]

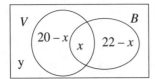

That is, 12 play neither sport. [1]

ii. $(20 - x) + (x) + (22 - x) = 25 \Leftrightarrow 42 - x = 25$ [2]

$$\Leftrightarrow x = 17 \text{ [1]}$$

Therefore, $p(V') = 1 - p(V) = 1 - \dfrac{20}{37} = \dfrac{17}{37}$ [1]

iii. $p(V \cap B') = \dfrac{20 - 17}{37} = \dfrac{3}{37}$. [2]

CHAPTER 7
LEVEL 1
For these questions make use of the standard trig. ratios for right–angled triangles.
1. 19.01cm **2.** 56cm **3.** 12.01cm **4.** 2.01cm **5.** 1.56cm **6.** 27° **7.** 56° **8.** 53°
LEVEL 2
1. $\dfrac{x}{\sin 56°} = \dfrac{3.14}{\sin 47°} \Rightarrow x = \dfrac{3.14 \sin 56°}{\sin 47°} = 3.5593967$ or approx. 3.56cm. The other problems
are solved in the same way: **2.** 1.41cm **3.** 7.27cm **4.** 23.7cm **5.** 4.92cm **6.** 6.03cm **7.** 50.86cm
8. 119.94cm
LEVEL 3
1.

$$x^2 = 1^2 + 1^2 - 2 \times 1 \times 1 \times \cos 120°$$

$$\Leftrightarrow x^2 = 2 - 2 \cos 120°$$

$$\Leftrightarrow x^2 = 3$$

$$\therefore x = \sqrt{3} \text{ (as } x > 0)$$

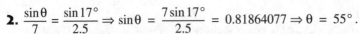

2. $\dfrac{\sin\theta}{7} = \dfrac{\sin 17°}{2.5} \Rightarrow \sin\theta = \dfrac{7 \sin 17°}{2.5} = 0.81864077 \Rightarrow \theta = 55°$.

The other angle is $= 180° - 55° = 125°$.

3. The data (two sides and the included angle) compels the use of the cosine rule.

$$c^2 = a^2 + b^2 - 2ab\cos C = 2^2 + 1.7^2 - 2(2)(1.7)\cos(63°) = 3.8028646$$

$$\Rightarrow c = \sqrt{3.8028646} = 1.95 \text{ cm}$$

Now, $\dfrac{\sin A}{a} = \dfrac{\sin C}{c} \Rightarrow \dfrac{\sin A}{2} = \dfrac{\sin 63°}{1.95} \Rightarrow \sin A = \dfrac{(2)\sin 63°}{1.95} = 0.91380904 \Rightarrow A = 66°$

(no ambiguity). Finally, $B = 180 - 66 - 63 = 51°$

4. $\tan 30° = \dfrac{x}{z} - (1)$ $\tan 60° = \dfrac{x+y}{z} - (2)$

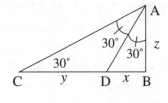

Dividing (1) by (2): $\dfrac{\left(\dfrac{1}{\sqrt{3}}\right)}{\left(\dfrac{\sqrt{3}}{1}\right)} = \dfrac{\left(\dfrac{x}{z}\right)}{\left(\dfrac{x+y}{z}\right)} \Leftrightarrow \dfrac{1}{3} = \dfrac{x}{x+y}$

$$\Leftrightarrow x + y = 3x \Leftrightarrow y = 2x \Leftrightarrow \dfrac{x}{y} = \dfrac{1}{2}$$

5. $\angle RQP = 180° - 45° - 105° = 30° \therefore \dfrac{a}{\sin 30°} = \dfrac{RQ}{\sin 45°} \Leftrightarrow RQ = \dfrac{\sin 45°}{\sin 30°} \times a = 1.4142a$.

Next, we have: $\dfrac{a}{\sin 30°} = \dfrac{PQ}{\sin 105°} \Leftrightarrow PQ = \dfrac{a}{\sin 30°} \times \sin 105° = 1.9318a$.

Therefore, perimeter is given by $a + 1.4142a + 1.9318a = 4.3460a$. i.e., perimeter $\sim 4.35a$.

LEVEL 4

1. $\dfrac{\sin C}{55} = \dfrac{\sin 45°}{70} \Rightarrow \sin C = 0.5555839 \Rightarrow C = 33.750942$ or $34°$

Therefore, $A = 180° - 45° - 34° = 101°$. This is a true bearing.
An alternative answer is east $11°$ south.

2. $\dfrac{180}{x} = \tan 79° \Rightarrow x = \dfrac{180}{\tan 79°} = 34.988456$

$\dfrac{180}{y} = \tan 44° \Rightarrow x = \dfrac{180}{\tan 44°} = 186.39546$

Helicopter has travelled $186.39546 - 34.988456 = 151.407$ m.

Speed $= \dfrac{151.407}{60} = 2.52345$ or 2.52 m/s to 3 S.F.

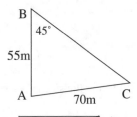

3. (a) $\tan \alpha = \dfrac{h}{AD} \Leftrightarrow AD = \dfrac{h}{\tan \alpha} - (1)$

(b) $AD = AB - BD = x - BD$, but, $\tan \beta = \dfrac{h}{BD} \Leftrightarrow BD = \dfrac{h}{\tan \beta} \therefore AD = x - \dfrac{h}{\tan \beta} - (2)$

(c) From (1) & (2): $\dfrac{h}{\tan \alpha} = x - \dfrac{h}{\tan \beta} \Leftrightarrow x = \dfrac{h}{\tan \alpha} + \dfrac{h}{\tan \beta} = h\left(\dfrac{1}{\tan \alpha} + \dfrac{1}{\tan \beta}\right)$

$$\Leftrightarrow x = h\left(\dfrac{\tan \alpha + \tan \beta}{\tan \alpha \tan \beta}\right) \Leftrightarrow h = \dfrac{x \tan \alpha \tan \beta}{\tan \alpha + \tan \beta}$$

EXAMINATION STYLE QUESTIONS

1. i. Distance $= 650\cos 60° = 325$ metres north.

ii. Distance $= 650\sin 60° = 562.91651$ metres east.

iii. $220\cos 20° = 206.73238$ metres south.

$\quad 220\sin 20° = 75.244432$ metres west.

iv. $470\cos 60° = 235$ metres north.

$\quad 470\sin 60° = 407.03194$ metres west.

v. Total distance north $= 325 - 206.73238 + 235 = 353.26762$ m

Total distance east $= 562.91651 - 75.244432 - 407.03194 = 80.6401$ m

So the boat is 353 metres north and 81 metres east of its original position.

vi. By Pythagoras, distance $= \sqrt{353.26762^2 + 80.6401^2} = 362.35458 = 362$m

vii. $\tan A = \dfrac{80.6401}{362.35458} \Rightarrow A = 12.546415°$ The return bearing is 192.5° true.

2. $A = \dfrac{1}{2}bc\sin A = \dfrac{1}{2}(5)(5)\sin 25° = 5.2827283 = 5.28\text{mm}^2 = \dfrac{5.28}{10^2}\text{cm}^2 = 0.0528\text{cm}^2$

3. (a)

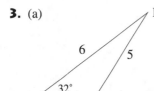
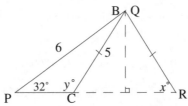

(b) Using the sine rule we have: $\dfrac{\sin x}{6} = \dfrac{\sin 32°}{5} \Leftrightarrow \sin x = \dfrac{6}{5}\sin 32°$

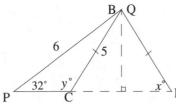

$\therefore \sin x = 0.6359 \Rightarrow x = 39.4869°$

$\qquad\qquad\qquad\qquad = 39°\,29'$

Therefore, $y = 180 - 39°29' = 140°31'$.

The two triangles are:

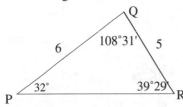
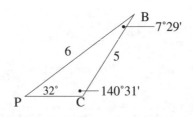

For $\triangle PQR$: $PR^2 = 6^2 + 5^2 - 2 \times 6 \times 5 \times \cos 108°31' = 80.054 \therefore PR = 8.947$ (8.95 cm)

For $\triangle ABC$: $AC^2 = 6^2 + 5^2 - 2 \times 6 \times 5 \times \cos 7°29' = 1.5110 \therefore AC = 1.229$ (1.23 cm)

(c) $A_{\triangle PQR} = \dfrac{1}{2} \times 6 \times 8.947 \times \sin 32° = 14.22$ (14.2 cm²)

$A_{\triangle ABC} = \dfrac{1}{2} \times 6 \times 1.229 \times \sin 32° = 1.954$ (1.95 cm²)

So, difference is $14.22 - 1.95 = 12.27$ i.e., approx. 12.3 cm²

4. (a)

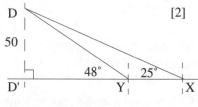

(b) $x^2 = 450^2 + 620^2 - 2 \times 450 \times 620 \times \cos 140°$

$\therefore x = 1007.1508$ i.e., 1007 m (to nearest metre).

(c) i. $T_1 = \dfrac{450}{v} + \dfrac{620}{u}$

ii. $T_2 = \dfrac{x}{\left(\dfrac{u+v}{2}\right)} = \dfrac{2x}{u+v} = \dfrac{2014.3}{u+v}$

So that the time difference is $T_1 - T_2 = \dfrac{450}{v} + \dfrac{620}{u} - \dfrac{2014.3}{u+v}$.

TEST

1. Use of tan [1]. Height $= 120\tan 31° = 72.103274$ or 72.1 metres [1].

2. Use of the sine rule [1]. $\dfrac{a}{\sin 30°} = \dfrac{7}{\sin 55°} \Rightarrow a = \dfrac{7\sin 30°}{\sin 55°} = 4.2727$ to 5 S.F.

3. Use of the formula $\frac{1}{2}bc\sin A$ [1]. Area $= \frac{1}{2}(5)(9)\sin 73° = 21.52\text{cm}^2$ to 4 S.F. [1].

4. Use of the cosine rule [1].

$13^2 = 11^2 + 12^2 - 2(11)(12)\cos\theta \Rightarrow \cos\theta = \dfrac{11^2 + 12^2 - 13^2}{2(11)(12)} = 0.36363636$ [1]

$\theta = \arccos(0.36363636) = 68.676314$ or $69°$ to the nearest degree [1].

5.

```
D
|
50 |
  |_____
      48°      25°
D' |        Y |           | X
```

[2]

For $\triangle XDD'$: $\tan 25° = \dfrac{50}{D'X} \therefore D'X = \dfrac{50}{\tan 25°}$. [1]

For $\triangle D'YD$: $\tan 48° = \dfrac{50}{D'Y} \therefore D'Y = \dfrac{50}{\tan 48°}$. [1]

$XY = D'X - D'Y = 50\left(\dfrac{1}{\tan 25°} - \dfrac{1}{\tan 48°}\right) = 62.21$ [2]

CHAPTER 8
LEVEL 1

1. Using the form $y = mx + c$, with m as the gradient and c as the y–intercept, we have:

(a) $m = 3, c = -1$; (b) $m = -1, c = -1$ (c) $2y = x + 4 \Leftrightarrow y = \frac{1}{2}x + 2$, therefore, $m = \frac{1}{2}, c = 2$.

2. i. (a) $d = \sqrt{(3-2)^2 + (4-4)^2} = \sqrt{1+0} = 1$ (b) $\sqrt{109}$ (c) $2\sqrt{13}$

ii. (a) $m = \dfrac{4-4}{2-3} = \dfrac{0}{-1} = 0$ (b) $\dfrac{10}{3}$ (c) $\dfrac{6}{4}\left(= \dfrac{3}{2}\right)$

iii. (a) $M \equiv \left(\frac{1}{2}(3+2), \frac{1}{2}(4+4)\right) \equiv \left(\frac{5}{2}, 4\right)$ (b) $\left(\frac{7}{2}, 3\right)$ (c) (0,0)

3. i. (a) $d = \sqrt{(6-2)^2 + (4-4)^2 + (2-6)^2} = \sqrt{4^2 + 0^2 + (-4)^2} = \sqrt{32} = 4\sqrt{2}$ (b) $\sqrt{19}$

ii. (a) $M \equiv \left(\dfrac{2+6}{2}, \dfrac{4+4}{2}, \dfrac{6+2}{2}\right) \equiv (4, 4, 4)$ (b) $\left(-\frac{1}{2}, \frac{1}{2}, -\frac{1}{2}\right)$

LEVEL 2

1. Let m_2 be the gradient of the perpendicular line.

i. $m_1 = 2 : m_1 \times m_2 = -1 \therefore 2m_2 = -1 \Leftrightarrow m_2 = -\frac{1}{2}$. ii. $m_1 = -\frac{1}{3} \therefore m_2 = 3$

iii. $5y = 2x + 10 \Leftrightarrow y = \frac{2}{5}x + 2 \therefore m_1 = \frac{2}{5} \therefore m_2 = -\frac{5}{2}$. **2.** $y - 3 = 3(x-2) \therefore y = 3x - 3$

3. $2x + 3y + 1 = 0 \Leftrightarrow y = -\frac{2}{3}x - \frac{1}{3}$. So, $-\frac{2}{3} \times m = -1 \Leftrightarrow m = \frac{3}{2} \therefore \perp$ line is given by:

$y - 2 = \frac{3}{2}(x-1) \Leftrightarrow 2y - 3x - 1 = 0$. **4.** $x - 2y - 1 = 0 \Leftrightarrow y = \frac{1}{2}x - \frac{1}{2}$. As lines are parallel,

we have that $m = \frac{1}{2} \therefore (y-2) = \frac{1}{2}(x-1) \Leftrightarrow 2y - x - 3 = 0$.

5. (a) $m = -\frac{3}{2}, c = 3 \therefore y = -\frac{3}{2}x + 3$ (b) $m = \frac{5-1}{2-(-1)} = \frac{4}{3} \therefore y = \frac{4}{3}x + c$.

Using (2,5): $5 = \frac{8}{3} + c \Leftrightarrow c = \frac{7}{3}$.Therefore, $y = \frac{4}{3}x + \frac{7}{3}$ or $3y = 4x + 7$.

(c) $m = \frac{a^2 - 0}{2a - a} = a \therefore y = ax + c$. Using (a,0): $0 = a^2 + c \Leftrightarrow c = -a^2$. Therefore,

$y = ax - a^2$. **6.** (a) $y = x + 2$ —(1), $y = -x + 4$ —(2); (1) + (2): $2y = 6 \Leftrightarrow y = 3$. Sub into (1)

$3 = x + 2 \Leftrightarrow x = 1$. i.e., (1, 3). (b) $x + y = 6$ —(1), $2x - y = 3$ —(2);

(1) + (2): $3x = 9 \Leftrightarrow x = 3$. Sub into (1) $x + 3 = 6 \Leftrightarrow x = 3$. i.e., (3,3).

(c) $-x + y - 1 = 0$—(1), $2x + y + 2 = 0$—(2); (2) – (1): $3x + 3 = 0 \Leftrightarrow x = -1$

$\therefore 1 + y - 1 = 0 \Leftrightarrow y = 0$. i.e., (–1, 0)

LEVEL 3
1. (a) Because the lines have different y–intercepts, there will be no solution if they are parallel.
i.e., $m = 2$. (b) As long as they aren't parallel, there will always exist a unique solution $\therefore m \neq 2$.
That is $m \in \mathbb{R} \setminus \{2\}$
2. We can set this up using a graphics calc. with X as the time t hours, and Y as the volume, V ml:
(a)   (b)   (c)

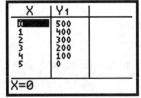

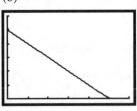

The gradient, $m = -\frac{500}{5} = -100$

and $c = 500$.
Therefore, using $V(t) = mt + c$, we have
that
$V(t) = -100t + 500, 0 \le t \le 5$.

3. (a) $kx - y = 9 \Leftrightarrow y = kx - 9$ —(1) $y = 3x + 5$—(2); i. (1) || (2) $\Rightarrow k = 3$.

ii. (1) $\perp$ (2) $\Rightarrow 3 \times k = -1 \therefore k = -\frac{1}{3}$ (b) $2x + ky = 4 \Leftrightarrow y = -\frac{2}{k}x + \frac{4}{k}$ —(1) $y = 3x + 5$—(2);

i. (1) || (2) $\Rightarrow -\frac{2}{k} = 3 \Leftrightarrow k = -\frac{2}{3}$. ii. (1) $\perp$ (2) $\Rightarrow 3 \times -\frac{2}{k} = -1 \therefore k = 6$.

4. $4a - 5b = 2c \Leftrightarrow c = \frac{1}{2}(4a - 5b)$ –(1) & $3a + b = 3c \Leftrightarrow c = \frac{1}{3}(3a + b)$ –(2)

As (1) = (2): $\frac{1}{2}(4a - 5b) = \frac{1}{3}(3a + b) \Leftrightarrow 12a - 15b = 6a + 2b \Leftrightarrow 6a = 17b \therefore \frac{a}{b} = \frac{17}{6}$

5. Let the endpoint have coordinates (x,y), then, $1 = \frac{x-2}{2}$ and $2 = \frac{4+y}{2}$

Therefore, $x - 2 = 2 \Leftrightarrow x = 4$ & $4 = y = 4 \Leftrightarrow y = 0$. So, $A \equiv (4, 0)$.

•(–2,4)
(1,2)
•A(x,y)

6. (a) & (b) $\qquad$ (c) $PQ = \sqrt{3^2 + 2^2 + 3^2} = \sqrt{22}$ (d) (3.5, 1, 0)

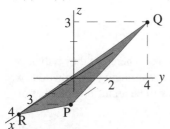

LEVEL 4

1. $m_{AB} = m_{AC} \therefore \dfrac{1-2}{m-3} = \dfrac{-4-2}{1-3} \Leftrightarrow \dfrac{-1}{m-3} = \dfrac{-6}{-2} \Leftrightarrow -1 = 3(m-3) \therefore -1 = 3m-9 \therefore m = \dfrac{8}{3}$

2. (a) $y = ax - 1$ —(1) $y = -x + a$ —(2);

(1) – (2): $0 = (a+1)x - 1 - a \Leftrightarrow (a+1)x = a + 1 \Leftrightarrow x = 1$.

Substituting into (1): $y = a - 1$. So, point of int. is $(1, a - 1)$.

(b) $2ax + y = 1$ —(1) $x - ay = 1$ —(2): $a \times (1) + (2)$: $(2a^2 + 1)x = a + 1 \Leftrightarrow x = \dfrac{a+1}{2a^2+1}$.

Substituting into (1): $y = 1 - 2a \times \dfrac{a+1}{2a^2+1} = \dfrac{2a^2+1-2a^2-2a}{2a^2+1} = \dfrac{1-2a}{2a^2+1}$. Int. pt.

is $\left(\dfrac{a+1}{2a^2+1}, \dfrac{1-2a}{2a^2+1}\right)$. (c) $ay = x + a$ —(1) $x - y = -1$ —(2);

(1) + (2): $(a-1)y = a - 1 \Leftrightarrow y = 1$. From (2): $x - 1 = -1 \therefore x = 0$. (0, 1).

3. i.

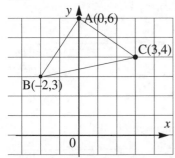

ii. $m_{AB} = \dfrac{6-3}{0-(-2)} = \dfrac{3}{2}$ and $m_{AC} = \dfrac{4-6}{3-0} = -\dfrac{2}{3}$

So, as $m_{AB} \times m_{AC} = \dfrac{3}{2} \times -\dfrac{2}{3} = -1 \Rightarrow \overline{AB} \perp \overline{AC}$.

Next, $AB = \sqrt{3^2 + 2^2} = \sqrt{13}$ & $AC = \sqrt{2^2 + 3^2} = \sqrt{13}$

Therefore, $\triangle ABC$ is a right-angled, isosceles triangle.

iii. $D \equiv B + (3, -2) \equiv (-2, 3) + (3, -2) \equiv (1, 1)$

4. $bx + y = ab$ —(1) $ax - by = a^2$ —(2); $b \times (1) + (2)$:

$(b^2 + a)x = ab^2 + a^2 \Leftrightarrow (b^2 + a)x = a(b^2 + a)$.

So that $x = a$. Substituting into (1): $y = ab - ab = 0$. That is, point of intersection is $(a, 0)$.

5. $ax + 3y = 5 \Leftrightarrow y = -\dfrac{a}{3}x + \dfrac{5}{3}$ —(1) & $2x + (a+1)y = 6 \Leftrightarrow y = -\dfrac{2}{a+1}x + \dfrac{6}{a+1}$ —(2).

(a) If (1) $\parallel$ (2) then $-\dfrac{a}{3} = -\dfrac{2}{a+1} \Leftrightarrow a(a+1) = 6$. So that

$a^2 + a - 6 = 0 \Leftrightarrow (a+3)(a-2) = 0 \therefore a = 2, -3$.

(b) If (1) $\perp$ (2) then $-\dfrac{a}{3} \times -\dfrac{2}{a+1} = -1 \Leftrightarrow 2a = -3a - 3$. So that $5a = -3 \Leftrightarrow a = -\dfrac{3}{5}$.

6. (a) $a = 2$: $x + y = 1$—(1) $4x + y = 2$—(2); (2) – (1): $3x = 1 \Leftrightarrow x = \dfrac{1}{3}$. Sub into (1): $y = \dfrac{2}{3}$.

i.e., $\left(\dfrac{1}{3}, \dfrac{2}{3}\right)$. (b) $a = -4$: $-2x + y = -2$—(1) $-2x + y = 2$—(2); or (1) is $y = 2x - 2$ and (2) is

$y = 2x + 2$. That is, the lines are parallel and have different y–intercepts. Therefore they will never intersect and so there are no real solutions. (c) $a = 4$: This time, upon rearranging the equations we end up with the same equation, $y = -2x + 2$. This means that there will be an infinite number of solutions (as they coincide for all values of x).

7. i.

ii. mid-points: $O \equiv (0, 0)$ i.e.,

$$P \equiv \left(\frac{2b + (-2a)}{2}, \frac{2c + 0}{2}\right) \equiv (b - a, c)$$

$$Q \equiv \left(\frac{2a + 2b}{2}, \frac{2c + 0}{2}\right) \equiv (a + b, c)$$

iii. (a) $m_{OC} = \dfrac{2c}{2b} = \dfrac{c}{b}$: $(y - 0) = \dfrac{c}{b}(x - 0) \Leftrightarrow y = \dfrac{c}{b}x$.

(b) $m = \dfrac{c - 0}{(a + b) - (-2a)} = \dfrac{c}{3a + b}$: $y - 0 = \dfrac{c}{3a + b}(x - (-2a)) \Leftrightarrow (3a + b)y - cx - 2ac = 0$.

iv. $\overleftrightarrow{AQ} \cap \overleftrightarrow{OC}$: $(3a + b)\left(\dfrac{c}{b}x\right) - cx - 2ac = 0 \Leftrightarrow (3a + b)cx - bcx - 2abc = 0$

$$3acx - 2abc = 0 \Leftrightarrow x = \frac{2}{3}b$$

Sub into $y = \dfrac{c}{b}x$: $y = \dfrac{c}{b}\left(\dfrac{2}{3}b\right) = \dfrac{2}{3}c$. Therefore, $\overleftrightarrow{AQ} \cap \overleftrightarrow{OC} = \left(\dfrac{2}{3}b, \dfrac{2}{3}c\right)$.

Equation $\overleftrightarrow{BP}$: $m_{BP} = \dfrac{c - 0}{b - a - 2a} = \dfrac{c}{b - 3a}$; $y - 0 = \dfrac{c}{b - 3a}(x - 2a) \Leftrightarrow y = \dfrac{c}{b - 3a}(x - 2a)$.

When $x = \dfrac{2}{3}b$, $y = \dfrac{c}{b - 3a}\left(\dfrac{2}{3}b - 2a\right) = \dfrac{c}{b - 3a} \times \dfrac{2}{3}(b - 3a) = \dfrac{2}{3}c$.

Therefore, $\overleftrightarrow{AQ} \cap \overleftrightarrow{OC} \cap \overleftrightarrow{BP} \equiv \left(\dfrac{2}{3}b, \dfrac{2}{3}c\right) \Rightarrow \overleftrightarrow{AQ}, \overleftrightarrow{OC}, \overleftrightarrow{BP}$ are concurrent.

EXAMINATION STYLE QUESTIONS

1. i. (a) $y - 0 = -\dfrac{1}{3}(x - 1) \Leftrightarrow y = -\dfrac{1}{3}(x - 1)$

(b) $-\dfrac{1}{3} \times m_{AC} = -1 \therefore m_{AC} = 3 \therefore (y - 0) = 3(x - (-3))$. i.e., $y = 3(x + 3)$.

ii. $X \equiv \overleftrightarrow{BX} \cap \overleftrightarrow{AC}$: $-\dfrac{1}{3}(x - 1) = 3(x + 3) \Leftrightarrow -x + 1 = 9x + 27 \Leftrightarrow x = 2.6 \therefore y = 1.2$.

i.e., $X \equiv (-2.6, 1.2)$.

iii. Let C have coordinates (a, b): $\dfrac{1}{2}(a - 3) = -2.6 \Leftrightarrow a = -2.2$ & $\dfrac{1}{2}(b + 0) = 1.2 \Leftrightarrow b = 2.4$.

i.e., $C \equiv (-2.2, 2.4)$. Therefore, Area $\triangle ABC = \dfrac{1}{2} \times 4 \times 2.4 = 4.8$ sq. units

2. Using $(-1, 2)$, we have: $-a + 2b + 10 = 0$——(1). Also, after rearranging: $y = \frac{8}{12}x + \frac{16}{12}$ &

$y = -\frac{a}{b}x - \frac{10}{b}$. As the lines are perp. $\frac{8}{12} \times -\frac{a}{b} = -1 \Leftrightarrow a = \frac{3}{2}b$ ——(2). Sub (2) into (1):

$-\frac{3}{2}b + 2b = -10 \Leftrightarrow b = -20$ & $a = -30$.

3. i. (a)

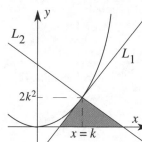

L_2

L_1

$2k^2$

$x = k$

y

x

(b) $y = 2x^2 \therefore y' = 4x$. So, at $x = k$, $y' = 4k$. i.e., gradient $= 4k$.

At $(k, 2k^2)$, $m = 4k \therefore (y - 2k^2) = 4k(x - k) \Rightarrow y = 4kx - 2k^2$

iii. $4y + x = 16 \Leftrightarrow y = -\frac{1}{4}x + 4 \therefore -\frac{1}{4} \times 4k = -1 \Rightarrow k = 1$.

iv. For L_1: $y = 0 \Rightarrow 0 = 4kx - 2k^2 \Leftrightarrow x = \frac{2k^2}{4k} = \frac{1}{2}k$.

For L_2: $y = 0 \Rightarrow 4 \times 0 + x = 16 \Leftrightarrow x = 16$.

$\therefore$ Area $= \frac{1}{2} \times \left(16 - \frac{1}{2}\right) \times 2(1)^2 = \frac{1}{2} \times \frac{31}{2} \times 2 = \frac{31}{2}$ sq. units

TEST

1. For $2y - x = 8$: $x = 0$, $y = 4$ i.e., $(0, 4)$. When $y = 0$, $x = -8$ i.e., $(-8, 0)$. [1]

For $y = 4 - x$: $x = 0$, $y = 4$ i.e., $(0, 4)$.

When $y = 0$, $x = 4$, i.e., $(4, 0)$. [1]

Therefore, $AB = 4 - (-8) = 12$. [2]

[1]

[1]

4

−8

4

0

A

B

2. i. $AB = \sqrt{(5-3)^2 + (1-5)^2} = 2\sqrt{5}$ ii. $m = \frac{1-5}{5-3} = -2$ iii. $\left(\frac{1}{2}(3 + 5), \frac{1}{2}(5 + 1)\right) \equiv (4, 3)$

3. $6x = 5y + 3$——(1) $8y = 12x + 6$——(2);

$2 \times (1) + (2)$: $8y + 12x = 10y + 6 + 12x + 6 \Leftrightarrow -2y = 12 \Leftrightarrow y = -6$ [2]

Substituting into (1): $6x = -30 + 3 \Leftrightarrow x = -\frac{9}{2}$. [1]

4. $px - 3y = 8 \Leftrightarrow y = \frac{p}{3}x - \frac{8}{3}$ ——(1) and $qx + y = 4 \Leftrightarrow y = -qx + 4$ ——(2)

(a) If (1) $\perp$ (2) then $\frac{p}{3} \times -q = -1 \Leftrightarrow pq = 3$ [2]

(b) If there are no solutions, then the lines are parallel. So, $\frac{p}{3} = -q \Leftrightarrow p = -3q$. [2]

5. (a) [2] (b) [1]

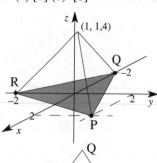

(c) $PQ = \sqrt{4^2 + 2^2 + 0^2} = \sqrt{20} = 2\sqrt{5}$ [2]

(d) $\left(\frac{1}{2}(2), \frac{1}{2}(0), \frac{1}{2}(0)\right) \equiv (1, 0, 0)$ [2]

(e) $Vol = (\text{base area}) \times 4 \times \frac{1}{3}$

$PR = \sqrt{4 + 16 + 0} = \sqrt{20}$, $QR = \sqrt{4 + 4 + 0} = \sqrt{8}$ [1]

$(\sqrt{8})^2 = (\sqrt{20})^2 + (\sqrt{20})^2 - 2\sqrt{20}\sqrt{20}\cos\theta$

$\therefore \cos\theta = \frac{4}{5}\left(\therefore \sin\theta = \frac{3}{5}\right)$ [1]

$\therefore Vol = \frac{1}{3} \times 4 \times \left(\frac{1}{2} \times \sqrt{20} \times \sqrt{20} \times \frac{3}{5}\right) = 8$ cubic units. [2]

6. i. $B \equiv (a + b, 0 + c) \equiv (a + b, c)$ [2]

ii. For $\overline{AC}: \left(\frac{1}{2}(a+b), \frac{1}{2}(0+c)\right) \equiv \left(\frac{1}{2}(a+b), \frac{1}{2}c\right)$. [2]

$\overline{OB}: \left(\frac{1}{2}(0+a+b), \frac{1}{2}(0+c)\right) \equiv \left(\frac{1}{2}(a+b), \frac{1}{2}c\right)$. [2]

iii. They bisect. [1] iv. Rhombus implies OA = OC, so $a = \sqrt{b^2 + c^2} \therefore B \equiv (b + \sqrt{b^2 + c^2}, c)$. [1]

v. $m_{OB} = \dfrac{c}{b + \sqrt{b^2 + c^2}}$, $m_{AC} = \dfrac{-c}{\sqrt{b^2 + c^2} - b}$ [2] [1]

vi. $m_{OB} \times m_{AC} = \dfrac{c}{b + \sqrt{b^2 + c^2}} \times \dfrac{-c}{\sqrt{b^2 + c^2} - b} = \dfrac{-c^2}{(b^2 + c^2) - b^2} = -\dfrac{c^2}{c^2} = -1$. [2]

Therefore, diagonals are perpendicular. [1]

CHAPTER 9
LEVEL 1

1. i. Base: $BD^2 = 8^2 + 8^2 \therefore BD = 8\sqrt{2} \approx 11.31$ cm

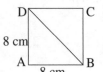

ii.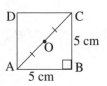

$\tan\theta = \dfrac{8}{8\sqrt{2}} \therefore \theta = arctan\left(\dfrac{1}{\sqrt{2}}\right) = 35.26°$

That is, $\theta = 35°16'$

2. i.

$AC^2 = 5^2 + 5^2$

$= 2 \times 5^2$

$\therefore AC = 5\sqrt{2}$

$= 7.07$

ii.

$AO = \dfrac{1}{2}AC = \dfrac{5}{2}\sqrt{2}$

So, $\tan\theta = \dfrac{OV}{AO} = \dfrac{15}{\dfrac{5}{2}\sqrt{2}} = \dfrac{6}{\sqrt{2}}$

$\therefore\theta = arctan\left(\dfrac{6}{\sqrt{2}}\right) = 76.737°$

That is, $76°44'$

LEVEL 2

1. i. First we need to find EF:

Next we find BE:

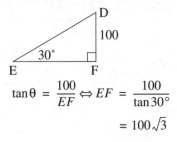

$\tan\theta = \dfrac{100}{EF} \Leftrightarrow EF = \dfrac{100}{\tan 30°}$

$= 100\sqrt{3}$

$BE^2 = 200^2 + (100\sqrt{3})^2$

$= 70000$

$\therefore BE = 264.58$

That is, 264.58 cm

ii.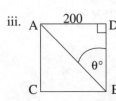

$\tan\alpha = \dfrac{100}{100\sqrt{7}} = \dfrac{1}{\sqrt{7}} \therefore\alpha = \tan^{-1}\left(\dfrac{1}{\sqrt{7}}\right) = 20.40°$

That is, $\alpha = 20°42'$

iii.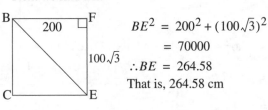

First we need to find ED: $\sin 30° = \dfrac{100}{ED} \Leftrightarrow ED = \dfrac{100}{0.5} = 200$.

Therefore, $\tan\theta = \dfrac{200}{200} = 1 \therefore\theta = 45°$

2. We first need to determine AC:

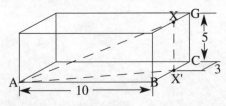

$AC^2 = AB^2 + (BX')^2 = 100 + 9 = 109$

$\therefore AC = \sqrt{109}$

So, $\tan\alpha = \dfrac{5}{\sqrt{109}} \therefore\alpha = 25.59° = 25°35'$

3.

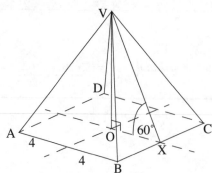

Using ΔOVX: $\tan 60° = \dfrac{OV}{OX}$

$$\therefore OV = 4 \times \tan 60°$$
$$= 4\sqrt{3}$$
$$= 6.9282$$

Therefore, height is 6.93 cm

4.

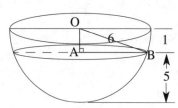

Using ΔOAB: $6^2 = 1^2 + AB^2 \therefore AB = \sqrt{35} = 5.916$.
That is, radius is 5.92 cm.

5. i.

$$x^2 = 17.6^2 + 17.6^2 - 2 \times 17.6 \times 17.6 \cos 30°$$

$$= 2 \times 17.6^2 - 2 \times 17.6^2 \times \dfrac{\sqrt{3}}{2}$$

$$\therefore x = 9.11$$

ii.

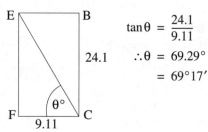

$$\tan \theta = \dfrac{24.1}{9.11}$$

$$\therefore \theta = 69.29°$$
$$= 69°17'$$

LEVEL 3

1. **Step 1:**

$$XZ^2 = 1^2 + 2^2$$

$$\therefore XZ = \sqrt{5}$$

Step 3:

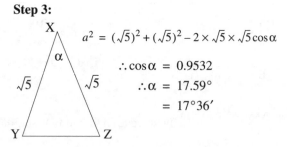

$$a^2 = (\sqrt{5})^2 + (\sqrt{5})^2 - 2 \times \sqrt{5} \times \sqrt{5} \cos \alpha$$

$$\therefore \cos \alpha = 0.9532$$

$$\therefore \alpha = 17.59°$$
$$= 17°36'$$

Step 2:

$$a^2 = 1^2 + 1^2 - 2 \times 1 \times 1 \cos 40°$$

$$a = 0.6840$$

2. i. OV $= 3r + 2r = 5r$ ii.

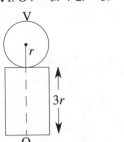

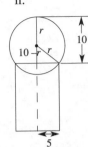

$$r^2 = (10 - r)^2 + 5^2 \therefore r^2 = 100 - 2r + r^2 + 25$$
$$\therefore 20r = 125$$
$$\Leftrightarrow r = \frac{125}{20}$$

Diameter $= 2r = 12.5$ cm

3.

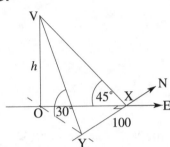

$\Delta OXV: \tan 45° = \dfrac{h}{OX} \Leftrightarrow OX = \dfrac{h}{\tan 45°} = \dfrac{h}{1} = h$

$\Delta OYV: \tan 30° = \dfrac{h}{OY} \Leftrightarrow OY = \dfrac{h}{\tan 30°} = \dfrac{h}{1/\sqrt{3}} = h\sqrt{3}$

$\Delta OXY: 100^2 + h^2 = (h\sqrt{3})^2$

$\therefore 100^2 + h^2 = 3h^2 \Leftrightarrow h^2 = \dfrac{100^2}{2} \therefore h = 50\sqrt{2}$

i.e., height is 70.71 m

4. i. $\sin 20° = \dfrac{4}{x} \Leftrightarrow x = \dfrac{4}{\sin 20°} = 11.6952$ ii. BV $=$ OV $-$ OB $= 11.70 - 4$

$$= 7.70 \text{ cm}$$

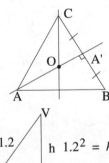

5.

i.

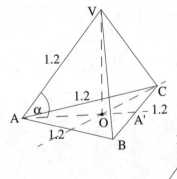

$AO = \dfrac{2}{3}AA' = \dfrac{2}{3}\sqrt{AB^2 - BA'^2}$

$= \dfrac{2}{3}\sqrt{1.2^2 - 0.6^2}$

$= \dfrac{2}{3}\sqrt{1.08}$

$1.2^2 = h^2 + \left(\dfrac{2}{3}\sqrt{1.08}\right)^2 \Leftrightarrow h^2 = 0.96$

$\therefore h = 0.9797$

Therefore, height is 0.98 m

ii. $\sin\alpha = \dfrac{OV}{AV} = \dfrac{0.9797}{1.2} \therefore \alpha = \sin^{-1}(0.8165) = 54.73°$. i.e., $54°44'$.

LEVEL 4

1. Let AO' & BO' be the altitudes of $\triangle ACV$ and $\triangle BCV$ respectively. So that the angle between $\triangle ACV$ and $\triangle BCV$ is the same as the angle between AO' & BO'.

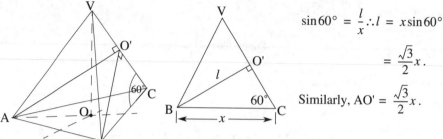

$$\sin 60° = \frac{l}{x} \therefore l = x\sin 60°$$

$$= \frac{\sqrt{3}}{2}x.$$

Similarly, AO' $= \frac{\sqrt{3}}{2}x.$

B   Using $\triangle$ ABO':

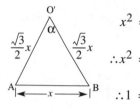

$$x^2 = \left(\frac{\sqrt{3}}{2}x\right)^2 + \left(\frac{\sqrt{3}}{2}x\right)^2 - 2\left(\frac{\sqrt{3}}{2}x\right)^2\cos\alpha$$

$$\therefore x^2 = \frac{3}{4}x^2 + \frac{3}{4}x^2 - 2 \times \frac{3}{4}x^2\cos\alpha$$

$$\therefore 1 = \frac{3}{4} + \frac{3}{4} - \frac{6}{4}\cos\alpha \Leftrightarrow \cos\alpha = \frac{1}{3} \therefore \alpha = 70.5287°\quad \text{i.e.,}\ \alpha = 70°32'$$

2.

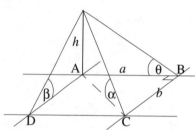

$$\tan\alpha = \frac{h}{AC} \Leftrightarrow h = AC \cdot \tan\alpha = \sqrt{a^2 + b^2}\tan\alpha$$

$$\&\ \tan\theta = \frac{h}{a} = \frac{\sqrt{a^2 + b^2}\tan\alpha}{a} = \left(\sqrt{1 + \left(\frac{b}{a}\right)^2}\right)\tan\alpha$$

$$\therefore \theta = \tan^{-1}\left(\left(\sqrt{1 + \left(\frac{b}{a}\right)^2}\right)\tan\alpha\right)$$

Similarly, $\tan\beta = \frac{h}{b} = \frac{\sqrt{a^2 + b^2}\tan\alpha}{b} = \left(\sqrt{\left(\frac{a}{b}\right)^2 + 1}\right)\tan\alpha \therefore \beta = \tan^{-1}\left(\left(\sqrt{\left(\frac{a}{b}\right)^2 + 1}\right)\tan\alpha\right).$

3.

Aerial view:

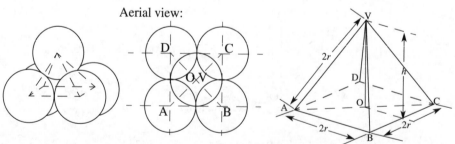

$$AC^2 = (2r)^2 + (2r)^2 = 8r^2 \therefore AC = 2\sqrt{2}r \Rightarrow AO = \frac{1}{2} \times 2\sqrt{2}r = \sqrt{2}r$$

Using $\triangle AOV$: $AV^2 = AO^2 + OV^2 \therefore (2r)^2 = (\sqrt{2}r)^2 + h^2 \Leftrightarrow h^2 = 2r^2 \therefore h = \sqrt{2}r.$

Therefore, height $= r + \sqrt{2}r = (1 + \sqrt{2})r.$

EXAMINATION STYLE QUESTIONS

1. i. (a)

Aerial view:

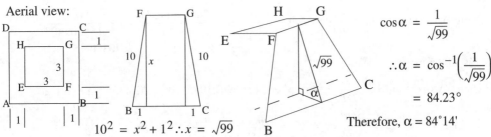

$$10^2 = x^2 + 1^2 \therefore x = \sqrt{99}$$

$$\cos\alpha = \frac{1}{\sqrt{99}}$$

$$\therefore \alpha = \cos^{-1}\left(\frac{1}{\sqrt{99}}\right)$$

$$= 84.23°$$

Therefore, $\alpha = 84°14'$

(b)

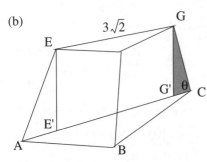

$$CG' = \frac{1}{2}(AC - E'G') = \frac{1}{2}(AC - EG)$$

$$= \frac{1}{2}(5\sqrt{2} - 3\sqrt{2})$$

$$= \sqrt{2}$$

$$\cos\theta = \frac{CG'}{CG} = \frac{\sqrt{2}}{10} \therefore \theta = \cos^{-1}\left(\frac{\sqrt{2}}{10}\right) = 81.869°$$

That is, $\theta = 81°52'$.

ii. $\sin\theta = \dfrac{G'G}{10} \Leftrightarrow G'G = 10\sin\theta = 10 \times \dfrac{\sqrt{98}}{10} = 9.899$. i.e., $G'G = 9.90$ m.

iii. Using $\triangle FGV$:

$$5^2 = y^2 + 1.5^2 \therefore y = \frac{1}{2}\sqrt{91}$$

$$3^2 = \left(\frac{1}{2}\sqrt{91}\right)^2 + \left(\frac{1}{2}\sqrt{91}\right)^2 - 2\left(\frac{1}{2}\sqrt{91}\right)\cos\alpha$$

$$\therefore 18 = 91 - 91\cos\alpha \Leftrightarrow \alpha = \cos^{-1}\left(\frac{73}{91}\right)$$

$$= 36.659°$$

i.e., $36°39'$.

iv. From iii.: $\left(\dfrac{1}{2}\sqrt{91}\right)^2 = h^2 + 1.5^2 \Leftrightarrow h^2 = \dfrac{41}{2} \therefore h = 4.5276$. i.e., 4.53 m

Therefore, height above ABCD $= 9.899 + 4.527 = 14.4271$ i.e., 14.43 m

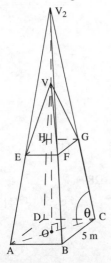

From (b), $\theta = 81°52'$ or $\cos\theta = \dfrac{\sqrt{2}}{10}$

From $\triangle ABC$: $AC = 5\sqrt{2} \therefore OC = \dfrac{5}{2}\sqrt{2}$.

$$\tan\theta = \frac{OV_2}{OC} \Leftrightarrow OV_2 = OC \times \tan\theta = \frac{5}{2}\sqrt{2} \times \sqrt{\frac{98}{2}} = 24.7487$$

Therefore, as $OV_2 > OV$, tallest is when a square pyramid is completed (using 5m square base).

Higher by 24.7487 m $-$ 14.4271 m $= 10.3216$ cm. i.e., by 10.32 m.

2. (a) i. $\sin 15° = \dfrac{CF}{BC} \Leftrightarrow BC = \dfrac{CF}{\sin 15°} = \dfrac{80}{\sin 15°} = 309.096$. i.e., 309.1 m

ii. Using ΔBCD: $\cos 40° = \dfrac{BC}{BD} \Leftrightarrow BD = \dfrac{BC}{\cos 40°} = \dfrac{80/(\sin 15°)}{\cos 40°} = \dfrac{80}{\sin 15° \cos 40°}$

$= 403.4965$

That is, 403.5 m

iii. Using ΔBED: $\sin\theta = \dfrac{80}{DB} = \sin 15° \cos 40° = 0.1982 \therefore \theta = 11.4356°$. i.e., $11°26'$

(b) i. $\Delta A'E'D'$: $\tan\alpha = \dfrac{D'E'}{A'E'} \Leftrightarrow A'E' = \dfrac{h}{\tan\alpha} = \dfrac{h}{(1/12)} \therefore A'E' = 12h$.

$\Delta B'E'D'$: $\tan\beta = \dfrac{D'E'}{B'E'} \Leftrightarrow B'E' = \dfrac{h}{\tan\beta} = \dfrac{h}{(1/14)} \therefore B'E' = 14h$

$\Delta G'E'D'$: $\tan\gamma = \dfrac{D'E'}{E'G'} \Leftrightarrow E'G' = \dfrac{h}{\tan\gamma} = \dfrac{h}{(1/18)} \therefore E'G' = 18h$

ii.

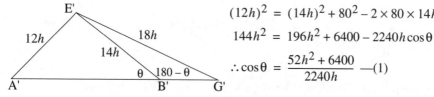

$(12h)^2 = (14h)^2 + 80^2 - 2 \times 80 \times 14h\cos\theta$

$144h^2 = 196h^2 + 6400 - 2240h\cos\theta$

$\therefore \cos\theta = \dfrac{52h^2 + 6400}{2240h}$ —(1)

Similarly, $(18h)^2 = (14h)^2 + 40^2 - 2 \times 40 \times 14h\cos(180 - \theta)$, but $\cos(180 - \theta) = -\cos\theta$.

$\therefore 324h^2 = 196h^2 + 1600 + 1120\cos\theta$

$\therefore \cos\theta = \dfrac{128h^2 - 1600}{1120h}$ —(2)

Equating (1) and (2): $\dfrac{52h^2 + 6400}{2240h} = \dfrac{128h^2 - 1600}{1120h} \Leftrightarrow 3200 + 26h^2 = 128h^2 - 1600$

$\Leftrightarrow 102h^2 = 4800$

$\therefore h = 6.8599$

That is, height is 6.86 m.

TEST

1. Using ΔABX: $\sin 30° = \dfrac{BX}{30} \Leftrightarrow BX = 30\sin 30° = 15$ [1]

From ΔBCX: $XC^2 = 20^2 + 15^2 = 625$ [1] $\therefore XC = 25$ i.e., 25 cm [1]

2. i. Using ΔABV:

$VV_1 = \sqrt{15^2 - 4.5^2}$

$= \sqrt{204.75}$ [1]

$\cos\theta = \dfrac{9}{\sqrt{204.75}}$ [1]

$\therefore \theta = \cos^{-1}(0.6289)$

$= 51.0257°$ i.e., $51°1'$ [1]

108

ii.

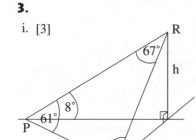

$$AC = \sqrt{18^2 + 9^2}$$
$$= \sqrt{405} \quad [1]$$
$$\therefore AO = \frac{1}{2}\sqrt{405}$$
$$\cos\alpha = 0.5\sqrt{405}/15$$
$$= \frac{\sqrt{405}}{30} \quad [1]$$

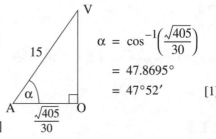

$$\alpha = \cos^{-1}\left(\frac{\sqrt{405}}{30}\right)$$
$$= 47.8695°$$
$$= 47°52' \quad [1]$$

iii.

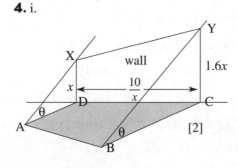

$$18^2 = (\sqrt{204.75})^2 + (\sqrt{204.75})^2 - 2(\sqrt{204.75})^2 \cos\beta \quad [1]$$
$$\therefore \cos\beta = \frac{2 \times 204.75 - 324}{2 \times 204.75} \quad [1]$$
$$\beta = \cos^{-1}(0.2087)$$
$$= 77.9484° \quad \text{i.e., } 77°57' \quad [1]$$

3.

i. [3]

ii. $\angle PRQ = 180° - 61° - 52° = 67°$ [1]

We have that $\sin 8° = \dfrac{h}{PR} \Leftrightarrow h = PR \times \sin 8°$ [1]

But, $\dfrac{PR}{\sin 52°} = \dfrac{15}{\sin 67°} \Leftrightarrow PR = \dfrac{1.5 \sin 52°}{\sin 67°}$ [1]

$\therefore h = \dfrac{1.5 \sin 52°}{\sin 67°} \times \sin 8° = 0.1787$. i.e., 178.71 m [1]

4. i.

ii.

$$\tan\theta = \frac{XD}{AD} \therefore AD = \frac{x}{\tan\theta} \quad [1]$$
$$\tan\theta = \frac{YC}{BC} \therefore BC = \frac{1.6x}{\tan\theta} \quad [1]$$
$$\text{Area} = \frac{1}{2}(AD + BC) \times DC$$
$$= \frac{1}{2}\left[\frac{x}{\tan\theta} + \frac{1.6x}{\tan\theta}\right] \times \frac{10}{x} \quad [1] = \frac{13}{\tan\theta} \quad [1]$$

CHAPTER 10
LEVEL 1

1. i. $\begin{pmatrix} -5 \\ 9 \end{pmatrix}$ ii. $\begin{vmatrix} -2a \\ b + 2a \\ c + a \end{vmatrix}$ iii. $\begin{pmatrix} 4 \\ -2 \end{pmatrix}$ **2.** i. $5i + 3j$ ii. $4i + 12j$ iii. $-ai - 6bj$ iv. $i - 6j$

3. i. $\overrightarrow{OC} = \overrightarrow{OA} + \overrightarrow{AC} = a + b$ ii. $\overrightarrow{BA} = \overrightarrow{BO} + \overrightarrow{OA} = -b + a$.

LEVEL 2

1. i. $\sqrt{2^2 + (-4)^2} = \sqrt{4 + 16} = \sqrt{20} = 2\sqrt{5}$ ii. $\sqrt{25 + 1 + x^2} = \sqrt{26 + x^2}$ iii. $\sqrt{9 + 4} = \sqrt{13}$

2. i. $\left|\binom{2}{3}\right| = \sqrt{4+9} = \sqrt{13}$. Therefore, unit vector is $\frac{1}{\sqrt{13}}\binom{2}{3}$.

ii. $|7i + 2j - k| = \sqrt{49+4+1} = 3\sqrt{6}$. Therefore, unit vector is $\frac{1}{3\sqrt{6}}(7i + 2j - k)$.

iii. $|-2i + 7j| = \sqrt{4+49} = \sqrt{53}$. Therefore, unit vector is $\frac{1}{\sqrt{53}}(-2i + 7j)$.

LEVEL 3

1. $\overrightarrow{OM} = \overrightarrow{OA} + \overrightarrow{AM} = a + \frac{1}{2}\overrightarrow{AB} = a + \frac{1}{2}(\overrightarrow{AO} + \overrightarrow{OB}) = a + \frac{1}{2}(-a + b) = \frac{1}{2}(a + b)$.

2. $a = kb \therefore (6i + 9j) = kxi + k(x+1)j \Leftrightarrow 6 = kx - (1)$ and $9 = k(x+1) - (2)$

(2) divided by (1): $\frac{9}{6} = \frac{k(x+1)}{kx} \Leftrightarrow 9x = 6x + 6 \Leftrightarrow x = 2$.

LEVEL 4

1.

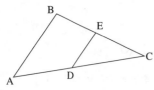

$\overrightarrow{DE} = \overrightarrow{DC} + \overrightarrow{CE} = \frac{1}{2}\overrightarrow{AC} + \frac{1}{2}\overrightarrow{CB} = \frac{1}{2}(\overrightarrow{AC} + \overrightarrow{CB})$

$= \frac{1}{2}\overrightarrow{AB}$

Therefore, DE is parallel to AB and half its length.

2.

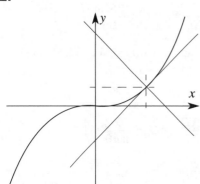

$y = x^3 \Rightarrow \frac{dy}{dx} = 3x^2 \therefore$ at $x = 1$, $\frac{dy}{dx} = 3$.

So, a vector in the direction of tangent would be

$a = i + 3j \therefore \hat{a} = \frac{1}{\sqrt{10}}(i + 3j)$

Gradient of normal at $(1, 1)$ is $-\frac{1}{3}$.

Therefore, vector in direction of normal would be

$b = -3i + j \therefore \hat{b} = \frac{1}{\sqrt{10}}(-3i + j)$

EXAMINATION STYLE QUESTIONS

1. i. $A = 400\cos 60°i + 400\sin 60°j = 200i + 200\sqrt{3}j$, $B = 300\cos 20°i + 300\sin 20°j$.

ii. $R = A + B = (200 + 300\cos 20°)i + (200\sqrt{3} + 300\sin 20°)j$

iii. $|R| = \sqrt{(200 + 300\cos 20°)^2 + (200\sqrt{3} + 300\sin 20°)^2} \approx 658.67$

$\tan\theta = \frac{200\sqrt{3} + 300\sin 20°}{200 + 300\cos 20°} = 0.9317 \therefore \theta = 42.9764° = 42°58'$

2. (a) i. $\overrightarrow{OY} = \overrightarrow{OB} + \overrightarrow{BY} = y + \frac{1}{2}\overrightarrow{BA} = y + \frac{1}{2}(\overrightarrow{BO} + \overrightarrow{OA}) = y + \frac{1}{2}(-y + x) = \frac{1}{2}(x + y)$

ii. $\overrightarrow{XY} = \overrightarrow{XB} + \overrightarrow{BY} = \frac{1}{4}\overrightarrow{OB} + \frac{1}{2}\overrightarrow{BA} = \frac{1}{4}y + \frac{1}{2}(x - y) = \frac{1}{2}x - \frac{1}{4}y$

iii. $\overrightarrow{YZ} = \overrightarrow{YA} + \overrightarrow{AZ} = \frac{1}{2}\overrightarrow{BA} + \frac{1}{2}\overrightarrow{OA} = \frac{1}{2}(x - y) + \frac{1}{2}x = x - \frac{1}{2}y$

(b) $\overrightarrow{XY} = \frac{1}{2}x - \frac{1}{4}y = \frac{1}{2}\left(x - \frac{1}{2}y\right) = \frac{1}{2}\overrightarrow{YZ} \therefore \overrightarrow{XY}$ is $\parallel \overrightarrow{YZ}$ & as Y is common to both $\overrightarrow{XY}$ & $\overrightarrow{YZ}$

then X, Y and Z are collinear.

TEST

1. i. $a + b = 9i - 3j$ [1]   ii. $|a - b| = |-3i + 7j| = \sqrt{9 + 49} = \sqrt{58}$ [1] [1] [1]

iii. $5a - 2b = 15i + 10j - (12i - 10j) = 3i + 20j$ [1] [1]

2. $\left|\begin{pmatrix} 5 \\ -2 \end{pmatrix}\right| = \sqrt{25 + 4} = \sqrt{29} \therefore$ unit vector $= \frac{1}{\sqrt{29}}\begin{pmatrix} 5 \\ -2 \end{pmatrix}$ [1][1]

3. i. $\overrightarrow{AB} = 2\overrightarrow{OC} = 2c$ [1]   ii. $\overrightarrow{OB} = \overrightarrow{OA} + \overrightarrow{AB} = a + 2c$ [1]   iii. $\overrightarrow{CB} = \overrightarrow{CO} + \overrightarrow{OA} + \overrightarrow{AB}$ [1]
$$= -c + a + 2c$$
$$= a + c$$
[2]

4. i. $A = 6\cos 20°i + 6\sin 20°j$ [2], $B = 2\cos 10°i - 2\sin 10°j$ [1] [1]

ii. $R = (6\cos 20°i + 6\sin 20°j) + (2\cos 10°i - 2\sin 10°j) \therefore |R| = 7.7964$, i.e., 7.80 [1] [1]

5. Let E, F, G and H be the midpoints of $\overline{AB}, \overline{BC}, \overline{CD}$ & $\overline{DA}$ as shown.

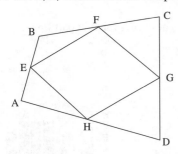

$\overrightarrow{EF} = \overrightarrow{EB} + \overrightarrow{BF} = \frac{1}{2}\overrightarrow{AB} + \frac{1}{2}\overrightarrow{BC} = \frac{1}{2}(\overrightarrow{AB} + \overrightarrow{BC})$ [1]

$$= \frac{1}{2}AC$$

$$= \frac{1}{2}(\overrightarrow{AD} + \overrightarrow{DC})$$

$$= \frac{1}{2}(2\overrightarrow{HD} + 2\overrightarrow{DG})$$

$$= \overrightarrow{HG}$$ [2]

As $\overrightarrow{EF} = \overrightarrow{HG}$, then $\overline{EF} \parallel \overline{HG}$ & $|\overrightarrow{EF}| = |\overrightarrow{HG}|$ [2]. Then, as EFGH forms a quadrilateral EFGH must be a parallelogram. [1]

CHAPTER 11
LEVEL 1
1. i. 1 ii. 13 iii. 1.3 iv. 40% **2.** i. 1 ii. 3 iii. 10-14 & 20-24. **3.** 75
LEVEL 2
1. i. 2.09 ii. 13.7 iii. 4.05 iv. 9.28 v. 52.6 **2.** i. 4 ii. 3 iii. 12 iv. 13 v. 16 & 17
3. i. 17 ii. 31 iii. 4.2 iv. 49.1 v. 0.8
LEVEL 3
1. i. 2 & 7 ii. 22 & 82 iii. 23.5 & 84.2 iv. 5.5 & 20 (take the mid points between 5 & 6 and 19 & 21) v. 3.4 & 6.8 **2.** i. 2.57 ii. 30.1 iii. 2.91 iv. 279 v. 0.296
LEVEL 4
1. The median as this is the measure that is least affected by the small number of outliers (the luxury homes).
2. This question is best answered using a graphic calculator. You need to know the correct syntax to use with your model of calculator. These screens were produced using a Texas TI-83.

i.
```
normalcdf(-1000,
347,345,2.8)
        .7624748125
```
or 76%

ii.
```
normalcdf(345.5,
1000,345,2.8)
        .4291371201
```
or 43%

iii.
```
normalcdf(343,34
6,345,2.8)
        .4019823224
```
or 40%

iv.

```
invNorm(.01,345,
2.8)
      338.4862259
```
or 338.5 gms

3. i. 50 ii. 5 iii. 2 iv. The mean is likely to be about 5 as there is a positive skew. v. The range is $9 - 2 = 7$. A complete distribution usually covers 6 standard deviations. On this basis the standard deviation might be expected to be about 7/6 or 1.2 marks.

EXAMINATION STYLE

1. i.

Weight:	0-.9	1-1.9	2-2.9	3-3.9	4-4.9	....	8-8.9	9-9.9	10-10.9	11-11.9	12-12.9
Frequency:	0	1	1	2	3		3	3	1	2	3	0	01

ii. Mean = 6.35gms iii. 2.615gms

iv.
```
normalcdf(5,9,6.
35,2.615)
      .5417226198
```
or 0.542

v.
```
normalcdf(3.5,10
00,6.35,2.615)
      .8621139094
```
or 86%

vi.
```
invNorm(.9,6.35,
2.615)
      9.701257347
```
or 9.7gms

2. i. Number of employees: $4 + 2 + 1 + 4 + 3 + 3 + 2 = 19$

ii. Total wage estimate (using class mid-points) =

$4(50) + 2(250) + 1(350) + 4(450) + 3(550) + 3(650) + 2(750) = 7950$

Estimate of mean = $\dfrac{7950}{19} = 418.42105 \approx \$420$ iii. \$450 iv. These are probably part time or casual workers. v. The mean.

TEST

1. i.

Height	175	176	177	178	179	180	181
Frequency	1	0	3	4	4	5	3

Method [1] answers [1]

ii.
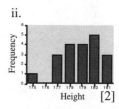

iii.
Height	175-179	180-184
Frequency	12	8

[1] First method is best.

iv. Mode = 180cm [1] Mean = 178.85 [1] Median = 179cm [1]
v. Standard deviation method [1] Answer = 1.558cm [1]
Quartiles are 178 & 180cm [1] Interquartile range = 2cm [1]

2. i. Standard deviation = $\sqrt{1.44} = 1.2$ cm [1] ii. 80% [2] iii. 5% [2] iv. 75% [2]

CHAPTER 12
LEVEL 1

1. $\dfrac{2}{52} = \dfrac{1}{26}$ **2.** $\dfrac{4}{9}$ **3.** $\dfrac{1}{8}$ **4.** $\dfrac{2}{6} = \dfrac{1}{3}$ **5.** $\dfrac{1}{4}$ **6.** $\dfrac{1}{2}$

LEVEL 2

1. 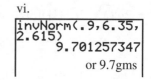 i. $p(A \cup B) = 0.7$ ii. $p(B') = 0.5$ iii. $p(A' \cap B) = 0.4$

2. i. $2^4 = 16$ ii. $\dfrac{1}{16}$ iii. $\dfrac{3}{8}$ iv. $\dfrac{1}{16} + \dfrac{1}{4} = \dfrac{5}{16}$ **3.** i. $\dfrac{1}{9} \times \dfrac{1}{9} = \dfrac{1}{81}$ ii. $\dfrac{1}{9} \times \dfrac{1}{8} = \dfrac{1}{72}$

4. i. 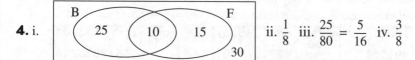 ii. $\dfrac{1}{8}$ iii. $\dfrac{25}{80} = \dfrac{5}{16}$ iv. $\dfrac{3}{8}$

LEVEL 3

1.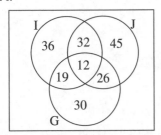

i. $p(A|B) = \dfrac{p(A \cap B)}{p(B)} = \dfrac{0.3}{0.4} = \dfrac{3}{4}$ ii. $\dfrac{0.3}{0.5} = \dfrac{3}{5}$

iii. $p(A) \times p(B) = 0.5(0.4) = 0.2$, $p(A \cap B) = 0.3$ so the events are not independent.

2. i. $\dfrac{4}{51}$ ii. No iii. $\dfrac{4}{52} = \dfrac{1}{13}$ **3.** (a) i. Yes ii. $\dfrac{3}{8} \times \dfrac{2}{7} = \dfrac{3}{28}$ iii. $\dfrac{4}{8} \times \dfrac{3}{7} = \dfrac{3}{14}$

(b) i. No ii. $\dfrac{3}{8} \times \dfrac{2}{8} = \dfrac{3}{32}$ iii. $\dfrac{3}{16}$.

LEVEL 4

1.
A: 0.36 0.24 0.16 :B
0.24

i. $p(A \cup B) = 0.76$ ii. $p(A \cap B) = 0.24$

iii. $p(A|B') = \dfrac{0.36}{0.36 + 0.24} = 0.6$

2. i.

I: 36 32 45 :J
12
19 26
30
G

ii. $\dfrac{12}{200} = \dfrac{3}{50}$ iii. $\dfrac{32 + 19 + 26}{200} = \dfrac{77}{200}$

iv. $\dfrac{32 + 12}{32 + 12 + 26 + 45} = \dfrac{44}{115}$

v. No, selections made without replacement are always dependent.

EXAMINATION STYLE

1. i.

Number of eggs	2	3	4	5	6	7	8	9	10	11
Frequency	5	1	5	8	3	4	2	6	2	4

ii. $\dfrac{6}{40} = \dfrac{3}{20}$ iii. 6.325 eggs per bird iv. $\dfrac{18}{40} = \dfrac{9}{20}$ v. 2.787 eggs vi. The interval is 3.5376 to

9.11236 or in whole numbers 4 to 9. vii. The probability is: $\dfrac{28}{40} = \dfrac{7}{10}$

2. i. Each spin is physically separate from the others. The result of the first spin will not affect the second.
ii.

Heads	Probability
0	0.064
1	0.288
2	0.432
3	0.216

iii. $0.6^2 = 0.36$

iv. $(0.6^{10})0.4 = 0.00241865$. You must include the probability of the tail that ends the sequence.

TEST.

1. i. $\dfrac{2}{10} = \dfrac{1}{5}$ [1] ii. There are 4 vowels [1] $\dfrac{4}{10} = \dfrac{2}{5}$ [1].

2. i. $\frac{1}{4}$ [1] ii. $\frac{1}{4} \times \frac{12}{51} = \frac{3}{51}$ [2] iii. $\frac{25}{51}$ [2]

3. i.

A   B

0.04   0.16   0.64   [2] ii. $0.04 + 0.16 + 0.64 = 0.84$ [2] iii. 0.16 [1]

0.16

iv. $\frac{0.16}{0.8} = \frac{1}{5}$ [2]

4. i. $\frac{3}{7}$ (the results are independent) [1] ii. $6\left(\frac{3}{7}\right)^2\left(\frac{4}{7}\right)^2$ [1] $\frac{864}{2401}$ [1] iii. $\left(\frac{3}{7}\right)^2$ [1] $\frac{9}{49}$ [1]

CHAPTER 13
LEVEL 1
1. (a) dom $= (-1, 4]$, ran $= [0, 5]$ (b) dom $= [0, 6]$, ran $= [0, 6]$ (c) dom $= \mathbb{R}\backslash\{2\}$, ran $= \mathbb{R}\backslash\{3\}$.
2. Using vertical line test, the only functions are (a) and (c).
3. (a) $y = 2 + 2 = 4$ (b) $y = (2 + 2)^2 + 2 = 18$ (c) $y = 2^2 + 2 = 6$
LEVEL 2

1. $4 = \frac{x}{x+2} \Leftrightarrow 4x + 8 = x \Leftrightarrow -3x = 8 \Leftrightarrow x = -\frac{8}{3}$ **2.** (a) $2 - x \geq 0 \Leftrightarrow x \leq 2$ (b) $x \geq 3$

(c) $x > -1$

3. (a) $g(f(x)) = \frac{1}{f(x)+1} = \frac{1}{(2x-1)+1} = \frac{1}{2x}$

(b) $f(g(x)) = 2g(x) - 1 = \frac{2}{x+1} - 1 = \frac{1-x}{1+x}$

4. (a) i.   ii.   (b) i. ran $= [1, \infty)$ ii. ran $= [1, 5]$

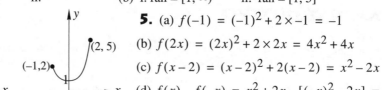

5. (a) $f(-1) = (-1)^2 + 2 \times -1 = -1$

(b) $f(2x) = (2x)^2 + 2 \times 2x = 4x^2 + 4x$

(c) $f(x-2) = (x-2)^2 + 2(x-2) = x^2 - 2x$

(d) $f(x) - f(-x) = x^2 + 2x - [(-x)^2 - 2x] = 4x$

6. (a)   (b)   (c)

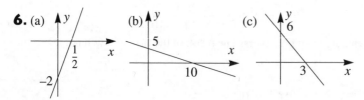

7. (a) i. $f(3) = 3(3-3) = 0$ ii. $f(h) = h(h-3) = h^2 - 3h$

(b) $f(3+h) - f(3) = (3+h)(3+h-3) - 0 = (3+h)h = 3h + h^2$
LEVEL 3
1. (a)   (b)

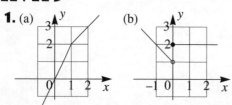

2. i. $f(3) = 3 + \dfrac{1}{3-2} = 3 + 1 = 4$

ii. $f\left(\dfrac{2x+1}{x}\right) = 3 + \dfrac{1}{\dfrac{2x+1}{x} - 2} = 3 + \dfrac{x}{2x+1-2x} = 3 + x$

3. $g(f(x)) = \dfrac{1}{f(x)} - 1 = \dfrac{1}{\left(\dfrac{1}{x+1}\right)} - 1 = (x+1) - 1 = x$;

$f(g(x)) = \dfrac{1}{g(x)+1} = \dfrac{1}{\left(\dfrac{1}{x}-1\right)+1} = \dfrac{1}{\left(\dfrac{1}{x}\right)} = x$

4. Calculator check. **5.** $\dfrac{x}{x-1} = k \Leftrightarrow x = kx - k \Leftrightarrow k = x(k-1) \Leftrightarrow x = \dfrac{k}{k-1}$

6.

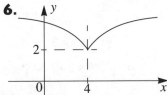

LEVEL 4

1. From the graph of $f(x) = 4x - x^2$, we have that the function is increasing if $S = (0, 2)$

2. $x^2 - 2 = \dfrac{1}{x^2-2} \Leftrightarrow (x^2-2)^2 = 1 \Leftrightarrow x^2 - 2 = \pm 1$, $x^2 - 2 = -1 \Leftrightarrow x^2 = 1 \Leftrightarrow x = \pm 1$.

Next, if $x^2 - 2 = 1 \Leftrightarrow x^2 = 3 \Leftrightarrow x = \pm\sqrt{3}$. Therefore, solution set is $\{\pm\sqrt{3}, \pm 1\}$.

3. Domain: $9 - x^2 > 0 \Leftrightarrow x^2 < 9 \Leftrightarrow -3 < x < 3$.

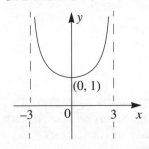

4. (a) $f(x+2) = 2(x+2)^2 - 2 = 2x^2 + 8x + 6 \equiv ax^2 + bx + c$, $\therefore a = 2, b = 8, c = 6$.

(b) $f(x) + 2 = f(x+2) \Leftrightarrow 2x^2 = 2x^2 + 8x + 6 \Leftrightarrow x = -3/4$.

5. (a) x–intercept $(y = 0)$: $0 = a + \dfrac{b}{x} \Leftrightarrow x = -\dfrac{b}{a}$ (b) i. & ii.

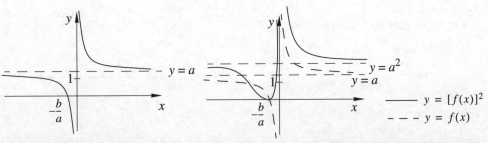

EXAMINATION STYLE QUESTIONS

1. (a)   (b) $I = [2, \infty)$ (c) i.   ii. range of $g = (\infty, 4]$

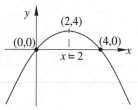

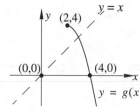

2. (a)   (b) range $= (0, 4]$ (c) $f'(x)$ doesn't exist at $x = 0$ (only)

3. (a) i. $k = 0$ ii. $k = 2$ iii. $k = -2$ (b) At $x = 2$:

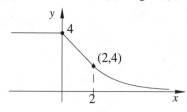

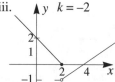

$$\frac{1}{2} \times 2 + k = 0$$

$$\therefore k = -1$$

4. (a) $f(g(x)) = 9 - (g(x))^2 = 9 - (\sqrt{x})^2 = 9 - x$ (b) i. $d_{f(g(x))} = d_{g(x)} = [0, \infty)$.

ii. 9   iii. range $= (-\infty, 9]$ **5.** (a) Yes. (b) 4   (c) i. $\left[0, \frac{16}{3}\right]$ ii. $[0, 4]$

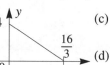

(d) $2 = 4 - \frac{3}{4}x \Leftrightarrow x = \frac{8}{3}$

TEST

1. i. $f(1) = 1 - 1 + 1 = 1$ [1] ii. $a^2 - \frac{1}{a} + 1 = 1 \Leftrightarrow a^2 - \frac{1}{a} = 0 \Leftrightarrow a^3 - 1 = 0 \Leftrightarrow a = 1$.[3]

2.   **3.** (a) From graph, range $= (-\infty, 16]$ [1](b) range $= (-\infty, 16+k]$. [1]

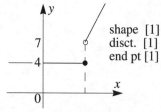

shape [1]
disct. [1]
end pt [1]

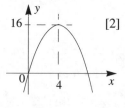

[2]

This occurs because all that has happened is that 'k' has been added to the function in (a) and so the graph in (a) is moved up 'k' units.

4. (a) At $x = 1$, $f(1) = 2^{-k}$.

For f to be continuous at $x = 1$ then

$$b = 2^{-k} \Leftrightarrow b = \frac{1}{2^k} \Leftrightarrow b \times 2^k = 1 .[3]$$

(b)

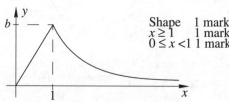

Shape   1 mark
$x \geq 1$ 1 mark
$0 \leq x < 1$ 1 mark

5. (a) [1]

t min	1	3	7	14	29	59
$T\,°C$	60	45	37.5	34	32	31

(b)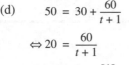

shape [1]
Asymp [1]

(c) $T \to 30$ [1]

(d) $50 = 30 + \dfrac{60}{t+1}$

$\Leftrightarrow 20 = \dfrac{60}{t+1}$

$\Leftrightarrow t = 2$ [1]

6. Steps [2], end pts. [1] values [1]

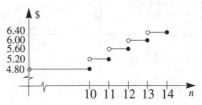

7. (a) $y = \begin{cases} \dfrac{1}{2}x+1 & \text{if } -2 \le x < 0 \\[2mm] 1 - \dfrac{1}{2}x & \text{if } 0 \le x \le 2 \end{cases}$ [1] [1] [1]

(b) $y = \begin{cases} -1 & \text{if } -3 < x \le -1 \\ 0 & \text{if } -1 < x \le 1 \\ 1 & \text{if } 1 < x \le 3 \end{cases}$ [1] [1] [1]

CHAPTER 14
LEVEL 1

1. i. 1   ii. $\dfrac{\sqrt{3}}{2}$ iii. $\dfrac{1}{\sqrt{2}} = \dfrac{\sqrt{2}}{2}$ iv. $-\dfrac{1}{\sqrt{2}}$ v. $\dfrac{\sqrt{3}}{2}$ vi. $\sin(300°) = -\sin(60°) = -\dfrac{\sqrt{3}}{2}$

2. i. $\sin(23°) = 0.3907$ ii. 0.5736   iii. 0.9848   iv. –0.3420   v. $\cos(-500°) = -0.7660$ vi. 0.2720

LEVEL 2

1. i. 2   ii. max value of $\cos x = 1$ and min $= -1$, therefore max. value is $1 - (-1) = 2$ iii. 7   iv. 1
v. 1   vi. max. value of $\cos(4x)$ is 1. Therefore, max value of $3 + \cos(4x) = 3 + 1 = 4$.

2. i. $360°$ ii. $\dfrac{360°}{0.5} = 720°$ iii. $\dfrac{360°}{3} = 120°$ iv. $360°$ v. $\dfrac{360°}{(1/3)} = 1080°$ vi. $\dfrac{360°}{3/4} = 480°$

3. i. $y = 1$ ii. $y = 2$ iii. $y = -3$

LEVEL 3

1. i.

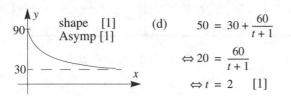

ii.

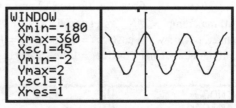

iii.

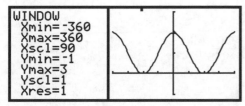

iv.

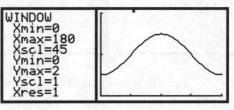

v.

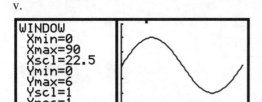

vi.

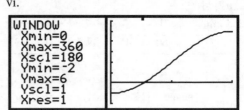

2. i. $\cos 2x = 0 \therefore 2x = 90° \Leftrightarrow x = 45°$ **ii.** $\sin 3x = 0 \therefore 3x = 180° \Leftrightarrow x = 60°$

iii. $\cos\left(\dfrac{x}{3}\right) = 0 \therefore \dfrac{x}{3} = 90° \Leftrightarrow x = 270°$

LEVEL 4

1. i. period $= 360°$ & inverted sin $\therefore -\sin x$; Amp $= \dfrac{1}{2} \times 4 = 2$ & transl is $+1 \therefore f(x) = 1 - 2\sin x$.

ii. period $= 180°$ $\therefore \cos 2x$; Amp $= \dfrac{1}{2} \times 4 = 2 \therefore 2\cos 2x$; transl is $+1 \therefore f(x) = 1 + 2\cos 2x$.

iii. period $= 180°$ & inverted $\therefore -\cos 2x$; Amp $= \dfrac{1}{2} \times 2 = 1$ & transl is $+2 \therefore f(x) = 2 - \cos 2x$

iv. period $= 90°$ $\therefore \cos 4x$; Amp $= \dfrac{1}{2} \times 2 = 1$ & transl is $+1 \therefore f(x) = 1 + \cos 4x$

2. i. $\therefore x = 30°, 180° - 30°, -360° + 30°, -180° - 30° = 30°, 150°, -330°, -210°$.
ii. $\therefore x = 30°, 360° - 30°, -30°, -360° + 30° = 30°, 330°, -30°, -330°$. i.e., only $30°, 330°$.
iii. $2x = 72°32', 360° - 72°32', 360° + 72°32', 720° - 72°32'$
   $\therefore x = 36°16', 180° - 36°16', 180° + 36°16', 360 - 36°16'$
     $= 36°16', 143°44', 216°16', 343°44'$
     $= 36°, 144°, 216°, 344°$ (to nearest degree)
iv. $2x = 69°30', 360° - 69°30' \therefore x = 34°45', 180° - 34°45' = 35°, 145°$ (to nearest degree).
v. $x = 180° + 19°28', 360° - 19°28' = 199°28', 340°32' = 199°, 341°$ (to nearest degree).

vi. $\sin(2x) = \pm\dfrac{\sqrt{3}}{2} \therefore 2x = 60°, 120°$ or $2x = 240°, 300°$ i.e., $x = 30°, 60°, 120°, 150°$.

3. i. (a) $C(0) = 18 - 6\cos(0) = 12$ **(b)** $C(2\text{ pm}) = C(14) = 18 - 6\cos(5 \times 14) = 23.1961$ i.e., $23.2°$C.
ii. (a) max temp. $= 24°$C, min temp. $12°$C
(b) max. occurs when $\cos(15t) = -1$, i.e., $15t = 180$, so $t = 12$.
   min. occurs when $\cos(15t) = 1$, i.e., $15t = 0, 360$, so $t = 0, 24$.
iii.

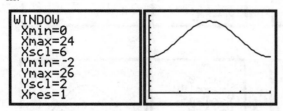

iv. $C = 20 \Leftrightarrow 20 = 18 - 6\cos(15t)$ $\Leftrightarrow \cos(15t) = -\dfrac{1}{3}$

$$15t = 180° - Cos^{-1}\left(-\dfrac{1}{3}\right), 180° + Cos^{-1}\left(-\dfrac{1}{3}\right)$$

$$= 109.47°, 250.52°$$

$$\therefore t = 7.2981, 16.7019$$

That is, 7:18 am & 16:42 (4:42pm). Therefore, between 7:18 am and 4:42pm.

v. Rising most rapidly at t = 6 (i.e., 6 am). Using the gradient of the tangent or graphics calculator we have largest rate = 1.57°C/hr.

EXAMINATION STYLE QUESTIONS

1. i. (a) $\frac{360}{360} = 1$ (b) 3.   ii.

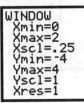

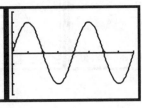

iii. $f\left(\frac{1}{3}\right) = 3\sin 120° = \frac{3\sqrt{3}}{2}$

$$\therefore A \equiv \left(\frac{1}{3}, \frac{3\sqrt{3}}{2}\right)$$

$$f\left(\frac{1}{2}\right) = 3\sin 180° = 0 \therefore B \equiv \left(\frac{1}{2}, 0\right). \therefore \bar{f}_{AB} = \frac{\frac{3\sqrt{3}}{2} - 0}{\left(\frac{1}{3} - \frac{1}{2}\right)} = -9\sqrt{3}.$$

2. i.

t hours	0	1	2	3	4	5	6	7	8
h metres	5.5	6.6	7	6.6	5.5	4.4	4	4.4	5.5

ii.   iii.

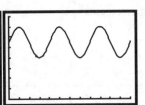

iv. $h = 4 \therefore t = 6, 6 + 8, 6 + 2 \times 8 = 6, 14, 22$

3. i (a) 5 m [max. of $2\cos(120t°)$ is 2, so max. of $3 + 2\cos(120t°)$ is $3 + 2 = 5$]

(b) 1 m [min. of $2\cos(120t°)$ is –2, so min. of $3 + 2\cos(120t°)$ is $3 - 2 = 1$]

ii. $4 = 3 + 2\cos(120t°) \Leftrightarrow \cos(120t°) = 0.5 \therefore 120t = 60, 300, 420, 660$

$$\text{i.e.,} t = \frac{1}{2}, \frac{5}{2}, \frac{7}{2}, \frac{11}{2}$$

iii.

iv. Using part ii., we have that

$$x \geq 4 \Leftrightarrow t \in \left[0, \frac{1}{2}\right] \cup \left[\frac{5}{2}, \frac{7}{2}\right] \cup \left[\frac{11}{2}, 6\right]$$

Therefore, total time $= \frac{1}{2} + \frac{2}{2} + \frac{1}{2} = 2$

That is, $\frac{2}{6} \times 100\% = 33.33\%$.

4. i. $\dfrac{360}{k} = 12 \therefore k = 30$ **ii.** By observation, we have: $b = 11$ and $a = -10$.

iii.

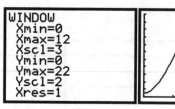

```
WINDOW
Xmin=0
Xmax=12
Xscl=3
Ymin=0
Ymax=22
Yscl=2
Xres=1
```

iv. $H = 16 \Rightarrow 16 = -10\cos(30t°) + 11$

$\Leftrightarrow \cos(30t°) = -0.5$

$\therefore 30t = 180 - 60,\ 180 + 60$

$30t = 120,\ 240$

i.e., $t = 4,\ 8$

v. Therefore, above 16 m for 4 seconds.

i.e., $\dfrac{4}{12} \times 100\ \% = 33.33\%$ of the time.

TEST

1. i. $\sin(-270°) = -\sin(270°) = 1$ [1]   **ii.** $\cos(135°) = -\cos(45°) = -\dfrac{1}{\sqrt{2}}$ [1]

2. i. 2 [1]   **ii.** $\dfrac{360°}{3} = 120°$ [1]   **iii.** $5 - 2 \times -1 = 7$ [1]   **3.** $\sin 3x° = \dfrac{1}{2} \therefore 3x = 30 \Leftrightarrow x = 10$ [3]

4. period $= \dfrac{360°}{60} = 6°$, Ampl $= 6$, transl. $+3$ [2]

x–intercepts $(y = 0)$: $\cos(60x°) = -\dfrac{1}{2} \therefore 60x = 120,\ 240 \Leftrightarrow x = 2,\ 4$ [2]

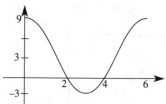

Shape [1]
Range [1]
Domain & intercepts [1]

5. $\dfrac{360}{k} = 180 \therefore k = 2$ [1], Ampl. $= 2$ [1], transl. $= +2$ [1], Equation: $f(x) = 2 + 2\sin(2x°)$ [1]

6. i. period $= \dfrac{360}{90/13} = 13 \times 4 = 52$ weeks. [1]   **ii.** $N_{max} = 7000$ [1] $N_{min} = 2000$ [1]

iii.

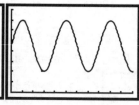

```
WINDOW
Xmin=0
Xmax=143
Xscl=13
Ymin=0
Ymax=8000
Yscl=1000
Xres=1
```

shape [1]
range [1]
endpoints & domain [2]

iv. (a) By observation, t $= 13$ [1]

(b) $6000 = 4500 + 2500\sin\left(\dfrac{90}{13}t°\right) \Leftrightarrow \sin\left(\dfrac{90}{13}t°\right) = \dfrac{3}{5} \therefore \dfrac{90}{13}t = 36.86$. [2]

So, $t = 5.33$ [1]

v. $3000 = 4500 + 2500\sin\left(\dfrac{90}{13}t°\right) \Leftrightarrow \sin\left(\dfrac{90}{13}t°\right) = -\dfrac{3}{5}$ [1]

$\therefore \dfrac{90}{13}t = 180 + 36.86,\ 360 - 36.86,\ 540 + 36.86,\ 720 - 36.86$ [1]

$= 216.86,\ 324.14,\ 576.86,\ 683.14$

That is $t = 31.32, 46.82, 83.32, 98.68$ [1]

Now, 31.32 weeks = 219 days, i.e., 9th August. While 46.82 weeks = 328 days, i.e., 24 Nov.
Therefore, population will be at least 3000 from August (9th) to November (24rd). [2]

CHAPTER 15
LEVEL 1
1. i. Window : [–2, 3] by [0,8]   ii. Window : [–2, 3] by [0,8]   iii. Window : [–2, 3] by [0,8]

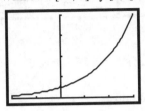 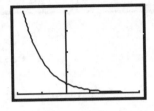 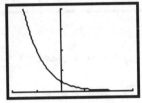

2. i. $y = 2 + 3 \times 5^1 = 17$ ii. $y = 3 - \frac{1}{3} \times 2^2 = \frac{5}{3}$

LEVEL 2
1. i. 3.6 [from graph]. Similarly, ii. 2.5   iii. 1.8

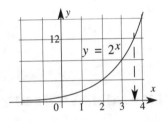

LEVEL 3
1. $f(1) = 1 \therefore 1 = 2^{-1} + k \Leftrightarrow k = 0.5 \therefore f(x) = 2^{-x} + 0.5$

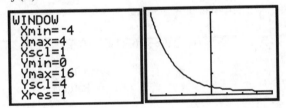 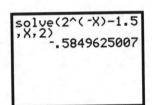

$f(x) = 2 \Leftrightarrow 2^{-x} + 0.5 = 2 \Leftrightarrow 2^{-x} = 1.5 \therefore x = -0.5849 \approx -0.59$

2. Asymptote at $y = 2$, therefore, $c = 2$. So, $y = k \times 3^x + 2$. As graph passes through (1, 0), we

have: $0 = 3k + 2 \Leftrightarrow k = -\frac{2}{3} \therefore y = -\frac{2}{3} \times 3^x + 2$.

3. i.

t seconds	0	15	30	45	60
N	2	4	8	16	32

ii.

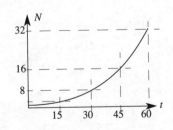

iii. $N = 2 \times 2^{t/15}$ iv. 5 mins = $5 \times 60 = 300$ seconds.

$$\therefore N = 2 \times 2^{20} = 2097152$$

LEVEL 4

1. i.

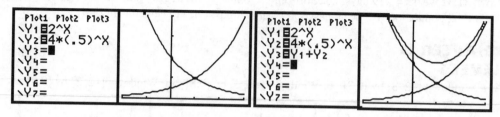

i

i. $f(x) + g(x) = 5 \Leftrightarrow 2^x + \dfrac{4}{2^x} = 5 \Leftrightarrow (2^x)^2 + 4 = 5 \times 2^x \Leftrightarrow (2^x)^2 - 5 \times 2^x + 4 = 0$.

iii. $(2^x - 4)(2^x - 1) = 0 \Leftrightarrow 2^x = 4$ or $2^x = 1 \Leftrightarrow x = 2$ or $x = 0$.

2. i, Max. rate occurs at $t = 0$, i.e., $R(0) = 5 \times (0.95)^0 = 5$.

ii. (a)   (b)   iii. $R = 2.5 \Rightarrow 2.5 = 5 \times (0.95)^t \therefore (0.95)^t = 0.5$

Now, sub. into $y = A(t)$:

$A = 98(1 - 0.5) = 49$

i.e., 49 mg.

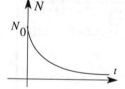

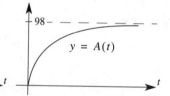

EXAMINATION STYLE QUESTIONS

1. i.

ii. $t = 12, N = N_0 \times (0.82)^{12} = 0.0924 N_0$.

i.e., 9.24% of N_0 is left over after 12 years.

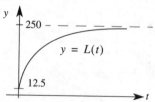

iii. $N = \dfrac{1}{2}N_0 \Rightarrow \dfrac{1}{2}N_0 = N_0 \times (0.82)^t \Leftrightarrow (0.82)^t = 0.5$

$t = 3.4927$

i.e., $t = 3.50$ (years)

iv. $L(6) = 250[1 - 0.95 \times (0.85)^6] = 160.42$

v. $20 = 250[1 - 0.95 \times (0.85)^t] \Leftrightarrow (0.85)^t = \dfrac{1}{0.95}\left[1 - \dfrac{2}{25}\right] \Leftrightarrow (0.85)^t = 0.9684$

Therefore, $t = 0.1974$ i.e., 70 days old.

vi.

TEST

1. shape [1], asymptote [1], endpoints [2], range [1]

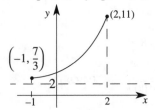

2. By obs., $a = 8$. [1] When $x = 0$, $y = 0$ $\therefore 0 = 8 - kb \Leftrightarrow kb = 8 - (1)$ [2]

When $x = -1$, $y = 4$ $\therefore 4 = 8 - kb^0 \Leftrightarrow k = 4 \therefore b = 2$ [1] [1]

3. (a) $2^x + 3 = 12 \Leftrightarrow 2^x = 9 \Leftrightarrow x = 3.1699$. i.e., $x = 3.170$ (to 3 dec. pl.) [2]

(b) $\frac{1}{2} - 4^{-x} = \frac{1}{8} \Leftrightarrow 4^x = \frac{3}{8} \Leftrightarrow x = -0.70751$. i.e., $x = -0.708$ (to 3 dec. pl.) [2]

4. i. $150 = 200 \times a^2 \therefore a^2 = 0.75 \therefore a = \sqrt{0.75} = 0.866$ [2]

ii. Decomposes by 60% means that there is only 40% left.

40% of $200 = 0.4 \times 200$ $\therefore 0.4 \times 200 = 200 \times (\sqrt{0.75})^t \Leftrightarrow 0.4 = (0.75)^{t/2} \Leftrightarrow \frac{t}{2} = 3.18508$

$$\therefore t = 6.37$$

That is, approx. 6.4 yrs. [2]

iii. $M = 200 \times (0.75)^{10/2} = 47.46$

iv. $A = 200 - M = 200 - 200(0.75)^{t/2}$

$$= 200\left[1 - \left(\frac{3}{4}\right)^{t/2}\right]$$

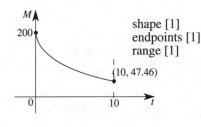

shape [1]
endpoints [1]
range [1]

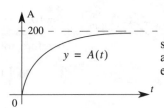

$y = A(t)$

shape [1]
asymptote [1]
equation [1]

5. From the graphs below, we have that $x \sim 1.9$ [1]

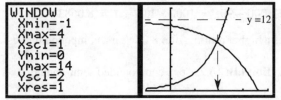

$y = 12$

Shapes [1], [1]
Asymptote [1].

CHAPTER 16
LEVEL 1

1. i. $\frac{x}{152.35} = \frac{25}{1} \Leftrightarrow x = 152.35 \times 25 = 3808.75$ i.e., US $ 25 = ¥ 3808.75$

ii. $\frac{x}{1.92} = \frac{50}{0.58} \Leftrightarrow x = \frac{1.92}{0.58} \times 50 = 165.51$ i.e., £50 = AUS $ 165.51.

iii. $\frac{x}{1.92} = \frac{150}{152.35} \Leftrightarrow x = \frac{1.92 \times 150}{152.35} = 1.89$ i.e., ¥150 = AUS $ 1.89

2. $I = \dfrac{PRT}{100} = 745 \times \dfrac{7}{100} \times 5 = 260.75$ i.e., $260.75

LEVEL 2

1. $25,000 + \dfrac{6}{100} \times 30000 = 25,000 + 1,800 = 26,800$. i.e., $26,800

2. $A = P\left(1 + \dfrac{r}{100}\right)^n$, $P = 4000$, $r = 6$, $n = 4 \therefore A = 4000\left(1 + \dfrac{6}{100}\right)^4 = 5049.907$

Therefore, interest earned $= 5049.91 - 4000 = \$1049.91$

LEVEL 3

1. $P = 650$, $r = 5$ p.a. $n = 15$. $A = 650\left(1 + \dfrac{5}{100}\right)^{15} = 1351.30$. i.e., £1351.30

Interest $= 1351.30 - 650 = £701.30$. Now, using $I = \dfrac{PRT}{100}$, $701.30 = \dfrac{650R \times 5}{100} \Leftrightarrow R = 7.1928$.

Therefore, equivalent rate, $R = 7.20\%$ p.a

2. i. monthly rate $= \dfrac{12}{12} = 1.0\%$ ii. (a) $I = \dfrac{25000 \times 1 \times 12}{100} = 3000$ (b) $I = \dfrac{25000 \times 1}{100} = 250$

iii. $9000 = \dfrac{25000 \times 1 \times T}{100} \Leftrightarrow T = 36$. i.e., 36 months (or 3 years).

3. $A = P\left(1 + \dfrac{r}{100}\right)^t \therefore 1892 = 1000(1.0075)^{12t} \Leftrightarrow 12t = 85.3364 \therefore t = 7.113$ i.e., ~ 7 yrs

and 5 weeks.

LEVEL 4

1.

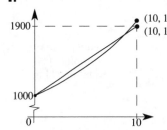

$T = 10$, $I = \dfrac{PRT}{100} = \dfrac{1000 \times 9 \times 10}{100} = 900$

Therefore, total $= 1000 + 900 = \$1900$

$A = 1000\left(1 + \dfrac{7}{100}\right)^{10} = 1967.15$. i.e., $1967.15

Make use of a graphics calculator to solve the following:

At A: $1000 + \dfrac{1000 \times 9t}{100} = 1000 \times 1.07^t \Leftrightarrow 1000 + 90t = 1000 \times 1.07^t \therefore t = 8.0683$

Therefore, for $0 \le t \le 8.07$ simple interest has a higher return. After 8.07 years, compound interest does better.

2. Bond A: 16% p.a. compounded monthly. **Bond B:** 16.2% p.a. compounded semi-annually.

Let r_e be the effective rate: Then, for

Bond A: $P(1 + r_e) = P\left(1 + \dfrac{16/12}{100}\right)^{12} \Leftrightarrow r_e = \left(1 + \dfrac{16/12}{100}\right)^{12} - 1 = 0.17227$

So, effective rate is 17.23%.

Bond B: $P(1 + r_e) = P\left(1 + \dfrac{16.2/2}{100}\right)^2 \Leftrightarrow r_e = \left(1 + \dfrac{16.2/2}{100}\right)^2 - 1 = 0.16856$

So, effective rate is 16.86%.

Therefore, Bond A is the better investment.

EXAMINATION STYLE QUESTIONS

1. (a) i. £1 = AUS \$x, but AUS \$1 = £0.38 ∴$x = \dfrac{1}{0.38} = 2.631$. i.e., £1 = AUS \$2.631.

ii. $y = \dfrac{1}{1.42} = 0.704$ ∴$y = 0.70$ iii. ∴$\dfrac{z}{0.38} = 1.42 \Leftrightarrow z = 0.38 \times 1.42 = 0.5396$ ∴$z = 0.54$

i.e., AUD\$1 = US\$0.54

(b) i. $\text{AUD}\left(500 \times \dfrac{1}{0.38}\right) = 1315.7895$ ∴AUD = \$1315.79

ii. Commission = $\dfrac{2}{100} \times 1315.7895 = 26.3158$.

Therefore, Debbie receives 1315.79 − 26.3158 = \$1289.47

(c) 50% of \$1289.47 = \$644.7368 i. $A = 644.7368 \times \left(1 + \dfrac{6.5}{100}\right)^5 = 883.3453$

Therefore, interest = 883.3453 − 644.7368 = \$238.61 ii. Interest = 2×644.7368 .

So, $644.7368 + 2 \times 644.7368 = 644.7368\left(1 + \dfrac{6.5}{100}\right)^t \Leftrightarrow 3 = 1.065^t$ ∴$t = 17.4452$ (17.45 yrs).

TEST

1. i. $50 \times 0.70 = 35$ (USD) [1] ii. $90 \times \dfrac{1}{0.70} = 128.57$ (SING) [2]

2. i. $I = \dfrac{2500 \times 4.8 \times 8}{100} = 960$ [1] ii. $A = 2500\left(1 + \dfrac{4.8/12}{100}\right)^{12 \times 8} = 3667.5533$ [2]

Therefore, interest = 3667.5533 − 2500 = 1167.55 crowns [1]

3. Customer receives $3.6848 \times 1500 = 5527.2$ (\$5527) [1]. Buying rate from bank is now

3.7979, therefore customer receives $\dfrac{5527.2}{3.7979} = 1455.33$ (=\$1455) [2]

Therefore, commission is 1500 − 1455 = \$45 on the 2 transactions. [1]

4. $14000 = 12000\left(1 + \dfrac{8/4}{100}\right)^{4t} \Leftrightarrow \dfrac{14}{12} = (1.02)^{4t} \Leftrightarrow 4t = 7.784$ ∴$t = 1.946 \sim 1.95$ years. [3]

5. Let the effective rate be r_e :

Option A: $P(1 + r_e) = P\left(1 + \dfrac{8/12}{100}\right)^{12} \Leftrightarrow r_e = \left(1 + \dfrac{8/12}{100}\right)^{12} - 1 = 0.08299$ i.e., 8.299% [2]

Option B: $P(1 + r_e) = P\left(1 + \dfrac{8.1/2}{100}\right)^{2} \Leftrightarrow r_e = \left(1 + \dfrac{8.1/2}{100}\right)^{2} - 1 = 0.08264$ i.e., 8.264% [2]

Therefore, Option A is the better investment. [1]

CHAPTER 17
LEVEL 1
1. i. $x \geq 0, y \leq 4, y \geq x$ ii. $x \geq 1, 0 \leq y \leq 2, x + y \leq 4$ iii. $x + 2y \geq 8, y \leq x + 4, x + y \leq 8, x \geq 0$
LEVEL 2
1. i. Test points: (0,4), (4,4), (0,0); $P(0, 4) = 0 + 5 \times 4 = 20$, $P(4, 4) = 2 \times 4 + 5 \times 4 = 28$

$P(0, 0) = 0 + 0 = 0$. ∴$P_{max} = 28$.

ii. Test points: (1, 0), (1, 2), (2,2), (4,0); $P(1, 0) = 2 + 0 = 2$, $P(1, 2) = 2 + 10 = 12$

$P(2, 2) = 4 + 10 = 14$, $P(4, 0) = 8 + 0 = 8$. ∴$P_{max} = 14$.

iii. Test points: $(0,4)$, $(8,0)$, $(2,6)$; $P(0, 4) = 0 + 20 = 20$, $P(8, 0) = 16 + 0 = 16$, $P(2, 6) = 4 + 30 = 34$. $\therefore P_{max} = 34$.

2. i.

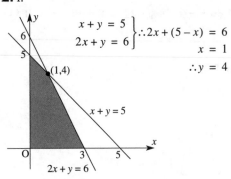

$\left.\begin{array}{l} x + y = 5 \\ 2x + y = 6 \end{array}\right\} \therefore 2x + (5 - x) = 6$

$x = 1$

$\therefore y = 4$

ii.

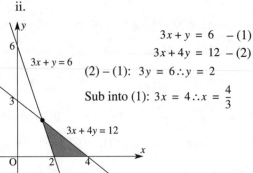

$3x + y = 6 \quad - (1)$

$3x + 4y = 12 \quad - (2)$

$(2) - (1): \ 3y = 6 \therefore y = 2$

Sub into (1): $3x = 4 \therefore x = \dfrac{4}{3}$

iii.

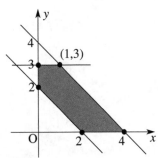

iv.

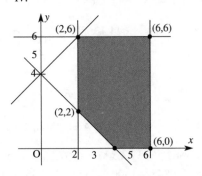

LEVEL 3

1. Solving for A: Sub. $x + 2y = 6$ (or $x = 6 - 2y$) into $3x + y = 8$: $3(6 - 2y) + y = 8$

$18 - 6y + y = 8$

$\therefore 10 = 5y \Leftrightarrow y = 2$

$\therefore x = 2$

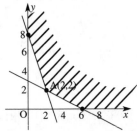

Test points: $(0,8)$, $(2,2)$, $(6,0)$;

$(0,8): p = 0 + 16 = 16$

$(2,2): p = 6 + 4 = 10$

$(6,0): p = 18 + 0 = 18$. $\therefore p_{min} = 10$

No, there is no maximum because there exist test points (a,b) where $a, b \rightarrow \infty$ and so, $p \rightarrow \infty$.

2. i. $x \geq 0$, $y \geq 0$, $25x + 35y \geq 25$, $15x + 15y \geq 12$, $15x + 35y \geq 16$.

ii.

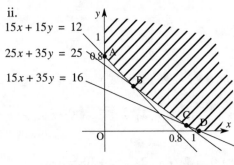

$15x + 15y = 12$

$25x + 35y = 25$

$15x + 35y = 16$

Intercepts:

$25x + 35y = 25:$ $\quad x = 0, y = \dfrac{25}{35} \therefore \left(0, \dfrac{5}{7}\right)$

$y = 0, x = 1 \therefore (1, 0)$

$15x + 15y = 12:$ $\quad x = 0, y = \dfrac{12}{15} \therefore \left(0, \dfrac{12}{15}\right)$

$y = 0, x = \dfrac{12}{15} \therefore \left(\dfrac{12}{15}, 0\right)$

$15x + 35y = 16:$ $\quad x = 0, y = \dfrac{16}{35} \therefore \left(0, \dfrac{16}{35}\right)$

$$y = 0, x = \frac{16}{15} \therefore \left(\frac{16}{15}, 0\right)$$

Test points:

A: $\left(0, \frac{12}{15}\right)$.　B: $15x + 15y = 12 \Rightarrow x + y = \frac{12}{15}$ –(1) $25x + 35y = 25$ –(2)

Sub. (1) into (2): $25x + 35\left(\frac{12}{15} - x\right) = 25 \Leftrightarrow 150x = 45 \therefore x = 0.3$.

Sub. into (1): $0.3 + y = 0.8 \therefore y = 0.5$. i.e., $(0.3, 0.5)$
C: $15x + 35y = 16$ –(1) $25x + 35y = 25$ –(2): (2) – (1): $10x = 9 \therefore x = 0.9$.

Sub. into (1): $13.5 + 35y = 16 \therefore y = \frac{2.5}{35} = \frac{1}{14}$. i.e., $\left(0.9, \frac{1}{14}\right)$.

D: $\left(\frac{16}{15}, 0\right)$ iii. $C = 12x + 8y$ iv. At $A\left(0, \frac{12}{15}\right)$: $C = 0 + 6.4 = 6.4$; At B(0.3, 0.5):

$C = 3.6 + 4 = 7.6$. At $C\left(0.9, \frac{1}{14}\right)$: $C = 10.8 + 0.57 = 11.37$; At $D\left(\frac{16}{15}, 0\right)$:

$C = 12.8 + 0 = 12.8$. Therefore, minimum daily cost is $6.4
3. Let x be the number of type A carriers and y the number of type B carriers.
So that $30x + 35y \geq 240$, $20x + 15y \geq 150$, $x \geq 0$, $y \geq 0$. Objective equation is $N = x + y$.
Solving simiultaneous equations, we have test points: (0, 10), (8, 0) and (6.6, 1.2)
At (0, 10), $N = 0 + 0 = 10$. At (8, 0), $N = 8 + 0 = 8$. At (6.6, 1.2) $N = 6.6 + 1.2 = 7.8$.

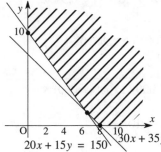

20x + 15y = 150　30x + 35y = 240

However, x and y must be positive integers. So, we need
to consider coordinates in the feasible region for which
the x and y values are positive integers.
When $x = 6$, $20 \times 6 + 15y = 150 \therefore y = 2$.
So, at (6, 2): $N = 6 + 2 = 8$

When $x = 7$, $20 \times 7 + 15y = 150 \therefore y = \frac{2}{3}$ and

$30 \times 7 + 35y = 240 \therefore y = \frac{6}{7}$ (neither are appropriate).

However, (7, 1) is appropriate so that $N = 7 + 1 = 8$
So, we have (6,2), (7,1) & (8,0) as appropriate test points, each giving a minimum $N = 8$.

LEVEL 4
1. i.

At A: $\left.\begin{matrix} x + y = 8 \\ y = 6x \end{matrix}\right\} \Rightarrow 7x = 8 \therefore x = \frac{8}{7} \Rightarrow y = \frac{48}{7}$ i.e., $\left(\frac{8}{7}, \frac{48}{7}\right)$.

At B: $\left.\begin{matrix} 6x + y = 24 \\ y = 6x \end{matrix}\right\} \Rightarrow 2y = 24 \therefore y = 12 \Rightarrow x = 2$ i.e., $(2, 12)$.

At C: $\left.\begin{matrix} 6x + y = 24 \\ x + y = 8 \end{matrix}\right\} \Rightarrow 5x = 16 \therefore x = \frac{16}{5} \Rightarrow y = \frac{24}{5}$ i.e., $\left(\frac{16}{5}, \frac{24}{5}\right)$.

At A: $z = \frac{8}{7}k + \frac{96}{7}$. At B: $z = 2k + 24$. At C: $z = \frac{16}{5}k + \frac{24}{5}$.

We now need to determine the range of values of k for which z is a maximum

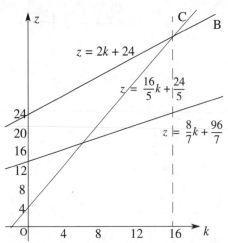

Solving for $B \cap C$:

$$2k + 24 = \frac{16}{5}k + \frac{24}{5}$$

$$\Leftrightarrow 10k + 120 = 16k + 24$$

$$\therefore k = 16$$

For $0 < k < 16$, $z_{max} = 2k + 24$

For $k > 16$, $z_{max} = \frac{16}{5}k + \frac{24}{5}$.

2. The two ratios are: A:B:C = 3:2:1 and A:B:C = 1:1:1, with $A \leq 6$, $B \leq 4.5$ and $C \leq 4$.
Let a = # of standard packets and b = # of delux packets.
i. Amounts of each type of ingredients:

	A	B	C
Standard	0.75 kg	0.50 kg	0.25 kg
Delux	0.50 kg	0.50 kg	0.50 kg

e.g., For standard, type A = $1.5 \times \frac{3}{6} = 0.75$ etc.. For delux, type A = $1.5 \times \frac{1}{3} = 0.5$ etc.

Therefore, constraints are:
$\quad 0.75a + 0.5b \leq 6000$, $0.5a + 0.5b \leq 4500$, $0.25a + 0.5b \leq 4000$, $a \geq 0$, $b \geq 0$.
or, $\quad 3a + 2b \leq 24000$, $a + b \leq 9000$, $a + 2b \leq 16000$, $a \geq 0$, $b \geq 0$

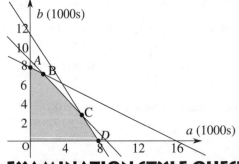

From the graph we have:
A(0,8000), B(2000,7000), C(6000,3000) &
D(8000,0)

iii. (a) $P(a, b) = 6a + 10b$
(b) At A: P = 80,000;
At B: P = 82,000
At C: P = 66,000
At D: P = 48,000
So, max. is $82,000 when 2000 standard & 7000
delux packets are sold.

EXAMINATION STYLE QUESTION

1. (a) i. The amounts of mix cannot be negative, so, $x \geq 0$ and $y \geq 0$.
ii. $3000x + 4000y \geq 36000 \therefore 3x + 4y \geq 36$ iii. $1000x + 4000y \geq 20000 \therefore x + 4y \geq 20$
(b) i. From graph, we have that $A \equiv (0, 9)$ & $C \equiv (20, 0)$. Solving for B:

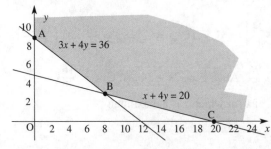

$\left. \begin{array}{l} x + 4y = 20 \\ 3x + 4y = 36 \end{array} \right\} \therefore 2x = 16 \Leftrightarrow x = 8 \therefore y = 3$

That is, $B \equiv (8, 3)$.
(c) i. $p(x, y) = 0.2x + 0.4y$
ii. At A: $p = 3.6$. At B: $p = 2.8$. At C: $p = 4$
Therefore, should only sell mix A.

2. i. Using $(0,10)$ & $(10,8)$: $y - 10 = -\frac{2}{10}(x - 0) \Leftrightarrow y = -0.2x + 10$.

Using $(0,10)$ & $(5,2)$: $y - 10 = -\frac{8}{5}(x - 0) \Leftrightarrow y = -1.6x + 10$.

Using $(10,8)$ & $(5,2)$: $y - 8 = \frac{6}{5}(x - 10) \Leftrightarrow y = 1.2x - 4$.

Therefore, constraints are: $y \le -0.2x + 10$, $y \ge -1.6x + 10$, $y \ge 1.2x - 4$.

ii. At $(0,10)$: $p(0, 10) = 5 \times 0 + 10 = 10$. At $(10,8)$: $p(10, 8) = 5 \times 10 + 8 = 58$.

At $(5,2)$: $p(5, 2) = 5 \times 5 + 2 = 27$

TEST

1. Test points are: $(0, 8) \Rightarrow z = 0 + 32 = 32$; $(0, 12) \Rightarrow z = 0 + 48 = 48$;

$(4, 3) \Rightarrow z = 28 + 12 = 40$; $(12, 0) \Rightarrow z = 84 + 0 = 84$. [1] $\therefore z_{min} = 32$. [1]

2. i.

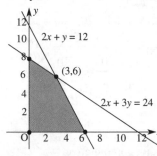

ii. At $(1,7)$: $p = 1 + 14 = 15$ [1]

At $(6,7)$: $p = 6 + 14 = 20$

At $(6,2)$: $p = 6 + 14 = 10$

Therefore, $p_{max} = 20$ & $p_{min} = 10$. [1]

[3]

3. $x \ge 0$, $y \ge 0$ [1], $x + y \le 12$ [1] [1], $y \ge -\frac{5}{4}x + 8$ [1] [1], $y \ge -\frac{3}{8}x + \frac{9}{2}$ [1] [1]

4. By observation, lines intersect at $(3,6)$ [or use simultaneous equations] [1]

[2]

At $(0,0)$: $z = 0$. At $(0,8)$: $z = 72$. At $(3,6)$: $z = 69$. At $(6,0)$: $z = 30$.

Therefore, $z_{max} = 72$ [1]

5. i.

	EL	LE
Earl G	$\frac{2}{3}x$	$\frac{1}{3}y$
Lady G	$\frac{1}{3}x$	$\frac{2}{3}y$

$\therefore \frac{2}{3}x + \frac{1}{3}y \le 10 \Rightarrow 2x + y \le 30$ – (1) [1] [1]

$\therefore \frac{1}{3}x + \frac{2}{3}y \le 6 \Rightarrow x + 2y \le 18$ – (2) [1] [1]

$x \ge 0$, $y \ge 0$ [1]

ii.

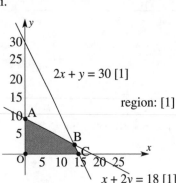

$2x + y = 30$ [1]

region: [1]

$x + 2y = 18$ [1]

iii. By obs. $O \equiv (0, 0)$, $A \equiv (0, 9)$, $C \equiv (15, 0)$ [1]

Solving for B: $2x + 4y = 36$ – (1)

$2x + y = 30$ – (2)

$(1) - (2)$: $3y = 6 \therefore y = 2$

$\Rightarrow x + 4 = 18 \therefore x = 14$

Therefore, $B \equiv (14, 2)$. Method [1] Ans. [1]

iv. (a) $I = 25x + 30y$ [1]

(b) At O, $I = 0$. At A, $I = 270$. At C, $I = 375$. At B, $I = 410$.

Therefore, maximum income generated = \$410 [1]

CHAPTER 18
LEVEL 1

1. i. $\begin{bmatrix} 5 & 1 \\ 1 & -6 \end{bmatrix}$ ii. $\begin{bmatrix} 5 & -3 \\ 3 & 0 \end{bmatrix}$ iii. $\begin{bmatrix} -4 & 3 \\ 1 & -3 \end{bmatrix}$ iv. $\begin{bmatrix} 10 & -4 \\ 5 & -3 \end{bmatrix}$ v. $\begin{bmatrix} 13 & -3 \\ -2 & -3 \end{bmatrix}$ vi. $\begin{bmatrix} 9 & 0 \\ -1 & -6 \end{bmatrix}$ vii. $\begin{bmatrix} -23 & 5 \\ -2 & 9 \end{bmatrix}$

viii. $\begin{bmatrix} -5 & 2 \\ 16 & -9 \end{bmatrix}$ **2.** (a) i. 4 ii. 7 iii. 2 (b) i. 6 ii. 8 iii. 1

3. i. ii. iii. **4.** i. yes ii. no iii. yes

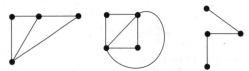

5. **6.** (a) flow = 50 + 40 = 90 (b) flow = 50 + 70 + 40 = 160

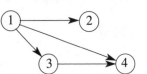 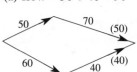 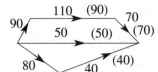

LEVEL 2

1. i. $\begin{bmatrix} -3 & 11 \\ 3 & 3 \end{bmatrix}$ ii. $\begin{bmatrix} 4 & -2 \\ -13 & -4 \end{bmatrix}$ Remember that matrix multiplication is not commutative.

iii. $\begin{bmatrix} -19 & 30 & -12 \\ 16 & 9 & -29 \\ 2 & 6 & 1 \end{bmatrix}$ iv. $\begin{bmatrix} 12 & -4 & -12 \\ 6 & -2 & -6 \\ 15 & -5 & -15 \end{bmatrix}$ v. $\begin{bmatrix} 12 & -14 & 3 \end{bmatrix}$

2. i. $\begin{array}{c} \\ A \\ A' \end{array} \begin{array}{c} A \quad A' \\ \begin{bmatrix} 0.4 & 0.6 \\ 0.3 & 0.7 \end{bmatrix} \end{array}$ ii. $\begin{array}{c} \\ P \\ Q \\ R \end{array} \begin{array}{c} P \quad Q \quad R \\ \begin{bmatrix} 1 & 0 & 0 \\ 0.1 & 0.7 & 0.2 \\ 0 & 0 & 1 \end{bmatrix} \end{array}$ 3. i. $\begin{array}{c} \\ A \\ B \\ C \end{array} \begin{array}{c} A \ B \ C \\ \begin{bmatrix} 0 & 1 & 0 \\ 1 & 0 & 1 \\ 1 & 0 & 0 \end{bmatrix} \end{array}$ ii. $\begin{bmatrix} 0 & 1 & 0 \\ 1 & 0 & 1 \\ 1 & 0 & 0 \end{bmatrix} \begin{bmatrix} 0 & 1 & 0 \\ 1 & 0 & 1 \\ 1 & 0 & 0 \end{bmatrix} = \begin{bmatrix} 1 & 0 & 1 \\ 0 & 1 & 0 \\ 0 & 1 & 0 \end{bmatrix}$

LEVEL 3

1. (a) i. $\begin{vmatrix} 1 & 2 \\ -1 & 7 \end{vmatrix} = 7 - (-2) = 9$ ii. $\begin{vmatrix} 1 & 2 \\ 0 & 4 \end{vmatrix} = 1 \times 4 - 2 \times 0 = 4$ iii. $\begin{vmatrix} 6 & 2 \\ -3 & 2 \end{vmatrix} = 12 - (-6) = 18$

(b) i. $\dfrac{1}{9}\begin{bmatrix} 7 & -2 \\ 1 & 1 \end{bmatrix}$ ii. $\dfrac{1}{4}\begin{bmatrix} 4 & -2 \\ 0 & 1 \end{bmatrix}$ iii. $\dfrac{1}{18}\begin{bmatrix} 2 & -2 \\ 3 & 6 \end{bmatrix}$ **2.** $\begin{array}{c}\;\;\;1\;\;\;2\\ \dfrac{1}{2}\begin{bmatrix} 1 & -1 \\ -1 & 1 \end{bmatrix}\end{array}$ = pay-off matrix for A.

3. i. $S = \begin{array}{c} \quad T \quad\;\; T' \\ \begin{matrix} T \\ T' \end{matrix}\begin{bmatrix} 0.85 & 0.15 \\ 0.40 & 0.60 \end{bmatrix}\end{array}$ ii. (a) The Monday to Wednesday transition matrix is given by S^2:

$S^2 = \begin{bmatrix} 0.85 & 0.15 \\ 0.40 & 0.60 \end{bmatrix}\begin{bmatrix} 0.85 & 0.15 \\ 0.40 & 0.60 \end{bmatrix} = \begin{bmatrix} 0.7825 & 0.2175 \\ 0.58 & 0.42 \end{bmatrix}$. Therefore, required prob. = 0.7825

(b) Required transition matrix = $S^3 = S^2 \times S = \begin{bmatrix} 0.7825 & 0.2175 \\ 0.58 & 0.42 \end{bmatrix}\begin{bmatrix} 0.85 & 0.15 \\ 0.40 & 0.60 \end{bmatrix} = \begin{bmatrix} 0.752 & 0.248 \\ 0.661 & 0.339 \end{bmatrix}$

That is, required prob. = 0.248 [Make sure that you can carry out matrix multiplication using your graphics calculator – it's so much easier!]

LEVEL 4

1. i. $\begin{array}{c} \text{From} \\ \begin{array}{ccc} \;A\;\; & B\;\; & C \end{array} \\ \text{To } \begin{matrix} A \\ B \\ C \end{matrix}\begin{bmatrix} 0 & 4 & 5 \\ 2 & 0 & 4 \\ 2 & 3 & 0 \end{bmatrix}\begin{bmatrix} 60 \\ 50 \\ 55 \end{bmatrix}\end{array}$ ii. $\begin{bmatrix} 475 \\ 340 \\ 270 \end{bmatrix}$ iii. These are the delivery costs for each store.

2. $P^2 = \begin{bmatrix} 1-\alpha & \alpha \\ \beta & 1-\beta \end{bmatrix}\begin{bmatrix} 1-\alpha & \alpha \\ \beta & 1-\beta \end{bmatrix} = \begin{bmatrix} (1-\alpha)^2 + \alpha\beta & (1-\alpha)\alpha + (1-\beta)\alpha \\ (1-\alpha)\beta + (1-\beta)\beta & (1-\beta)^2 + \alpha\beta \end{bmatrix}$

$= \begin{bmatrix} (1-\alpha)^2 + \alpha\beta & (1-\alpha+1-\beta)\alpha \\ (1-\alpha+1-\beta)\beta & (1-\beta)^2 + \alpha\beta \end{bmatrix}$

$= \begin{bmatrix} (1-\alpha)^2 + \alpha\beta & \alpha \\ \beta & (1-\beta)^2 + \alpha\beta \end{bmatrix}$

As $\alpha + \beta = 1 \therefore (1-\alpha-\beta) = 0$.

3. $\begin{vmatrix} a & 2 \\ -1 & 2 \end{vmatrix} = 0 \Leftrightarrow 2a+2 = 0 \Leftrightarrow a = -1$. $\left.\begin{array}{l} ax + 2y = 3 \\ -x + 2y = 1 \end{array}\right\} \leftrightarrow \begin{bmatrix} a & 2 \\ -1 & 2 \end{bmatrix}\begin{bmatrix} x \\ y \end{bmatrix} = \begin{bmatrix} 3 \\ 1 \end{bmatrix}$.

That is, no unique solutions exist if $a = -1$.(i.e., lines are parallel and not coincident).

EXAMINATION STYLE QUESTIONS

1. i. $\begin{bmatrix} 5 & 3 & 2 \\ 7 & 9 & 1 \\ 11 & 3 & 2 \end{bmatrix}$ & $\begin{bmatrix} 16500 \\ 19000 \\ 23500 \end{bmatrix}$ ii. $\begin{bmatrix} 5 & 3 & 2 \\ 7 & 9 & 1 \\ 11 & 3 & 2 \end{bmatrix}\begin{bmatrix} 16500 \\ 19000 \\ 23500 \end{bmatrix} = \begin{bmatrix} 186500 \\ 310000 \\ 285500 \end{bmatrix}$ Total: \$782 000

TEST

1. i. $\begin{bmatrix} 1 & 1 & 3 \\ 7 & 2 & -3 \end{bmatrix}$ [1] ii. AB cannot be evaluated! [1] iii. $\begin{bmatrix} 9 & -3 & 12 \\ 9 & 0 & -6 \end{bmatrix} - \begin{bmatrix} -8 & 8 & -4 \\ 16 & 8 & -4 \end{bmatrix} = \begin{bmatrix} 17 & -11 & 16 \\ -7 & -8 & -2 \end{bmatrix}$ [2]

2. i. [3]

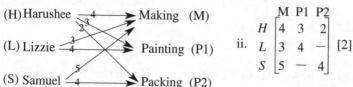

(H) Harushee →4→ Making (M)

(L) Lizzie →4→ Painting (P1)

(S) Samuel →4→ Packing (P2)

ii.
$$\begin{array}{c c c c} & M & P1 & P2 \\ H & 4 & 3 & 2 \\ L & 3 & 4 & - \\ S & 5 & - & 4 \end{array}$$ [2]

iii. There are a number of possibilities:

(HM) + (LP1) + (SP2) = 4 + 4 + 4 = 12
(HP2) + (LP1) + (SM) = 2 + 4 + 5 = 11
(HP1) + (LM) + (SP2) = 3 + 3 + 4 = 10

Therefore, scenario is Harushee paints, Lizzie makes and Samuel packs. [2]

3. Transition matrix for Wed. to Friday is given by X^2.

$$X^2 = \begin{bmatrix} 0.7 & 0.2 & 0.1 \\ 0.4 & 0.5 & 0.1 \\ 0.2 & 0.5 & 0.3 \end{bmatrix} \begin{bmatrix} 0.7 & 0.2 & 0.1 \\ 0.4 & 0.5 & 0.1 \\ 0.2 & 0.5 & 0.3 \end{bmatrix} = \begin{bmatrix} 0.59 & 0.29 & 0.12 \\ 0.5 & 0.38 & 0.12 \\ 0.4 & 0.44 & 0.16 \end{bmatrix}$$. Therefore, $p(W_C \cap F_F) = 0.5$ [2]

ii. For Saturday, use X^3: $X^3 = \begin{bmatrix} 0.553 & 0.323 & 0.124 \\ 0.526 & 0.35 & 0.124 \\ 0.488 & 0.38 & 0.132 \end{bmatrix}$. Therefore, $p(W_C \cap S_F) = 0.526$ [2]

iii. $p(F_F \cap S_F | W_C) = p(F_F | W_C) \times p(S_F | F_F) = 0.50 \times 0.7 = 0.35$ [3]

4. Least time to get from A to B is 5 $(A \rightarrow B)$: [1]

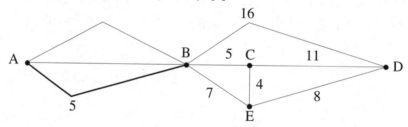

For $(A \rightarrow B \rightarrow E)$ there is one route: giving 5(AB) + 7(BE) = 12 [1]

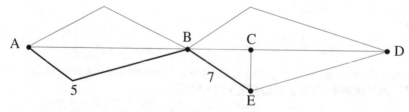

Similarly, for $(A \rightarrow C)$ there are two routes: [1]

Route 1 $(A \rightarrow B \rightarrow C)$ giving 5(AB) + 5(BC) = 10

Route 2 $(A \rightarrow B \rightarrow E \rightarrow C)$ giving 5(AB) + 7(BE) + 4(EC) = 16

For $(A \rightarrow D)$: [2]

Route 1: $(A \rightarrow B \rightarrow D)$ giving 5(AB) + 16(BD) = 21

Route 2: $A \rightarrow B \rightarrow C \rightarrow D$ giving 5(AB) + 5(BC) + 11(CD) = 21

Route 3: $A \rightarrow B \rightarrow E \rightarrow D$ giving 5(AB) + 7(BE) + 8(ED) = 20

Therefore, least amount of time taken is 20 min. [1]

CHAPTER 19
LEVEL 1
1. i. 0.1587   ii. 0.9772   iii. 0.4332

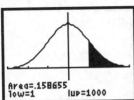   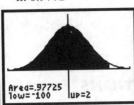 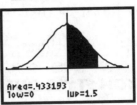

iv. 0.3829   **2.** i. 0.1587

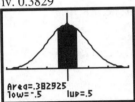

ii. $p(Z > 2 | Z > 1) = \dfrac{p(Z > 2)}{p(Z > 1)} = \dfrac{0.02275}{0.15865} = 0.1434$

LEVEL 2
1. Using the pdf,

$X \sim N(15, 9)$

i. 0.8413

ii. 0.1587

```
WINDOW
 Xmin=6
 Xmax=24
 Xscl=2
 Ymin=-.25
 Ymax=.25
 Yscl=1
 Xres=■
```

```
ShadeNorm(12,100
00,15,3)■
```

Area=.841345
low=12   up=10000

2. i. 0.7603   ii. 0.7603   **3.** i. $p(|X - 26| \le 2) = p(-2 \le X - 26 \le 2) = p(24 \le X \le 28) = 0.6247$

ii. $\dfrac{p(24 < X < 28)}{p(X < 28)} = \dfrac{0.624655}{0.933192} = 0.6694$

```
normalcdf(24,28,
25,2)
        .6246552391
normalcdf(-1000,
28,25,2
        .9331927713
```

LEVEL 3
1. $X \sim N(500, 125^2)$,

$p(650 < X < 700) = p\left(\dfrac{650 - 500}{125} < Z < \dfrac{700 - 500}{125}\right) = p(1.2 < Z < 1.6) = 0.06027$. i.e., 6%.

2. $X \sim N(145, 90^2)$ $p(X < 157) = p(Z < 0.1333) = 0.5530$. Therefore, student is ranked in the top 45%.

3. $p(X \ge c) = 1 - p(X \le c) = 0.25 \therefore p(X \le c) = 0.75 \therefore \dfrac{c - 50}{2} = \Phi^{-1}(0.75)$

$$\Rightarrow \dfrac{c - 50}{2} = 0.6745 \therefore c = 51.35$$

LEVEL 4
1. $X \sim N(35, 6.25)$ i. $p(X \ge 40) = p(Z \ge 2) = 0.0228$

ii. $p(X \ge c) = 0.1 \therefore \dfrac{c - 35}{2.5} = \Phi^{-1}(0.9) \Leftrightarrow c = 35 + 2.5 \times \Phi^{-1}(0.9) = 38.20$

2. $p(X > 4) = p\left(Z > \dfrac{4 - a}{b}\right) = 0.15 \Leftrightarrow \dfrac{4 - a}{b} = \Phi^{-1}(0.85) \therefore (4 - a) = b \times \Phi^{-1}(0.85) \text{—(1)}$

$$p(X \le 3) = p\left(Z \le \frac{3-a}{b}\right) = 0.7 \Leftrightarrow \frac{3-a}{b} = \Phi^{-1}(0.70) \therefore (3-a) = b \times \Phi^{-1}(0.70) \text{—(2)}$$

$$(1) - (2): 1 = b(\Phi^{-1}(0.85) - \Phi^{-1}(0.70)) \therefore b = \frac{1}{(\Phi^{-1}(0.85) - \Phi^{-1}(0.70))} = 1.953$$

Sub into (1): $a = 4 - \dfrac{\Phi^{-1}(0.85)}{(\Phi^{-1}(0.85) - \Phi^{-1}(0.70))} = 1.976$

EXAMINATION STYLE QUESTIONS

1. $X \sim N(2600, 450^2)$, i.e., $\mu = 2600, \sigma = 450$.

(a) i. $p(X > 3000) = p\left(Z > \dfrac{3000 - 2600}{450}\right) = p(Z > 0.8888) = 0.1870$. i.e., 18.70%

ii. $p(X < 2000) = p\left(Z < \dfrac{2000 - 2600}{450}\right) = p(Z < -1.3333) = 0.0912$ i.e., 9.12%

(b) $p(X > 3000 | X \ge 2700) = \dfrac{p(X \ge 3000)}{p(X \ge 2700)} = \dfrac{0.1870}{0.4121} = 0.4539$

2. (a) $X \sim N(3, 0.5^2)$ i. $p(X < 2.5) = 0.1587$ ii. $p(X > 3.5) = 0.1587$

(b) $1 - 2 \times 0.1587 = 0.6826$ (c) $p(X < a) = 0.95 \Rightarrow a = 3.82$

(d) i. $3 \times (0.8413) \times (0.1587)^2 + (0.1587)^3 = 0.0676$ ii. $(0.6827)^3 = 0.3182$

TEST

1. $p(X > 7.5) = p\left(Z > \dfrac{7.5 - 5}{\sqrt{1.21}}\right) = p(Z > 2.2727) = 0.0115$ [1]

2. $\dfrac{2a - a}{\sqrt{b}} = \Phi^{-1}(0.85) \Rightarrow a = \sqrt{b} \times \Phi^{-1}(0.85)$ —(1) [1]

$\dfrac{1 - a}{\sqrt{b}} = \Phi^{-1}(0.65) \Rightarrow 1 - a = \sqrt{b} \times \Phi^{-1}(0.65)$ —(2) [1]

$(1) + (2): 1 = \sqrt{b}(\Phi^{-1}(0.85) + \Phi^{-1}(0.65)) \therefore \sqrt{b} = \dfrac{1}{(\Phi^{-1}(0.85) + \Phi^{-1}(0.65))}$

$$\Rightarrow b = \dfrac{1}{(\Phi^{-1}(0.85) + \Phi^{-1}(0.65))^2}$$

Therefore, b = 0.4947 [1] Sub into (1): a = 0.729 [1]

3. $X \sim N(50, 1.25^2)$, $p(49 < X < 52) = p(-0.8 < Z < 1.6) = 0.7333$. That is, 73.33% [3]

4. (a) $X \sim N(497, 4.41)$ i. $p(X > 500) = 0.0765$ [2] ii. $p(X < 495) = 0.1705$ [2]

(b) $p(X > 500 | X > 498) = \dfrac{p(X > 500)}{p(X > 498)} = 0.2415$ [3]

(c) $3 \times (0.0765)^2 \times (1 - 0.0765) = 0.0162$ [2]

(d) $p(X < 495) = 0.01 \therefore p\left(Z < \dfrac{495 - 497}{\sigma}\right) = 0.01 \Rightarrow \dfrac{495 - 497}{\sigma} = -2.3263 \Rightarrow \sigma = 0.8597$

[3]

CHAPTER 20
LEVEL 1

1. (a) (b) +ve direction, strong linear relationship.   **2.** –ve direction, strong and linear relationship

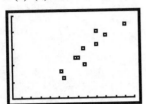

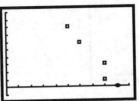

LEVEL 2

1. $r = 0.9213$ **2.** $r = 0.9686$

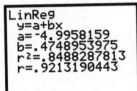

```
LinReg
  y=a+bx
  a=-4.9958159
  b=.4748953975
  r²=.8488287813
  r=.9213190443
```

```
LinReg
  y=a+bx
  a=-2.594594595
  b=.6486486486
  r²=.9382239382
  r=.9686196045
```

LEVEL 3

1. As the scatter plot indicates, there exists a strong positive linear relationship, r measures the strength of the relationship, whereas, r^2 represents the proportion of the variation in y which can be attributed to the variation in x.

2.(a)   (b) $y = -0.52x + 20.31$

```
LinReg
  y=ax+b
  a=-.5192307692
  b=20.30769231
  r²=.8411538462
  r=-.9171443977
```

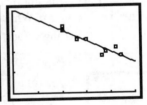

(c) $x = 14$, $y = 13.03$ **3.** (a)

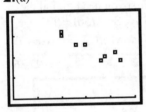

```
Y1=-.52X+20.31



X=14          Y=13.03
```

$$b = \frac{\sum xy - n\bar{x}\bar{y}}{\sum x^2 - n(\bar{x})^2} = \frac{13054 - \dfrac{900 \times 140}{10}}{81956 - \dfrac{900^2}{10}} = 0.4749 .$$

As $r = \dfrac{s_{xy}}{s_x s_y} = b \times \dfrac{s_x}{s_y} = b \times \sqrt{\dfrac{81956 - \dfrac{900^2}{10}}{2214 - \dfrac{140^2}{10}}} = 0.9213$

(b) Regression equation is: $(y - 14) = 0.4749(x - 90) \Rightarrow$ when $x = 40$, $y = -9.745$

4. $r^2 = 0.9 \therefore r = 0.9487$

LEVEL 4

1. (a) 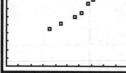   (b)

Yes. Scatter diagram
shows a strong +ve
linear relationship.

(c) i. $y = 0.1005x + 6.638$ ii.

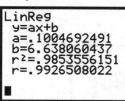

(d)

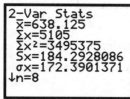

$$r = \frac{s_{xy}}{s_x s_y} = b \times \frac{s_x}{s_y} = 0.1005 \times \frac{184.2928}{18.6528}$$

$$= 0.993$$

(e) $x = 600$, $y = 66.94$ (f) Yes. But **not** by using $y = 0.1005x + 6.638$. First you need to find the regression of x on y, i.e., $x = by + c$. Which is given by $x = 9.808y - 55.76$. So, $x(56) = 493$.

2. (a)   (b) Using a transformed set of data, with $Y = lnd$ where $Y = -\alpha r + C$,

$C = lnk$, we have $Y = -0.2373r + 4.5471$. $\Rightarrow k = e^{4.5471} = 93.36$.

(c) i.

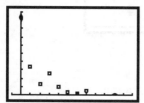  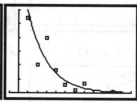

ii. $r = 16$, $d = 2.117$

Note: Using the exp regression function on the TI–83, gives the following result:

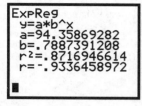 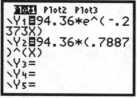 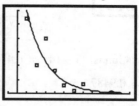

Notice, the graphs are superimposed. Which should have been expected, as $e^{-0.2373} = 0.7887$.

EXAMINATION STYLE

1. (a) i. The ZOOM command has been used in the second screen, which produces screen 3. This is to make sure that there is a strong +ve linear relationship between the two variables.

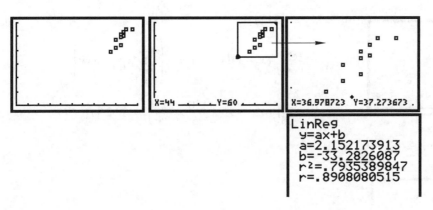

```
LinReg
y=ax+b
a=2.152173913
b=-33.2826087
r²=.7935389847
r=.8908080515
```

(a) ii. From last screen, $r = 0.8908$ (b) $r^2 = 0.7935$. That is, 79.35%   (c) $y = 2.15x - 33.28$
(d)   (e) $x = 37$, $y = 46.27$. Expenditure is \$4627

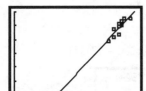

2. (a) i. 4.4; 11.97 ii. 14.06; 17.26 (b) $b = 0.4895$; $r = b \times \dfrac{s_x}{s_y} = 0.3397$

(c) $r^2 = (0.3397)^2 = 0.1154$.

(d) Regression equation is $(y - 14.06) = 0.4895(x - 4.4)$ ∴ when $x = 3.5$, $y = 13.6$

3. (a) i.   ii. $r = 0.9629$

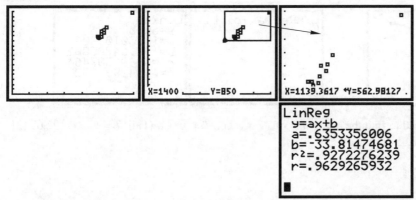

```
LinReg
y=ax+b
a=.6353356006
b=-33.81474681
r²=.9272276239
r=.9629265932
```

(b) $y = 0.635x - 33.815$
(c) Diagram shown alongside:
(d) When $x = 1040$, $y = 626.59$
The carcass weighs 626.59lbs

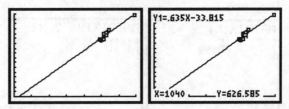

TEST

1. (a) [3] (b) i. –ve ii. linear iii. strong [3]
2. (a) $y - 9 = 0.4056(x - 6) \Leftrightarrow y = 0.4056x + 6.566$ [3]

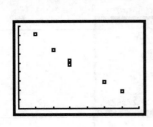

(b) $x = 8$, $y = 9.81$ [1]

(c) $s_{xy} = \dfrac{1}{n}\displaystyle\sum_{i=1}^{n}(x_i - \bar{x})(y_i - \bar{y}) = \dfrac{1}{n}\left(\displaystyle\sum_{i=1}^{n}x_iy_i - n\bar{x}\bar{y}\right)$

$\therefore s_{xy} = \dfrac{1}{25}\left(1423 - 25 \times \dfrac{150}{25} \times \dfrac{225}{25}\right) = 2.92$ [1]

3. $r^2 = 0.80 \therefore r = 0.8944$ [2]

4. (a)

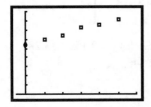

(b) From the given data: $6a + 150b = 408$ —(1) $150a + 5500b = 11200$ —(2) [1]

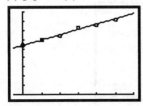

Solving for a and b; $150 \times (1) - 6 \times (2)$: $b = \dfrac{4}{7} \therefore a = \dfrac{376}{7}$ [2]

(c) [1]   (d) $T = 25$, $x = 68$ [1]

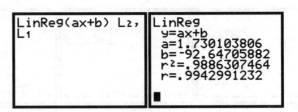

(e) i. First you need to find the regression of T on x, i.e., $T = bx + a$ [1] ii. $T = 1.73x - 92.65$ [2]
So, $x = 70$, $T = 28.45$ [1]

CHAPTER 21
LEVEL 1
1. (a) obs: exp:

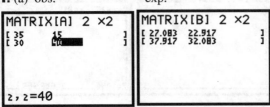

(b) obs: exp:

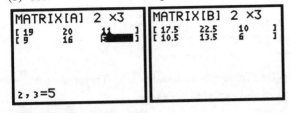

LEVEL 2

1. (a) Reject H_0 (i.e., assoc)   (b) Accept H_0. (no assoc)

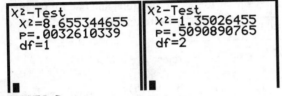

LEVEL 3

1. (a) obs: exp: (b)

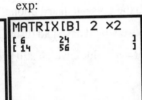 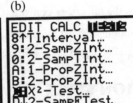

As p–value is $= 0.000013$ there is very little chance of rejecting H_0.

Therefore. there is a sig. difference.

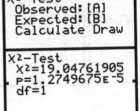

LEVEL 4

1. (a) i. $\bar{x} = \dfrac{0 + 19 + 22 + 24 + 20}{12 + 19 + 11 + 8 + 5} = \dfrac{85}{55} = \dfrac{17}{11}$. Therefore, $\mu_{est} = \dfrac{17}{11}$.

ii. Using $p(X = x) = e^{-17/11} \times \dfrac{\left(\dfrac{17}{11}\right)^x}{x!}$, we have, $p(X = 0) = e^{-17/11} \times \dfrac{\left(\dfrac{17}{11}\right)^0}{0!} = 0.2132$. We do the

same for $x = 1, 2, 3$ and then evaluate $p(X \geq 4) = 1 - p(X \leq 3)$. Or use the poisson distribution function on the TI–83:

x	0	1	2	3	≥ 4
$p(X = x)$	0.2132	0.3295	0.2546	0.1312	0.0715

```
Poissonpdf(17/11
,{0,1,2,3})
{.2132149333 .3…
1-Poissoncdf(17/
11,3)
        .071476465
```

(b) Based on the above probability table, we have the following expected values:

x	0	1	2	3	≥ 4
expected	11.73	18.12	14.00	7.22	3.93

(c) Note: The χ^2 is unreliable for small expected frequencies, (usually < 5). Therefore, we combine the last two classes. Our new observed and expected tables are:

x	0	1	2	≥ 3
observed	12	19	11	13
expected	11.73	18.12	14.00	11.15

Notice then, that the degrees of freedom is 2. That is, we have 4 classes, but two restrictions; one for the total and one for the mean. Therefore, $df = 4 - 2 = 2$.

At the 5% level, with 2 deg. of freedom, $\chi^2 = 5.99$. So, we reject H_0 if $U > 5.99$.

Now, $U = \dfrac{(12 - 11.73)^2}{11.73} + \dfrac{(19 - 18.12)^2}{18.12} + \dfrac{(11 - 14)^2}{14} + \dfrac{(13 - 11.15)^2}{11.15} = 0.9987$. Therefore,

accept H_0. That is, the data does conform to the poisson distribution.

Note: Without combining the last two classes, we would have had (using $5 - 2 = 3$ deg. of freedom): $U = 1.0723$ with $p(\chi^2 > 1.0733) = 0.7838$ ($= p$–value), which still provides the same conclusion.

EXAMINATION STYLE

1. (a)

```
MATRIX[A]  2 ×3
[ 25      22
[ 25      28        22      ]
R8:          ]

2,3=38
```

```
MATRIX[B]  2 ×3
[ 21.563  21.563  25.875 ]
[ 28.438  28.438  34.125 ]
```

We have assumed that there exists no association between the level of self-esteem and the smoking habit of males.

(b) value = 1.9994

```
X²-Test
X²=1.99946913
P=.3679771023
df=2
```

As, the p–value is > 0.05, we can safely say that there is no sig. difference.

(c) New exp values: As $p > 0.05$, still no sig. difference.

```
MATRIX[B]  2 ×2
[ 32.344  36.656      ]
[ 42.656  48.344      ]
```

```
X²-Test
X²=1.367921081
P=.2421693862
df=1
```

TEST

1. Initial assumption in working out expected values is that the two categories had no association (i.e., they were independent). [1] . For expected values table [2]

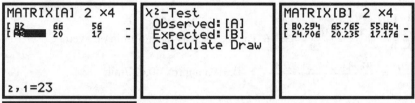

```
MATRIX[A] 2 ×4
[ 82      66    56
[ 43      20    17    -

2,1=23
```

```
X²-Test
Observed: [A]
Expected: [B]
Calculate Draw
```

```
MATRIX[B] 2 ×4
[ 80.294  65.765  55.824 -
[ 24.706  20.235  17.176 -
```

```
X²-Test
X²=.487913261
P=.9215386776
df=3
```

For χ^2_{cal} value [2]. As p–value > 0.05, accept H_0 i.e., there is no sig. difference. [1]

2. (a) $\bar{x} = 265$; $s = 57.4$ [2] Note: Use the mid-point of each interval as the x_i-value.

(b) Assuming that $\mu = 265, \sigma = 57.4$, we have: For method [2] For completed table [1]

obs	20	35	55	20	15	15
exp	20.60	32.46	43.44	36.47	19.20	7.86

To work out expected value:

Step 1: Find prob; $p(X < 200) = p\left(Z < \dfrac{200 - 265}{57.4}\right) = p(Z < -1.1324) = 0.1287$

Step 2: Expected no. $= 160 \times 0.1287 = 20.5971$

Similarly, evaluate $p(200 < X < 240) = 0.2028$ (exp no. $= 32.4564$)

$p(240 < X < 280) = 0.2715$ (exp no. $= 43.4389$)

$p(280 < X < 320) = 0.2279$ (exp no. $= 36.4699$)

$p(320 < X < 360) = 0.1200$ (exp no. $= 19.2043$)

$p(X > 360) = 0.0491$ (exp no. $= 7.856$)

```
normalcdf(200,24
0,265,57.4)
       .2028529354
Ans*160
       32.45646967
```

(c) We had to determine, total, mean and std. dev, so $df = 5 - 3 = 3$.

$$\chi^2_{calc} = \sum \frac{(obs - exp)^2}{exp} = \frac{(20 - 20.6)^2}{20.6} + \dots + \frac{(15 - 7.86)^2}{7.86} = 18.13 \text{ [2]}$$

(d) Now, with $df = 3$, $p(\chi^2 > 18.13) = 0.00041$ [1]. Therefore, as $p < 0.05$, results are significant at the 5% level. That is, wages are not normally distributed. [1].

CHAPTER 22
LEVEL 1

1. i. 2 ii. –1 iii. –0.5 **2.** (a) *av.* rate $= \dfrac{4 - 2}{4 - 0} = \dfrac{1}{2}$ (b) *av.* rate $= \dfrac{0 - 3}{4 - (-1)} = -\dfrac{3}{5}$

(c) *av.* rate $= \dfrac{3 - 3}{6 - 0} = 0$. **3.** i.A, D ii. B, C iii. C, D iv. A, B

LEVEL 2

1. (a) $x = 1 \Rightarrow f(1) = 5 - 1 = 4$ & $x = 3 \Rightarrow f(3) = 5 - 9 = -4$,

av. rate $= \dfrac{4 - (-4)}{1 - 3} = -\dfrac{8}{2} = -4$. (b) $t = 2 \Rightarrow h(2) = \dfrac{20}{2} + 2 = 12$,

$t = 5 \Rightarrow h(5) = \dfrac{20}{5} + 2 = 6$, *av.* rate $= \dfrac{6 - 12}{5 - 2} = -\dfrac{6}{3} = -2$.

2. $x = 3 \Rightarrow f(3) = \sqrt{4} - 1 = 1$, $x = 8 \Rightarrow f(8) = \sqrt{9} - 1 = 2$, av. rate $= m = \dfrac{2-1}{8-3} = \dfrac{1}{5}$. It

measures the average rate of increase of $f(x)$ over the interval [3, 8].

3. i. $\bar{T} = \dfrac{\left(30 + \dfrac{60}{10}\right) - \left(30 + \dfrac{60}{1}\right)}{9 - 0} = \dfrac{36 - 90}{9} = -6$ That is, decreasing at 6°/min on average.

ii. $\bar{T} = \dfrac{T(60) - T(50)}{10} = \dfrac{30.983607 - 31.176471}{10} = -0.0193$ approx $-0.02°$/min

4. i. $f(x + h) - f(x) = (x + h)^2 - x^2 = 2xh + h^2$

ii. $\dfrac{1}{h}(f(x + h) - f(x)) = \dfrac{2xh + h^2}{h} = 2x + h$ **5.**

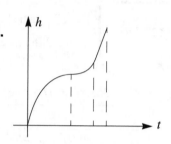

LEVEL 3

1. (a) $\dfrac{\left(\dfrac{1}{\dfrac{1}{2} + h}\right) - \dfrac{1}{\left(\dfrac{1}{2}\right)}}{h} = \dfrac{\left(\dfrac{2}{1 + 2h}\right) - 2}{h} = \dfrac{2 - 2(1 + 2h)}{(1 + 2h)h} = -\dfrac{4}{1 + 2h}$

(b) $\dfrac{(1 + h)(h + 1 - 1) - 0}{h} = \dfrac{h(1 + h)}{h} = 1 + h$ **2. (a)** $\displaystyle\lim_{h \to 0} -\dfrac{4}{1 + 2h} = -4$ **(b)** $\displaystyle\lim_{h \to 0} (1 + h) = 1$

3. $x = a \Rightarrow h(a) = a - a^3$, $x = a + h \Rightarrow h(a + h) = a - (a + h)^3$.

Therefore, gradient of secant $= \dfrac{a - (a + h)^3 - [a - a^3]}{a + h - a} = \dfrac{-(3a^2h + 3ah^2)}{h} = -3a^2 - 3ah$.

Therefore, gradient at $x = a$ is given by $\displaystyle\lim_{h \to 0} (-3a^2 - 3ah) = -3a^2$.

4. (a) $f'(x) = \displaystyle\lim_{h \to 0} \dfrac{f(x + h) - f(x)}{h} = \lim_{h \to 0} \dfrac{(x + h)^3 - x^3}{h} = \lim_{h \to 0} \dfrac{3x^2h + 3xh^2 + h^3}{h}$

$= \displaystyle\lim_{h \to 0} (3x^2 + 3xh + h^2) = 3x^2$

(b) $g'(x) = \displaystyle\lim_{h \to 0} \dfrac{g(x + h) - g(x)}{h} = \lim_{h \to 0} \dfrac{\dfrac{1}{x + h} + 2 - \left(\dfrac{1}{x} + 2\right)}{h} = \lim_{h \to 0} \dfrac{x - (x + h)}{h(x + h)x}$

$= \displaystyle\lim_{h \to 0} -\dfrac{1}{x(x + h)}$

$= -\dfrac{1}{x^2}$

LEVEL 4

1. (a) i. $R(x) > 0 \Leftrightarrow 0.03x(1000 - x) > 0 \Leftrightarrow 0 < x < 1000$ (b)

ii.
```
WINDOW
Xmin=-100
Xmax=1100
Xscl=100
Ymin=0
Ymax=8000
Yscl=500
Xres=1
```

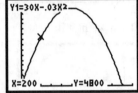

i.
```
Y1(400)-Y1(100)
              4500
Y1(900)-Y1(100)
                 0
```
ii.

(c) When $x = 200$, $R = 4800$ and so we need the largest x value (> 200) for which $R > 4800$. From the graph we observe that x (max) = 800. Therefore greatest increase is 599 (assuming that only an integer number of planters are produced)

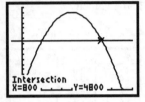

(d) $\lim\limits_{h \to 0} \dfrac{R(200 + h) - R(200)}{h} = \lim\limits_{h \to 0} \dfrac{30(200 + h) - 0.03(200 + h)^2 - [30 \times 200 - 0.03 \times 200^2]}{h}$

$$= \lim\limits_{h \to 0} \dfrac{18h - 0.03h^2}{h} = 18.$$

2. (a) i. $x(t + h) - x(t) = 10(t + h) - 2(t + h)^2 - [10t - 2t^2] = 10h - 4ht - 2h^2$

ii. $v = \lim\limits_{h \to 0} 10 - 4t - 2h = 2$ (c) $a = v'(t) = -4$ which is the constant for all t values. Therefore, when $v = 0$, $a = -4$.

3. $f'(x) = \lim\limits_{h \to 0} \dfrac{2^{x+h} - 2^x}{h} = \lim\limits_{h \to 0} \dfrac{2^x(2^h - 1)}{h} = 2^x \lim\limits_{h \to 0} \dfrac{(2^h - 1)}{h} = 2^x \times \log_e 2$.

Therefore, $f'(1.4) = 2^{1.4} \times \log_e 2 = 1.829$

EXAMINATION STYLE

1. (a)

(b) $av.$ rate $= \dfrac{50 - 90}{2 - 0} = -20 \,^{\circ}\text{C/min}$

(c) i.

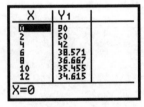

$av.$ rate $= \dfrac{T(2 + h) - T(2)}{h} = \dfrac{\frac{60}{3 + h} - \frac{60}{3}}{h} = \dfrac{60}{h}\left(-\dfrac{h}{3(h + 3)}\right) = -\dfrac{20}{h + 3}$.

ii. when $t = 2$, rate of change $= \lim\limits_{h \to 0} -\dfrac{20}{h + 3} = -\dfrac{20}{3} \,^{\circ}\text{C/min}$

(d) i.

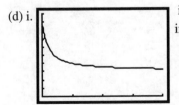

ii. The graph has an asymptote at $T = 30$, therefore as time increases, $T \to 30$

TEST

1.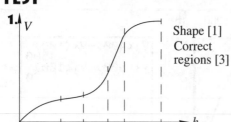

Shape [1]
Correct
regions [3]

2. $g'(2) = \lim\limits_{h \to 0} \dfrac{g(2+h) - g(2)}{h} = \lim\limits_{h \to 0} \dfrac{2^{2+h} - 2^2}{h}$ [1]

$$= 2^2 \lim\limits_{h \to 0} \dfrac{(2^h - 1)}{h} \text{ [1]}$$

$$= 4 \times 0.693 \text{ [1]}$$

$$= 2.77 \text{ [1]}$$

Note: Use a table of values to determine limit value.

3. *av.* velocity $= \dfrac{x(2) - x(0)}{2 - 0}$ [1] $= \dfrac{2 \times 2^2 - 4 \times 2 - 0}{2} = 0$ [2]

4. (a) We create a list: [1]   Then we plot it: [1]

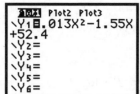

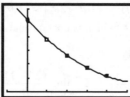

(b) $t = 10$ (1970) and $t = 30$ (1990)

av. rate $= \dfrac{17.6 - 38.2}{30 - 10}$ [1] $= -1.03$ [1]

(c) Difference in each decade:
$-14.2, -11.6, -9, -6.4$ [1]
Least difference occurs in the last decade. [1]

(d) i. This can be done by checking each point, or by simultaneous equation. However, we will sketch the graph and compare it with the set of points on our plot. This shows a good fit.

Plot1 Plot2 Plot3
\Y1◻.013X²-1.55X
+52.4
\Y2=
\Y3=
\Y4=
\Y5=
\Y6=

[3]
ii. In 2010, $t = 50$, therefore, $N(50) = 7.4$ [1]
That is, 7.4 deaths per 100,000. [1]

(e) i. $N(t + h) - N(t) = a(t + h)^2 - b(t + h) + c - [at^2 - bt + c] = 2aht - bh + ah^2$ [1] [1]

ii. $N'(t) = \lim\limits_{h \to 0} \dfrac{N(t+h) - N(t)}{h} = \lim\limits_{h \to 0} \dfrac{2aht - bh + ah^2}{h}$

$$= \lim\limits_{h \to 0} (2at - b + ah) = 2at - b \text{ [2]}$$

When $t = 35$, $N'(35) = 2 \times 0.013 \times 35 - 1.55 = -0.64$ [1]

CHAPTER 23
LEVEL 1

1. i. $7x^6$ ii. $12x$ iii. -1 **2.** i. $\dfrac{d}{dx}(x^2 - 1) = 2x$ ii. $\dfrac{d}{dx}(6x^2 - x - 2) = 12x - 1$

iii. $\dfrac{d}{dx}(x^2 - 1) = 2x$ **3.** i. $\dfrac{d}{dx}(x^3 - x^2) = 3x^2 - 2x$ ii. $\dfrac{d}{dx}(2x^{1/2} - x) = x^{-1/2} - 1 = \dfrac{1}{\sqrt{x}} - 1$

iii. $\dfrac{d}{dx}(x^{5/2} - 3x^{1/3}) = \dfrac{5}{2}x^{3/2} - x^{-2/3} = \dfrac{5}{2}x\sqrt{x} - \dfrac{1}{\sqrt[3]{x^2}}$

iv. $\dfrac{d}{dx}\left(\dfrac{x^2 + 2x + 1}{x}\right) = \dfrac{d}{dx}(x + 2 + x^{-1}) = 1 - \dfrac{1}{x^2}$

v. $\dfrac{d}{dx}(81x^{1/2} - 18x + x^{3/2}) = \dfrac{81}{2\sqrt{x}} - 18 + \dfrac{3}{2}\sqrt{x}$

vi. $\dfrac{d}{dx}(x^{1/2} - x^{-1/2} + x^{3/2}) = \dfrac{1}{2}x^{-1/2} + \dfrac{1}{2}x^{-3/2} + \dfrac{3}{2}x^{1/2} = \dfrac{1}{2\sqrt{x}} + \dfrac{1}{2\sqrt{x^3}} + \dfrac{3}{2}\sqrt{x}$

LEVEL 2

1. (a) $\dfrac{dy}{dx} = 1 + \dfrac{2}{x^3}, x = 1 \Rightarrow \dfrac{dy}{dx} = 1 + 2 = 3$ (b) $f'(x) = -3x^2, x = 3 \Rightarrow f'(3) = -27$

2. $\dfrac{dy}{dx} = 4x^3 - 8x = 4x(x^2 - 2) = 0 \Leftrightarrow x = 0, x = \pm\sqrt{2}$.

3. (a) $x'(t) = 3t^2 - 8t + 1 \therefore x'(1) = 3 - 8 + 1 = -4$ (b) $v'(t) = 6t - 8, \therefore v'(2) = 12 - 8 = 4$

4. $\dfrac{dy}{dx} = 3x^2 - 1, x = -1 \Rightarrow \dfrac{dy}{dx} = 3 - 1 = 2$.

5. (a)   (b)   (c)

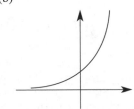
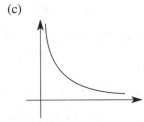

6. $R'(x) = 8 + \dfrac{8}{\sqrt{x}}, R'(25) = 8 + \dfrac{8}{\sqrt{25}} = 9.6$

LEVEL 3

1. (a) $\dfrac{dy}{dx} = 3x^2 - 3$ (b) at $x = 0, \dfrac{dy}{dx} = -3$ (c) $3x^2 - 3 = 0 \Leftrightarrow x = \pm 1$

2. By sketching the graph of s vs t, we have that $s_{max} = 2$.

3. $f'(x) = \lim_{h \to 0} \dfrac{f(x+h) - f(x)}{h} = \lim_{h \to 0} \dfrac{\left(2 - \dfrac{3}{(x+h)^2}\right) - \left(2 - \dfrac{3}{x^2}\right)}{h} = \lim_{h \to 0} \dfrac{3\left(\dfrac{1}{x^2} - \dfrac{1}{(x+h)^2}\right)}{h}$

$= \lim_{h \to 0} \dfrac{6xh + 3h^2}{0hx^2(x+h)^2}$

$= \lim_{h \to 0} \dfrac{6x + 3h}{0x^2(x+h)^2} = \dfrac{6x}{x^4} = \dfrac{6}{x^3}$

4. $f(1) = 10 \Rightarrow 10 = a + 2b + 4 \Leftrightarrow a + 2b = 6$ —(1)

$f'(x) = 2ax + 2b$, so $f'(2) = 0 \Leftrightarrow 4a + 2b = 0$ —(2)

(2) – (1): $3a = -6, a = -2$ sub. into (1): $b = 4$.

5. $f(x) = x^3 - 3x^2 \Rightarrow f'(x) = 3x^2 - 6x = 0 \Leftrightarrow 3x(x - 2) = 0 \Leftrightarrow x = 0$ or $x = 2$

6. $\dfrac{dC}{dv} = 2v - 6 = 0 \therefore v = 3$, when $v = 3, C = 3^2 - 6 \times 3 + 15 = 6$

LEVEL 4

1. $\dfrac{dA}{dx} = 200 - 4x = 0 \Leftrightarrow x = 50 \therefore A_{max} = 2 \times 50 \times 50 = 5000$

2. $S = 3x \times \dfrac{4V}{\sqrt{3}x^2} + \dfrac{\sqrt{3}}{2}x^2 = \dfrac{12V}{\sqrt{3}x} + \dfrac{\sqrt{3}}{2}x^2$.

$\dfrac{dS}{dx} = -\dfrac{12V}{\sqrt{3}x^2} + \sqrt{3}x = 0 \Leftrightarrow \dfrac{12V}{\sqrt{3}x^2} = \sqrt{3}x \Leftrightarrow x^3 = 4V = 512 \therefore x = 8$

Using sign test, at $x = 8$, S is a min.

So, $S_{min} = 64\sqrt{3} + 32\sqrt{3} = 96\sqrt{3}$.

3. i. $h + r = 6 \therefore h = 6 - r$. Now, $V = \pi r^2 h = \pi r^2 (6 - r) = \pi(6r^2 - r^3)$

ii. $\dfrac{dV}{dr} = \pi(12r - 3r^2) = 0 \Leftrightarrow 3r(4 - r) = 0 \Leftrightarrow r = 0$ or $r = 4$. When $r = 4$, $V = 32\pi$

iii.

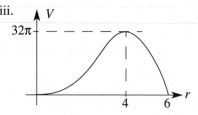

4. $2a + 2\pi\left(\dfrac{b}{2}\right) = 400 \therefore 2a + \pi b = 400 \Leftrightarrow a = \dfrac{1}{2}(400 - \pi b)$ —(1), $A = ab + \pi\left(\dfrac{b}{2}\right)^2$ —(2)

Sub (1) into (2):

$A = \dfrac{1}{2}(400 - \pi b)b + \dfrac{1}{4}\pi b^2 = 200b - \dfrac{1}{4}\pi b^2 \therefore \dfrac{dA}{db} = 200 - \dfrac{\pi}{2}b = 0 \Leftrightarrow b = \dfrac{400}{\pi}$, $a = 0$.

Using the sign test (or graph) shows that this provides a maximum. So, the track of largest area is

a circle, with $A_{max} = \pi \times \left(\dfrac{200}{\pi}\right)^2 = \dfrac{40000}{\pi}$.

EXAMINATION STYLE QUESTIONS

1. i. (a) global max. (b) $0 < x < a$

ii. (a)

h	0.1	0.01	0.001
PR	0.271	0.0297	0.002997

(c)

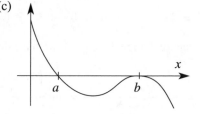

$x = 1.1, y = 1 - (-0.9)^3 = 1.729$

$x = 1.01, y = 1 - (-0.99)^3 = 1.970299$

$x = 1.001, y = 1 - (-0.999)^3 = 1.99700$

(b) $m_{0.1} = -\dfrac{0.271}{0.1} = -2.71$, $m_{0.01} = -\dfrac{0.0297}{0.01} = -2.97$, $m_{0.001} = -\dfrac{0.002997}{0.001} = -2.997$

Therefore, $m \to -3$. (c) $y' = -3(x - 2)^2$, $x = 1 \Rightarrow y' = -3$ (Hence, verified).

iii. (a) $SA = 400\pi = \pi r^2 + 2\pi rh \Leftrightarrow h = \dfrac{400 - r^2}{2r} = \left(\dfrac{200}{r} - \dfrac{r}{2}\right)$.

(b) $V = \pi r^2 h = \pi r^2\left(\dfrac{200}{r} - \dfrac{r}{2}\right) = \left(200r - \dfrac{1}{2}r^3\right)\pi$ (c) $\dfrac{dV}{dr} = \left(200 - \dfrac{3}{2}r^2\right)\pi = 0 \Leftrightarrow r = \dfrac{20}{\sqrt{3}}$.

Therefore, $V = \left[200 \times \dfrac{20}{3}\sqrt{3} - \dfrac{1}{2}\left(\dfrac{20}{3}\right)^3 \times 3\sqrt{3}\right]\pi = \dfrac{8000}{9}\sqrt{3}\pi$ cubic units.

(d)

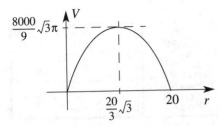

2. i. (a) $s(0) = 10$ (b) $s'(t) = 2 - 2t = v(t)$, $a = v'(t) = -2$. $t = 0$, $v(0) = -2$, $a(0) = -2$

(c) $v(t) = 0 \Leftrightarrow 2 - 2t = 0 \Leftrightarrow t = 1$.

ii.

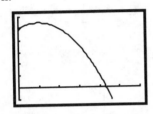

iii. $t = 4$, $s(4) = 10 + 8 - 16 = 2$.
Therefore, distance travelled $= 1 + 9 = 10$ m.

TEST

1. i. (a) i. $f(2) = 2(2)^2 + 1 = 9$ [1] ii. $f(2 + h) = 2(2 + h)^2 + 1 = 9 + 8h + 2h^2$ [2]

ii. $m_{av} = \dfrac{(9 + 8h + 2h^2) - 9}{(2 + h) - 2} = \dfrac{8h + 2h^2}{h} = 8 + 2h$ [2] iii. $\lim\limits_{h \to 0} (8 + 2h) = 8$ [1]

2. (a) $\dfrac{dy}{dx} = -6x^2 + 24$ [1] (b) $-6a^2 + 24$ [1] (c) $18 = -6a^2 + 24 \Leftrightarrow a^2 - 1 = 0 \Leftrightarrow a = \pm 1$

[1] Therefore, coordinates are: $(1, -10)$ & $(-1, -54)$ [1]

3. $f'(-1) = 0$ [1]and $f'(x) = 3x^2 - 2bx - 5 \therefore 0 = 3 + 2b - 5 \Leftrightarrow b = 1$ [2]

4. i.

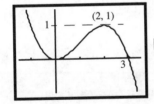

[1] [1] [1]

For stationary points:

$\dfrac{dy}{dx} = \dfrac{1}{4}[6x - 3x^2] = 0 \Leftrightarrow 3x(2 - x) = 0$ [1]

$\Leftrightarrow x = 0$ or $x = 2$

When $x = 0$, $y = 0$ and when $x = 2$, $y = 1$[1]

ii. $Y = 4k \times \dfrac{1}{4}x^2(3 - x) = 4ky$ [1]. Therefore, $Y_{max} = 4k \times y_{max} = 4k \times 1 = 4k$ [1]

5. i. $y + (x + 2) + x = 100 \Leftrightarrow y = 98 - 2x$ [2]

ii. $A = (x + 2)y = (x + 2)(98 - 2x) = 196 + 94x - 2x^2$ [2]

iii. Now, we have that $(x + 2)(98 - 2x) > 0 \Leftrightarrow -2 < x < 49$ [2]. But, $x > 0 \therefore 0 < x < 49$. [1]
However, we also have that $0 < y < 20 \Leftrightarrow 0 < 98 - 2x < 20 \therefore 39 < x < 49$. [1]

iv. $\dfrac{dA}{dx} = 94 - 4x$ [2]

v. A turning point would occur at $\dfrac{dA}{dx} = 0 \Leftrightarrow 94 - 4x = 0 \Leftrightarrow x = 23$. [2] However, this value

of x is outside the domain found in ii., therefore we need to look at the end points of the function:
When $x = 39$, $A = 820$. When $x = 49$, $A = 0$.[1] Therefore maximum area is 820m^2.[1]

6. i. $\dfrac{ds}{dt} = v = 3t^2 - 27$, $a = \dfrac{dv}{dt} = 6t$ [2] (a) -15 [1] (b) 12 [1]

ii. $v = 0 \Leftrightarrow 3t^2 - 27 = 0 \Leftrightarrow t = 3$ (as $t > 0$) [2] iii.

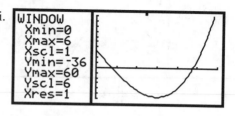

shape [2]; endpoints [1]; range [1]

iv. $20 + 2(34) = 88$ m [3]

CHAPTER 24
LEVEL 1

1. i. $\dfrac{3}{4}x^4 + x^2 + c$ ii. $\dfrac{1}{6}t^3 + 4t + c$ iii. $\dfrac{3}{4}t^2 - \dfrac{6}{5}t^5 + c$ iv. $5x + \dfrac{2}{x} + c$ **2. i.** $9x - \dfrac{1}{4}x^4 + c$

ii. $8x - \dfrac{2}{3}x^{3/2} + c$ iii. $\dfrac{1}{2}t^2 - \dfrac{1}{3}t^3 + c$

LEVEL 2

1. i. $\displaystyle\int (x^2 + 2x)dx = \dfrac{1}{3}x^3 + x^2 + c$ ii. $\displaystyle\int\left(\dfrac{1}{t^2} - \dfrac{1}{t^3}\right)dt = \int(t^{-2} - t^{-3})dt = -\dfrac{1}{t} + \dfrac{1}{2t^2} + c$

iii. $\displaystyle\int (2x^3 - 9x^2 + 9x)dx = \dfrac{1}{2}x^4 - 3x^3 + \dfrac{9}{2}x^2 + c$

iv. $\displaystyle\int x^{1/2}(1 - 2x^{1/2} + x)dx = \int(x^{1/2} - 2x + x^{3/2})dx = \dfrac{2}{3}x^{3/2} - x^2 + \dfrac{2}{5}x^{5/2} + c$

v. $\displaystyle\int (a^2x^2 - 2ax + 1)dx = \dfrac{1}{3}a^2x^3 - ax^2 + x + c$

vi. $\displaystyle\int\left(\dfrac{2}{t^2} - 4 + \dfrac{1}{t^3}\right)dt = \int(2t^{-2} - 4 + t^{-3})dt = -\dfrac{2}{t} - 4t - \dfrac{1}{2t^2} + c$

2. Antidifferentiating gives: $y = x^2 - \dfrac{2}{3}x^{3/2} + c = x^2 - \dfrac{2}{3}x\sqrt{x} + c$.

LEVEL 3

1. $f(x) = 4x - \dfrac{1}{3}x^3 + c$, $f(1) = 8 \Rightarrow 8 = 4 - \dfrac{1}{3} + c \Leftrightarrow c = \dfrac{13}{3}$ $\therefore f(x) = 4x - \dfrac{1}{3}x^3 + \dfrac{13}{3}$

2. $\dfrac{dy}{dx} = (x-2)^2 = x^2 - 4x + 4 \therefore y = \dfrac{1}{3}x^3 - 2x^2 + 4x + c$. When $x = 2$, $y = -4$, therefore,

$-4 = \dfrac{8}{3} - 8 + 8 + c \Leftrightarrow c = -\dfrac{20}{3}$ $\therefore y = \dfrac{1}{3}x^3 - 2x^2 + 4x - \dfrac{20}{3}$

3. $R = -\dfrac{100}{t} + c$ so that, $500 = -100 + c \Leftrightarrow c = 600 \therefore R = 600 - \dfrac{100}{t}$. So, $t = 2$, $R = 550$.

4. i. $C(x) = \dfrac{0.4}{3}x^3 + x^2 + c$. But $C(0) = 500$, so $c = 1500$ $\therefore C(x) = \dfrac{2}{15}x^3 + x^2 + 1500$.

ii. $C(10) = 1733\dfrac{1}{3}$.

LEVEL 4

1. $s = 6t^2 - 3t + c$. When $t = 0$, $s = 0$ $\therefore c = 0 \Rightarrow s = 6t^2 - 3t$, So, when $t = 5$, $s = 135$.

2. $N = 300t + 500 \times \dfrac{2}{3}t^{3/2} + c$. When $t = 0$, $N = 4000$ $\therefore c = 4000$.

That is, $N = 300t + 500 \times \frac{2}{3}t\sqrt{t} + 4000$. So, when $t = 16$, $N = 30133\frac{1}{3}$.

3. (a) $V = 12t - 3t^2 + c_1$. When $t = 0$, $v = 2$ $\therefore c_1 = 2$. So, $V = 12t - 3t^2 + 2$.

(b) $x = 6t^2 - t^3 + 2t + c_2$. When $t = 0$, $x = 0$ $\therefore c_2 = 0$, So, $x = 6t^2 - t^3 + 2t$. (c) $x(5) = 35$

4. $f'(4) = 0 \therefore a\sqrt{4} - 4b = 0 \Leftrightarrow a = 2b$ —(1) Also, $f(4) = 6$ and $f(0) = 2$.

Now, $f(x) = \frac{2}{3}ax^{3/2} - \frac{1}{2}bx^2 + c = \frac{2}{3}ax\sqrt{x} - \frac{1}{2}bx^2 + c$, Using $f(4) = 6$ we have that

$6 = \frac{2}{3}a \times 4\sqrt{4} - \frac{1}{2}b(4)^2 + c \Leftrightarrow 6 = \frac{16}{3}a - 8b + c$ —(2). Similarly, using the fact that $f(0) = 2$

we have, $2 = \frac{2}{3}a(0)\sqrt{0} - \frac{1}{2}b(0)^2 + c \Leftrightarrow c = 2$ —(3).

Substituting (3) and (1) into (2) we have: $6 = \frac{16}{3}(2b) - 8b + 2 \Leftrightarrow 4 = \frac{8}{3}b \therefore b = \frac{3}{2}$.

EXAMINATION STYLE QUESTIONS

1. i. $C'(0) = 55 \therefore 55 = 0 + 0 + 0 + c \Rightarrow c = 0$.
$C'(5) = 5 \therefore 5 = 25a + 5b + 55 \Rightarrow -10 = 5a + b$ — (1)
$C'(10) = 55 \therefore 55 = 100a + 10b + 55 \Rightarrow 0 = 10a + b$ — (2)
Now: (1) – (2) gives $-10 = -5a \Leftrightarrow a = 2$. Sub. into (2) $0 = 20 + b \Leftrightarrow b = -20$.

ii. $C(x) = \frac{a}{3}x^3 + \frac{b}{2}x^2 + cx + k = \frac{2}{3}x^3 - 10x^2 + 55x + k$. But, $x = 0$, $C = 25 \therefore k = 25$.

Therefore, $C(x) = \frac{2}{3}x^3 - 10x^2 + 55x + 25$. iii. $C(5) = 133\frac{1}{3}$. So, cost is approx. $133,333.

iv.

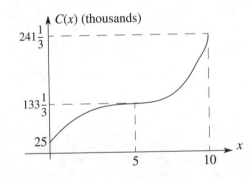

TEST

1. i. $x^9 - \frac{2}{3}x^{3/2} + c$ [2] ii. $-\frac{1}{x} + x^2 + c$ [2] iii. $\int(x^2 - 6x + 9)dx = \frac{1}{3}x^3 - 3x^2 + 9x + c$ [2]

2. $\frac{dV}{dt} = 0.2t^{3/2} \therefore V = 0.2 \times \frac{2}{5}t^{5/2} + c = 0.08t^{5/2} + c$ [2].

So, $5 = 0.08(4)^{5/2} \Rightarrow c = 2.44$ [1]. Therefore, $V = 0.08t^{5/2} + 2.44$ [1]

3. (a) i. $a = \frac{dv}{dt} = 8 - 2t \therefore v = 8t - t^2 + c$ [1]. Now, $t = 0$, $v = 0$, so, $c = 0$ [1]. $\therefore v = 8t - t^2$ [1]

ii. $v = \frac{dx}{dt} \therefore x = 4t^2 - \frac{1}{3}t^3 + k$ [1]. Now, $t = 0$, $x = 0$, so, $k = 0$. $\therefore x = 4t^2 - \frac{1}{3}t^3, t \geq 0$ [1]

(b) $v = 0 \Leftrightarrow 8t - t^2 = 0 \Leftrightarrow t(8 - t) = 0 \Leftrightarrow t = 0$ or $t = 8$ [1] [1]

4.

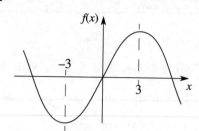

shape [1]
turning points [2]
positive regions [1]
negative regions [1]